Starting an Etsy® Business

for
dummies®

A Wiley Brand

Starting an Etsy® Business

3rd Edition

by Kate Shoup and Kate Gatski

A Wiley Brand

Starting an Etsy® Business For Dummies®, 3rd Edition

Published by: **John Wiley & Sons, Inc.,** 111 River Street, Hoboken, NJ 07030-5774, www.wiley.com

Copyright © 2017 by John Wiley & Sons, Inc., Hoboken, New Jersey

Published simultaneously in Canada

For general information on our other products and services, please contact our Customer Care Department within the U.S. at 877-762-2974, outside the U.S. at 317-572-3993, or fax 317-572-4002. For technical support, please visit https://hub.wiley.com/community/support/dummies.

Wiley publishes in a variety of print and electronic formats and by print-on-demand. Some material included with standard print versions of this book may not be included in e-books or in print-on-demand. If this book refers to media such as a CD or DVD that is not included in the version you purchased, you may download this material at http://booksupport.wiley.com. For more information about Wiley products, visit www.wiley.com.

Library of Congress Control Number: 2017946007

ISBN 978-1-119-37896-9 (pbk); ISBN 978-1-119-37901-0 (ebk); ISBN 978-1-119-37882-2 (ebk)

Manufactured in the United States of America

10 9 8 7 6 5 4 3 2 1

Contents at a Glance

Table of Contents

Introduction

D oes this sound like you? You hate your day job. You trained as a teacher, but what you really want to do all day is knit. Or you wait tables, but you dream of starting your own jewelry-making business. Or your background is in law, but what you *really* love is constructing handbags out of gum wrappers. There's just one problem: You have bills to pay. It's not like you can just ditch your day job to hand-craft sweaters or earrings or purses, right? Wrong. Thanks to Etsy (www.etsy.com), plenty of people have done just that. And armed with the information in *Starting an Etsy Business For Dummies,* 3rd Edition, you can, too!

What's Etsy? Etsy was created in 2005 to help artists and craftspeople sell their handmade wares online. (Since then, Etsy has evolved to allow the sale of vintage items and craft supplies.) Etsy allows creative types to channel their passion for their craft into their life's work. If your dream is to "make a living making things," then Etsy is for you!

About This Book

Starting an Etsy Business For Dummies, 3rd Edition, is a reference tool. You don't have to read it from beginning to end; instead, you can turn to any part of the book that gives you the information you need when you need it. And you can keep coming back to the book over and over. On the other hand, if you prefer to read things in order, you'll find that the information is presented in a natural, logical progression.

Sometimes we have information that we want to share with you, but it relates only tangentially to the topic at hand. When that happens, we place that information in a sidebar (a shaded gray box). Even though it may not be mission critical, we think you'll find it worth knowing. But you don't have to read it if you don't want to.

Within this book, you may note that some web addresses break across two lines of text. If you're reading this book in print and want to visit one of these web pages, simply key in the web address exactly as it's noted in the text, as though the line break doesn't exist. If you're reading this as an e-book, you've got it easy — just click the web address to be taken directly to the web page.

Foolish Assumptions

When writing this book, we made some assumptions about you, dear reader. We assume that you want to run your Etsy shop as a proper business. Sure, it's possible to build and manage an Etsy shop with minimal effort, but that will yield only minimal results. We're guessing that you're serious about making your Etsy shop a success and that you're willing to invest the time and energy to make that happen.

We also generally assume that you reside in the United States. Although most of the information discussed applies regardless of your geographic location, certain tidbits — such as matters related to taxation — are specific to U.S. residents.

Icons Used in This Book

Icons are those little pictures you see in the margins throughout this book, and they're meant to draw your attention to key points that can help you along the way. Here's a list of the icons we use and what they signify.

TIP

When you see this icon in the margin, the paragraph next to it contains valuable information on making your life as an Etsy seller easier.

REMEMBER

Some information is so important that it needs to be set apart for emphasis. This icon — like a string tied around your finger — is a friendly reminder of info that you'll want to commit to memory and use over the long haul.

WARNING

This icon highlights common mistakes that Etsy sellers make and pitfalls to avoid. An important part of achieving success is simply eliminating the mistakes; the information marked by this icon helps you do just that.

Beyond the Book

In addition to the material in the print or e-book you're reading right now, this product also comes with some access-anywhere goodies on the web. Check out the free Cheat Sheet at www.dummies.com/cheatsheet/startinganetsybusiness for tips on creating an eye-catching Etsy storefront, pricing your work, taking beautiful product photos, and more.

Where to Go from Here

Glance through the Table of Contents and find the part, chapter, or section that flips your switch. That's the best way to begin. If you're just trying to get a sense of what's available for purchase on Etsy, turn straight to Chapter 5. If you're itching to launch your own Etsy shop, Chapter 8 walks you through the process of building it from scratch. If your shop is up and running but you're not sure how to handle business matters — say, paying taxes or choosing the right structure for your business — then you'll want to flip right to Chapter 18.

When you're finished reading this book, invest some time reading the Etsy Blog (`https://blog.etsy.com/en/`), reading the Seller Handbook (`www.etsy.com/sellerhandbook`), and interacting with the larger Etsy community (get started at `www.etsy.com/community`). As your business grows, you'll undoubtedly encounter issues that this book doesn't discuss; when that happens, you're sure to appreciate these incredible resources.

1

Getting Started with Etsy

Chapter 1

Handmade for Each Other: Falling in Love with Etsy

M ost people think of Etsy as a website where artists and craftspeople can sell their wares online. But really, it's so much more. Indeed, Etsy describes itself as an economy — one where artists and designers "can find meaningful work selling their goods in both global and local markets" and "where thoughtful consumers can discover those goods and build relationships with the people who make and sell them." In short, Etsy enables creative types to channel their passion into their life's work!

This chapter offers you a bird's-eye view of Etsy — its purpose and business model, how to sign up for and navigate it, and all sorts of good stuff about opening and running your own shop.

Creative Crusade: Understanding Etsy's Purpose and Business Model

Many people think of Etsy as a sort of eBay for arts and crafts. And you can see why: People use both Etsy and eBay to buy stuff from other individuals. Also, both sites charge listing fees and make a small commission on every sale. Plus, members use feedback to rate their transactions.

But the sites have big differences, too:

>> Although Etsy is growing — as of this writing, the site boasts 1.7 million active sellers and 27.1 million active buyers, and in 2015 it facilitated more than $2.39 billion in transactions — it's still the proverbial mouse to eBay's proverbial elephant.

>> Etsy, which launched in 2005, doesn't use an auction format.

>> Whereas (almost) anything goes on eBay, Etsy was created specifically to enable artists and craftspeople to sell their handmade wares online. (Over time, the site has evolved to cater to so-called creative entrepreneurs; find out more about what you can and can't sell on Etsy in Chapter 7.) Etsy itself puts it this way:

> Our mission is to reimagine commerce in ways that build a more fulfilling and lasting world. We are building a human, authentic and community-centric global and local marketplace. We are committed to using the power of business to create a better world through our platform, our members, our employees and the communities we serve. As we grow, commitment to our mission remains at the core of our identity. It is woven into the decisions we make for the long-term health of our ecosystem, from the sourcing of our office supplies to our employee benefits to the items sold in our marketplace.

REMEMBER

So how does Etsy's business model work? Etsy stays afloat by charging sellers a fee for each item listed on the site. At this time, the listing fee is 20¢ per item. Etsy also collects a commission from the seller for each item sold — currently 3.5 percent of the total price of the item, not counting shipping. In addition, Etsy collects fees (3 percent of the total price of the item plus an additional 20¢) from shop-keepers in the United States who use its handy-dandy Etsy Payments feature, which enables buyers to pay using a credit card or Etsy gift card. These fees, which you can pay using a credit card that you put on file with Etsy or using your PayPal account, are due monthly.

MONIKER MYSTERY TOUR: PROBING THE SECRET BEHIND ETSY'S NAME

The origins of Etsy's name are as murky as a drifter's past, but theories abound. Some say that the name Etsy is a play on the Latin phrase *et si,* meaning "and if." Others suggest that the name comes from the Greek *etsi,* meaning "so," "thus," or "in this way." Still others posit that Etsy derives from the Unix directory /etc, pronounced "et-C," or that it's meant to call to mind the word *itsy,* as in "itsy-bitsy," or "cute," which, of course, many items on Etsy are.

Any attempts for clarification by Etsy are met with playful — but misleading — answers by Etsy's staff, ranging from "Etsy is an acronym for Expanded Truncated Structural Y" to "It means 'horny person' in Japanese.'" And although Etsy founder Rob Kalin once insinuated that the answer to this riddle could be found in Fellini's film *8½,* no one has yet managed to solve it.

World Up: Introducing the World of Etsy

Just what can you do on Etsy? And how do you use it? This section scratches the surface. (You find the nitty-gritty, step-by-step info about these topics in later chapters.)

Registering with Etsy

You don't need to register with Etsy to scope out what goodies are for sale. But if you're in the market to buy any of said goodies — or to communicate with other Etsy members or participate in the site's community features — you need to create an account with the site. Fortunately, creating an account is simple and free. All you need to do is enter your name and email address and choose a username and password. You don't even need to supply a credit card number!

If you plan to use Etsy to sell your own items (and we assume you do because you're reading this book), you need to take a few more steps as well as provide a major credit card (think MasterCard, Visa, Discover, or American Express) and other vitals, such as your address.

For step-by-step coverage of completing the registration process and signing in to your Etsy account, turn to Chapter 2. Chapter 8 covers the steps you need to take to become an Etsy seller.

Navigating the Etsy home page

Whether you're buying or selling, exploring or researching, Etsy's home page is your home base. It's the page that appears when you go to www.etsy.com. You can also access Etsy's home page from anywhere on the Etsy site by clicking the Etsy logo in the upper-left corner of each Etsy Marketplace page. (We explain why we say "Etsy Marketplace" here in a sec.) If you've created an account and are logged in to the site, you can also click the Home button in the upper-right area of the screen.

REMEMBER

The Etsy home page, shown in Figure 1-1, features several important sections. These include the following. (Note that this section assumes that you're *not* signed in to your Etsy account. The options change slightly if you are — and even more if you are a seller. For more information, see Chapters 3 and 8.)

>> A standard search box, for when you know what you're looking for

>> A set of links along the top, which you can click to browse items in various popular categories, including Clothing & Accessories and Jewelry

>> Editors' picks for top Etsy items

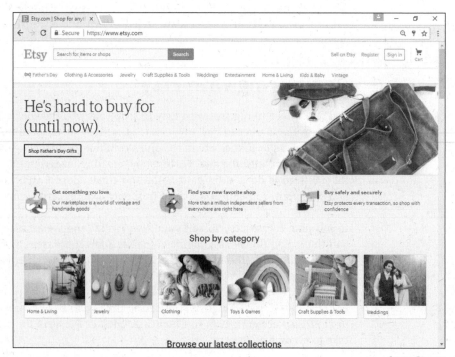

FIGURE 1-1:
Etsy's home page.

Source: Etsy.com

» Top shops that are worth a look

» Recent reviews from happy shoppers

» Access to various Etsy blogs

For more information about these and other home page features, check out Chapter 3.

Understanding your account and your shop

On Etsy, managing your account is easy. Etsy has grouped all the key settings and info in two easy-to-reach places: the You menu (see Figure 1-2) and the Shop Manager page (see Figure 1-3). You access the You menu and Shop Manager page by clicking the You and Shop Manager links, respectively, that appear along the top of every Etsy Marketplace page when you're logged in to your Etsy account. (If you haven't set up your Etsy shop yet, you may not see a Shop Manager link.) The You menu contains a series of links that provide access to all sorts of useful info — your public profile, conversations with other Etsy users, items you've bought, account settings, and teams you're on. The Shop Manager page contains links to various shop-related settings and more. For help with navigating You and Shop Manager, turn to Chapter 4.

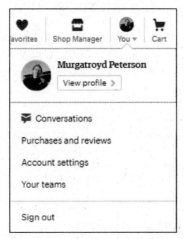

FIGURE 1-2:
The You menu.

Source: Etsy.com

REMEMBER

Notice in Figure 1-3 that there's no header bar on the Shop Manager page. That means there's no easy access to the various links on the header bar. To access those links, you have to switch from Shop Manager to the Etsy Marketplace. To do so, click the Shop Manager link in the upper-left corner of the Shop Manager page. Then choose Etsy Marketplace from the list that appears.

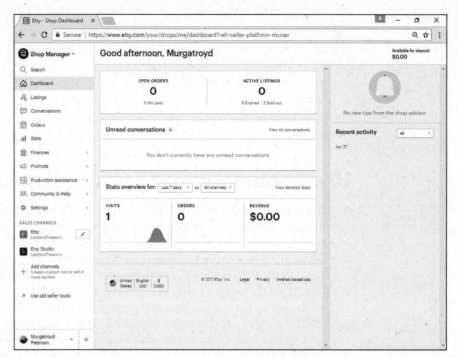

FIGURE 1-3:
The Shop
Manager page.

Source: Etsy.com

Discovering what's for sale on Etsy

Etsy features unique items — goodies you simply can't find anywhere else — along with supplies for crafting your own pieces. In fact, Etsy offers an incredible breadth of items for sale, from accessories to ceramics, jewelry to quilts, and everything in between.

TIP

To help you find a specific item, Etsy offers a robust Search tool. You can also use the Search tool to locate a particular shop. If you're just browsing, you'll appreciate Etsy's many browsing-related features. (Exactly which features are available depends on whether you're logged in to the site.) You access these tools from Etsy's home page. For additional help, turn to Chapter 5.

Ensuring your safety on Etsy

REMEMBER

No doubt about it, one of the highlights of Etsy is its thriving community of interesting, arty folk. But you may still find an occasional bad apple in the Etsy bunch. Take a few key steps to ensure your safety:

>> **To make sure that no one accesses your account without your authorization, choose a strong password.** Select one that meets all the following criteria:

- It's at least eight characters long.

- It doesn't contain your username or your real name.

- It doesn't contain a complete word.

- It differs from passwords that you've used in the past.

- It contains a mixture of uppercase letters, lowercase letters, numbers, symbols, and spaces.

For an added layer of protection, change your password every so often — say, every 30 to 60 days.

>> **Be on the lookout for scams.** These often involve the use of money orders or cashier's checks, along with an offer to pay significantly more than is necessary to expedite shipping or to cover some other weird request. If you do get taken on Etsy, contact your financial institution immediately. Then report the situation to Etsy. You may also opt to alert your local law enforcement.

>> **Before you jump into a forum or team discussion, monitor it for a while.** See whether the folks engaged in the discussion are people you really want to interact with. If a discussion goes south, simply disengage.

>> **Play it close to the vest.** Don't share your digits or other personal details, such as where you live or work, on Etsy's forums or other public spaces. Oh, and if you decide to meet up with someone you've met on Etsy in person, pick a neutral, public place, let a friend or family member know about your plans, and be sure to bring your phone with you in case you need to call for help.

Chapter 6 covers important safety issues in more detail.

Storefront and Center: Setting Up Your Storefront

When you set up your Etsy storefront, you can personalize it in several ways:

>> Uploading a cover photo and a shop icon

>> Including a shop title and shop announcement to describe your shop

>> Using sections to organize your goods

>> Populating your Etsy profile and your shop's About section, and choosing a profile picture

REMEMBER

As you set up your storefront, keep in mind that a major reason people shop on Etsy is to feel connected to the artists who make what they buy. If you want people to buy from *you*, make sure your Etsy shop reflects your personality! For example, do you have a serious bent? Then your shop should, too. Ditto if you're whimsical, modern, traditional, edgy, or frilly. Let your personality shine through in your choice of cover photo, shop icon, and other visual elements as well as in your bio and other text-based elements. Not only will this increase your sales, but it may just help you make some friends along the way. (For more on setting up your Etsy shop, check out Chapter 8.)

Oh, one more pointer: As you set up your Etsy shop, you'll want to clearly lay out your shop policies — how much you charge for shipping, whether you accept returns, and so on. We cover smart policies in Chapter 9.

Sell's Angels: Surveying the Etsy Selling Process

REMEMBER

Maybe you want to do more than buy on Etsy. Maybe you want to sell. Putting up an item for sale on Etsy is a simple process:

1. **Create (or curate, in the case of vintage pieces) the item you're selling and determine how much you want to charge for it (with the help of the pointers we provide in Chapter 10).**

2. **Photograph your piece.**

   You can include as many as five pictures of each piece in your Etsy shop. The photos you provide should convey the shape, size, color, and texture of your piece and also be easy on the eye.

3. **Compose a snappy title and description for your item listing.**

4. **List your item on the site and wait for someone to snatch it up.**

5. **When the item sells, ship it to the buyer (after you receive your payment, of course)!**

Okay, that's a broad overview. The process has a little more to it. But trust us: It's nothing you can't handle. Check out the chapters in Part 3 to get up to speed.

Takin' Care of Business: Handling Business Matters

For some sellers, running an Etsy shop is merely a hobby — a way to make a little extra money on the side. For others, it's their day job, or "what they do." Regardless of which camp you're in, you need to treat your Etsy shop as a proper small business — building a brand, marketing your shop, and providing excellent customer service.

If you're in the latter category — someone who seeks to earn a living by selling on Etsy — you may choose to do even more. For example, you may opt to incorporate your business, obtain a business checking account, streamline your supply chain, use special tools to analyze your business, and so on. Part 4 covers all these topics and more.

Community Collage: Engaging in the Etsy Community

Sure, Etsy is a great place to buy and sell all sorts of neat stuff. But it's more than that: It's a community of creative, crafty people that just begs for participation. Etsy offers several tools that help you jump right in, including these:

>> Public message boards, called *forums*

>> Teams, for connecting with like-minded Etsy members

>> A podcast, for tips on selling

>> Online Labs, in which Etsy staffers and members run online seminars, workshops, shop critiques, and other educational gatherings

You can also follow your favorite shops and sellers to keep up with their goings-on by adding them to your Favorites.

Other great resources for the Etsy community include the Etsy Blog (www.etsy.com/blog), which acts as a neighborhood newspaper of sorts. The Etsy Blog serves up fresh content daily and boasts material ranging from information to help you perfect various crafting techniques, to glimpses into the lives of other Etsy sellers, and more.

Etsy's email newsletters are another great source of information and inspiration. And if you're among the more than eleventy-jillion people who maintain a social media account — for example, on Facebook, Twitter, Instagram, or Pinterest — you can connect with Etsy there as well.

TIP

Etsy is super easy to use, but you'll still need a little help sometimes. Fortunately, Etsy maintains copious resources to help members find answers to all their burning Etsy-related questions, from Help files to an interactive Questions forum. Go to www.etsy.com/help for the scoop.

Ready to dive in? Flip to Part 5 for all the details on engaging in the Etsy community.

Chapter **2**

Let's Get This Party Started: Signing Up

The Father of Taoism Lao Tzu once said, "A journey of a thousand miles begins with one step." (He also said, "Silence is a source of great strength" and "The sage does not hoard"; we're still digesting those.) On Etsy, that one first step is becoming a registered user by signing up with the site. After that, you're ready to embark on your own Etsy journey! This chapter gives you all the info you need to register with Etsy.

Sign Me Up! Becoming a Registered User

Anyone can browse Etsy to see what goodies are for sale. But if you're in the market to buy, or if you eventually want to open your own shop, you need to create an account with the site by becoming a registered user. It's easy and free! Just follow the guidelines in this section.

TIP

In addition to being able to purchase items on the site, registered users can keep track of their best-loved items or shops by adding them to their Favorites, communicate with other Etsy members, and participate in the site's community features, such as the forums. Flip to Part 5 for more information about all these options.

Setting up your account

Assuming that you have access to a computer, tablet, or smartphone and an Internet connection, becoming a registered Etsy user is super easy. (Note that the screen images shown here were captured on a computer. They may look different on a tablet or smartphone.)

1. **In your web browser's address bar, type** `www.etsy.com` **and press Enter or Return.**

   Etsy's main page appears (see Figure 2-1).

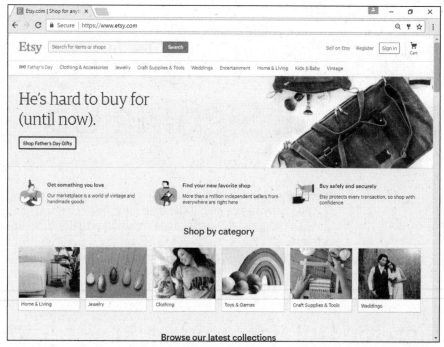

Source: Etsy.com

FIGURE 2-1:
Etsy's main page.

2. **Click the Register link in the top-right portion of your screen (refer to Figure 2-1).**

   The registration page appears (see Figure 2-2).

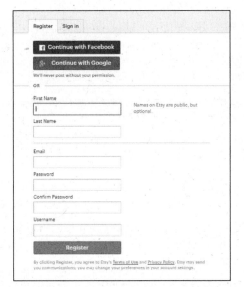

FIGURE 2-2:
The registration
page.

Source: Etsy.com

3. **Type your first name in the First Name field and your last name in the Last Name field.**

   Note that filling out these fields is strictly optional. If you do fill them out, your name will be publicly displayed throughout the site. If you want, you can add simply your first name or a nickname or your initials — whatever. If you decide to leave both of these fields blank, your username is the one that other Etsy users will see.

TIP

   You can save a few steps by clicking the Sign Up Using Facebook or Continue with Google button to create your Etsy account. If you do, some of your activity on Etsy — for example, when you favorite an item — may be posted on your Facebook page. This section walks you through signing up for Etsy the old-fashioned way: by entering your info directly on Etsy's site.

4. **Type your email address in the Email field.**

5. **In the Password field, type the password you want to use to access your Etsy account.**

   Create a password that's at least eight characters — one that you can remember easily but that won't be too obvious to anyone else.

6. **Retype the password in the Confirm Password field.**

7. **In the Username field, type the username you want to use on Etsy.**

   This name must contain fewer than 20 uppercase and/or lowercase letters or numbers (no spaces). Etsy notifies you if someone else has selected your username. In that case, try another one until you find one that's available.

REMEMBER

You can't change your username, so make sure that the name you choose is something you can live with as long as you're on Etsy and that you're cool with everyone you buy from and sell to seeing the username you choose. (In other words, "WinonaForever" may not be the way to go.)

8. **To read the terms of use, click the Terms of Use link, and to read Etsy's Privacy Policy, click the Privacy Policy link.**

   You find out more about the Terms of Use in the next section. Flip to Chapter 6 for more on Etsy's Privacy Policy.

9. **Click the Register button.**

   Etsy creates your account and sends a confirmation email to the address you supplied in Step 4.

TIP

If you don't receive the confirmation email right away, check your spam folder to make sure it wasn't intercepted.

10. **Open the email from Etsy and click the link that it contains to confirm your account.**

    You're ready to go!

Accessing Etsy's House Rules and reviewing its Terms of Use

Before registering with and using Etsy, take a moment to access the site's House Rules and review its Terms of Use. Follow these steps:

1. **Click the Help button in the bottom-right corner of any Etsy Marketplace page.**

   The Help page appears.

2. **Scroll down to the Still Have Questions? section and click the Read Our Site Policies link.**

   The Our House Rules page appears.

3. **Click the Terms of Use link.**

   The Terms of Use page appears, as shown in Figure 2-3.

Etsy's Terms of Use page is kind of like the site's constitution. It sets out your rights and responsibilities on the site. This 14-point document covers maintaining your privacy, content requirements, proper use of services, termination, warranties and liability, indemnification, handling disputes, and other important legal-type stuff.

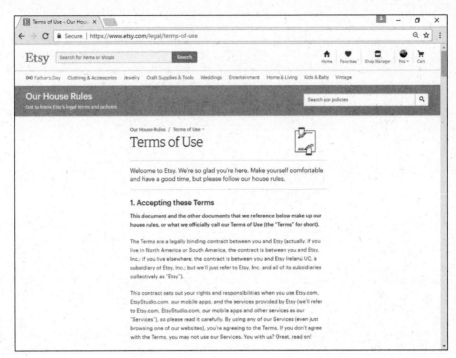

FIGURE 2-3:
Review Etsy's
Terms of Use.

REMEMBER

Maybe you're wondering why you need to read Etsy's Terms of Use. Here's our answer: Violating any of the policies spelled out in the Terms of Use is grounds for expulsion from the site. The "But I didn't know it was a policy!" defense doesn't fly.

In addition to its Terms of Use, Etsy has several more House Rules. We cover these in a bit more detail in Chapter 6.

It's a Sign: Signing In

After you've created your Etsy account, signing in is a snap. Just go to www.etsy. com and click the Sign In button in the upper-right corner of the screen. (You can see this button in Figure 2-1, just to the right of the Register link.) Then, in the pop-up window that appears, type your email address or username in the Email or Username field, type your password in the Password field, and click the Sign In button (see Figure 2-4).

TIP

Notice the Stay Signed In check box in Figure 2-4. If you select this check box, you can navigate away from the site and return without having to sign in all over again. However, we don't recommend you choose this setting if you're on a public computer (for example, at a library or Internet cafe). Otherwise, a complete stranger could access your account!

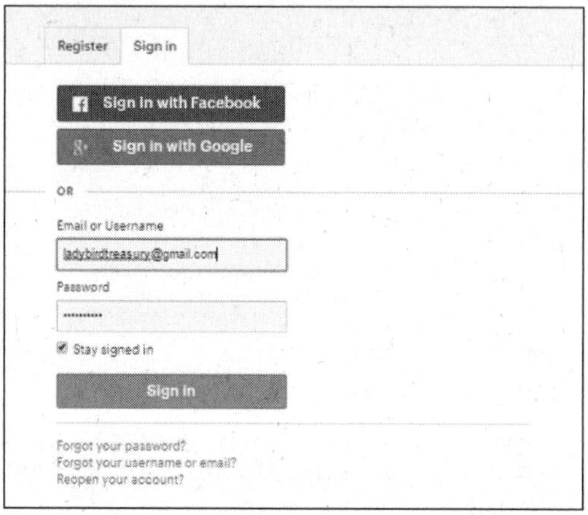

FIGURE 2-4:
Use your username or email address and your password to sign in to your Etsy account.

| Register | Sign in |

  f   Sign in with Facebook

  g+ Sign in with Google

OR

Email or Username

ladybintreasury@gmail.com

Password

●●●●●●●●●

☑ Stay signed in

Sign in

Forgot your password?
Forgot your username or email?
Reopen your account?

Source: Etsy.com

What about signing out? That's even easier than signing in. Simply click the You button that appears in the header bar when you're signed in and choose Sign Out from the menu that appears.

High Profile: Setting Up Your Public Profile

Everyone who joins Etsy has a public profile page. Why? A couple of reasons. For one, being able to check out other Etsy members helps to inspire confidence in the site. That is, it's not populated by a bunch of faceless buyers and sellers; it's populated by actual *people!* For another, it's fun to see who else is on the site.

An Etsy profile can (but doesn't have to) include the following tidbits:

» A profile picture

» Your name

- » Your gender
- » Your city
- » Your birthday
- » Your bio
- » A list of your favorite materials

Anyone who visits your Etsy shop can access your public profile by clicking your name or profile picture on any page in your Etsy shop.

To populate your Etsy public profile, follow these steps:

1. **Click the You menu along the top of any Etsy Marketplace page and choose View Profile.**

   Your profile page appears, as shown in Figure 2-5. Note the generic profile picture.

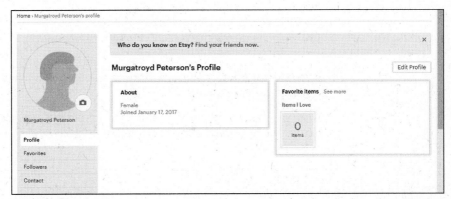

Source: Etsy.com

FIGURE 2-5: From here, you can populate your profile.

2. **To add a personalized profile picture, click the camera button in the bottom-right corner of the generic photo.**

   The Add a Profile Photo dialog box opens. It lists various photo specs, including the file type (JPG, GIF, or PNG), file size (smaller than 10 megabytes), and dimensions (at least 400 x 400 pixels).

3. **Click the Choose a File button.**

   A standard Open dialog box appears.

4. **Locate, select, and open the photo you want to use.**

Etsy shows you a preview of your photo (see Figure 2-6).

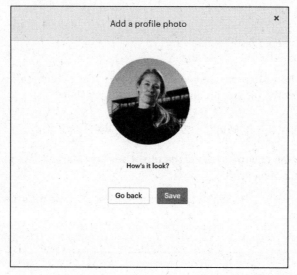

FIGURE 2-6:
Preview your
photo.

5. **If you like the photo, click Save. Otherwise, click Go Back and repeat Step 4 to use a different photo.**

When you save your photo, Etsy returns you to your profile page. The profile picture you chose replaces the generic one (see Figure 2-7).

FIGURE 2-7:
The photo you
chose replaces
the generic one.

AVATAR HERO: CHOOSING A PROFILE PICTURE

Your profile picture, or *avatar,* isn't just something people see when they peruse your profile page or visit your shop. It represents you across the site. When you post on a forum, your profile photo appears next to that post. Ditto when you comment on the Etsy Blog or participate in teams or online workshops. You want to select a profile photo that reflects well on you.

So what type of image do you want to choose? Etsy urges you to use one that shows your face. This helps to build trust. Just make sure the photo isn't blurry (no "Bigfoot sighting"–style photos), that it's well lit, and that your mug covers at least 70 percent of the frame.

6. **Click the Edit Profile button.**

   The Your Public Profile page opens. Here, you can enter additional information about yourself. (See Figure 2-8.)

FIGURE 2-8: You can populate your profile from the Your Public Profile page.

Source: Etsy.com

7. **If you want, indicate your gender.**

   If you prefer to keep that information private, select the Rather Not Say option button.

8. **Type your city in the City field.**

As you type, Etsy displays a list of matching locales; click your town in the list to select it.

By entering your city, you enable Etsy buyers near you to find your shop.

TIP

9. **Use the Month and Day drop-down lists to enter your birthday.**

10. **Type your bio in the About box.**

11. **In the Favorite Materials box, indicate which materials you like to use, separating entries with a comma and a space.**

You can add as many as 13.

12. **If you want your profile to include your shop, any favorite items or shops, and any teams you've joined, leave the check boxes at the bottom of the screen checked.**

If you see a Treasury Lists check box, ignore it. Etsy members used to be able to curate Treasuries — lists of their favorite items on the site — but that's no longer the case. Selecting this check box simply enables members who curated Treasuries in the past to continue to share them.

13. **Click the Save Changes button.**

Etsy saves the changes you made to your profile.

14. **To preview your profile, click the View Profile button in the top-right area of the page.**

Etsy shows you how your profile will appear to others (see Figure 2-9).

FIGURE 2-9:
Preview your profile.

Source: Etsy.com

BIOHAZARD: WRITING A WINNING BIO

For many people, the idea of writing anything — let alone about themselves — is about as enticing as spelunking in Yucca Mountain. But a succinct, clever, well-written bio is essential to the success of your Etsy shop. Why? Your bio enables buyers to see who they're buying from. It turns you into a bona-fide human being in your buyers' eyes.

If writing your bio seems a bit daunting, don't freak out. It's a process, like anything else. You can start by writing down the answers to a few key questions: Who are you? What's your educational and/or artistic background? What do you make and/or sell? What are you passionate about? Who or what inspires you?

With the answers to these questions in hand, you're ready to write your bio. Try to incorporate some of these tips:

- **Say hello.** If you were the proprietor of a real-world boutique, you'd certainly greet customers as they entered your store. Do the same for folks visiting your Etsy shop. While you're at it, thank them for stopping by. It's just good manners.

- **Be friendly and approachable.** This strategy will yield substantially better results than taking the opposite tack — being rude and inaccessible. Also, a little bit of humor can go a long way. Oh, and the tone of your bio needs to match the tone of your shop and products. If your business is about whimsy, a stuffy bio just won't do!

- **Stick with first person**. Some people write their bio in first person. Others opt for third person. Our view? Unless you're the queen or a professional athlete, go with first person.

- **Keep it short.** It's your Etsy bio, not *War and Peace*. A few short paragraphs will do. If you find your bio running a little long, try using sections, with titles, to break up your information.

- **Be professional . . . sort of.** No, you don't have to wear a pin-striped suit and practical pumps. But you do need to project an air of competence — even if your shop is all about fun. You want to be taken seriously as a seller, right?

- **Proofread.** Before you post your bio, triple-check it to make sure there aren't any spelling or grammatical errors. Better yet, ask your English-major friend to check it for you.

Chapter **3**

There's No Place Like Home: Discovering Etsy's Home Page

H ome. It's a word with many meanings. It's where you live. It's where your heart is. It's where you hang your hat. It's where the cows finally come. Simply put, it's a place to which you always long to return.

Etsy's home page is no different. As you use the site, you'll often find yourself returning home — to the home page, that is. Whether you're buying or selling, exploring or researching, Etsy's home page is your home base. In this chapter, you explore the various features of the page and find out how to navigate from it.

Home Sweet Home: Etsy's Home Page

Etsy's home page (see Figure 3-1) is the page that appears when you type "www.etsy.com" into your web browser. You can also access the home page by clicking the Etsy logo in the upper-left corner of each Etsy Marketplace page or by clicking the Home link in the header bar. The Etsy home page includes several sections. We delve into several of these sections in this chapter.

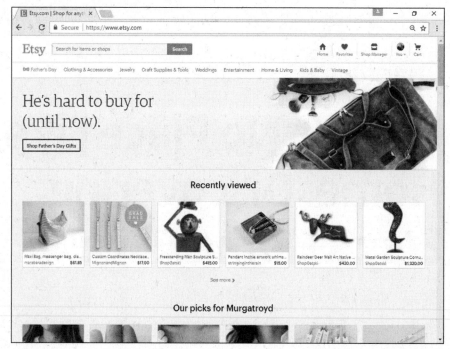

FIGURE 3-1:
The Etsy home page offers easy access to myriad site features, and it's easy on the eyes.

Source: Etsy.com

If your home page doesn't exactly match what we discuss here, don't freak out. Etsy regularly experiments with the layout of its home page.

REMEMBER

Tonight's Head(er)liner: Exploring the Header Bar

To enable you to easily access the tools you need, every Etsy Marketplace page, including the home page, contains a header bar with several links. The appearance of the header bar differs depending on whether you're signed in to your Etsy account. If you're *not* signed in, the header bar contains the following links:

>> **Etsy:** No matter where you are on the Etsy site, you can return to the home page by clicking the Etsy logo on the left side of the header bar.

>> **Sell on Etsy:** For quick access to tools and resources for sellers — including a helpful guide to how fees work and info about what you can and can't sell on Etsy — and to set up your own shop, click the Sell on Etsy link. (Parts 2 through 4 of this book are devoted to selling on Etsy.)

>> **Register:** Click this link to register with the site (see Chapter 2).

>> **Sign In:** If you already have an account, click the Sign In link to log on (see Chapter 2).

>> **Cart:** Click this link to view items in your shopping cart.

When you sign in to the site, the following links replace the Register and Sign In links (refer to Figure 3-1). (The Sell on Etsy link will remain until you create your Etsy shop, discussed in Chapter 8.)

>> **Home:** If you've navigated away from Etsy's home page to another page on the Etsy Marketplace site, you can click this link to return. (Or, as mentioned, you can click the Etsy logo in the upper-left corner of the header bar.)

>> **Favorites:** Etsy enables you to bookmark your favorite items and shops by adding them to your Favorites. To view your Favorites, click this link. For more on adding Favorites, see Chapter 22.

>> **Shop Manager:** After you set up your Etsy shop (see Chapter 8), this link appears in your header bar. It offers easy access to all the tools you need to manage your shop.

>> **You:** Access your Etsy account from this drop-down menu. Options include View Profile, Conversations, Purchases and Reviews, Account Settings, and

Your Teams. Or choose Sign Out to log off your Etsy account. (You get the scoop on managing your account in Chapter 4. For help with your profile, see Chapter 2.)

REMEMBER

The rest of this chapter assumes that you've signed in to your account and created your shop. (If you haven't yet, that's okay; just be aware that you may not see all the home-page features discussed here.)

Etsy's header bar includes one more important feature: a Search bar. When you know just what you're looking for — say, Kermit the Frog suspenders or a reclaimed barn wood unicycle — you can search for it here. Simply type in a relevant word or phrase and press Enter or Return on your keyboard or click the Search button. (For more info on searching, see Chapter 5.)

Category Eight: Browsing Etsy's Category Links

At last count, Etsy featured roughly 1.7 million active sellers, all with their own shops. Don't worry, though: The items in these shops are organized into broad categories — eight, to be exact — so you can easily find what you're looking for. Categories include Clothing & Accessories, Jewelry, Craft Supplies & Tools, Weddings, Entertainment, Home & Living, Kids & Baby, and Vintage.

Clicking a category reveals a menu of subcategories and even sub-subcategories to help you narrow the field, as shown in Figure 3-2. When you select one of these, Etsy displays listings for related items (see Figure 3-3). Whether you're after a bit of jewelry or some vintage awesomeness, Etsy's categories can help you find the item that's just right.

FIGURE 3-2: Drill down to the items you want to see.

Source: Etsy.com

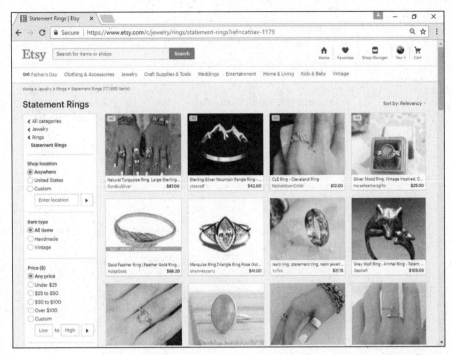

FIGURE 3-3:
Etsy displays
listings in the
chosen category,
subcategory, or
sub-subcategory.

Source: Etsy.com

But Wait! There's More! Exploring More Ways to Shop from Etsy's Home Page

Remember in *When Harry Met Sally. . .* how Sally had her own unique way of ordering at a restaurant? "I just want it the way I want it," she explained. The same is true with shopping on Etsy. Not everyone wants to do it in the same way! Fortunately, Etsy offers several ways to enhance your shopping experience, right from its home page.

Viewing personalized picks

Etsy's home page features a few special areas with listings just for you.

REMEMBER

Some of these areas may not appear, depending on whether you've viewed or favorited any listings or shops. If not, you may simply see an additional Categories section, which, like the links along the top of the page, offer easy access to various Etsy categories. The same goes if you're not signed in.

>> **Recently Viewed:** This section of the Etsy home page offers you quick access to the items you've viewed most recently. Simply click an item to open its listing. Or view additional items by clicking the See More link. (You'll see a similar link on several parts of the Etsy home page.)

>> **Recently Favorited:** Anything you've favorited lately appears in this part of the home page. Figure 3-4 shows the Recently Viewed and Recently Favorited parts of the Etsy home page.

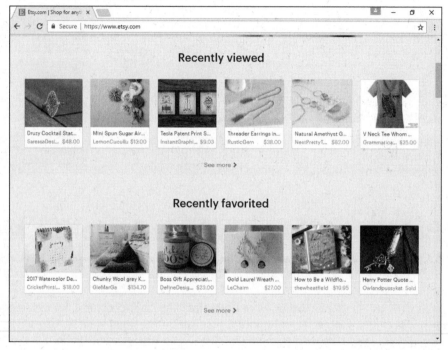

FIGURE 3-4:
Revisit recently viewed and recently favorited listings here.

>> **Our Picks for [You]:** Based on listings you've favorited, Etsy generates a personalized list of items that just may pique your interest.

>> **New from Your Favorite Shops:** Etsy doesn't limit you to favoriting listings. You can also favorite shops. When you do, fresh items from those shops appear on Etsy's home page. As always, simply click an item to open its listing.

TIP

You can also keep up with your favorite shops by perusing the Updates from Shops You Like feed. It's kind of like an Instagram feed. Shop owners use it to share news, reveal works in progress, highlight new items, and show different ways to use their products (among other things). Figure 3-5 shows the New from Your Favorite Shop and Updates from Shops You Like sections of the Etsy home page.

» **From People You Follow:** Etsy enables you to follow other site members, kind of like how you can follow people on, say, Twitter. For example, you could follow the owner of a shop you love or a friend you've made on the site. When someone you follow favorites an item on Etsy, that item appears in the From People You Follow area of the home page. (You can find out more about following people on Etsy in Chapter 22.)

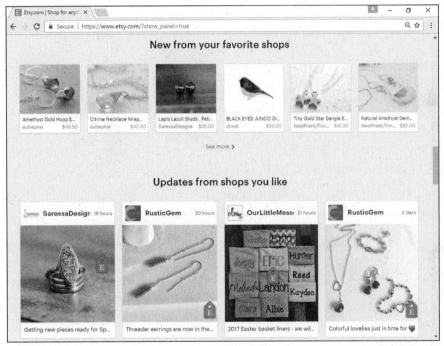

FIGURE 3-5: Keep up with shops you like.

Perusing more suggestions from Etsy

In addition to offering you personal picks, the Etsy home page includes sections with additional suggestions. You'll see the same suggestions regardless of who you are, whether you're signed in or not.

» **Shops Worth Exploring:** This section features a handful of shops that, in Etsy's estimation, deserve a look.

>> **Browse Our Latest Collections:** Here, you find links to collections compiled by Etsy's editors — or, as Etsy says, "daily discoveries from the most discerning and best-dressed people who work here." If the ones shown don't catch your interest, click the See More link.

>> **Shop for Gifts:** Not sure what to buy your dog for Valentine's Day? Check out the Shop for Gifts section. Here, you find links to yet more collections from Etsy's editors. Clicking See More reveals the One-of-a-Kind Gift Ideas page, which features several key gift-giving categories. Figure 3-6 shows the Browse Our Latest Collections and Shop for Gifts sections on the Etsy home page.

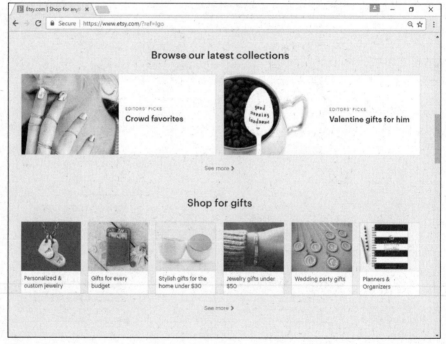

FIGURE 3-6: See listings hand-picked by Etsy's editors in the Browse Our Latest Collections and Shop for Gifts sections.

Source: Etsy.com

The Velvet Blog: Reading Etsy Blog Posts

To view new blog posts at a glance, scroll down to the Fresh from the Blog section of Etsy's home page (see Figure 3-7). There, you find headlines from newly posted content on the Etsy Blog, ranging from craft how-tos to tips for sellers and beyond. If you see a headline that looks interesting, click it to read the post.

Or click the Read the Blog link to land on the main page for the Etsy Blog, where you can access additional posts. (We discuss the Etsy Blog in more detail in Chapter 21).

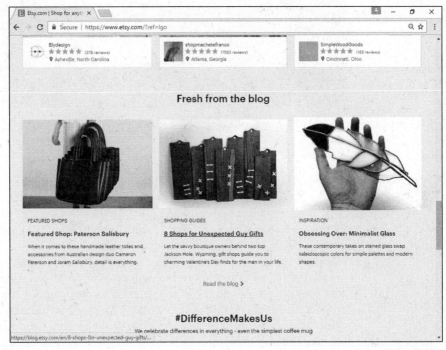

Source: Etsy.com

FIGURE 3-7: Keep up with the Etsy Blog.

Campaign Promises: Tracking Etsy Campaigns

From time to time, Etsy's home page features links to information about various campaign initiatives, like the one shown in Figure 3-8. This campaign, #DifferenceMakesUs, "celebrates the many ways that Etsy allows every one of us to express our originality." The campaign features a series of videos designed for dissemination on social media "to highlight how Etsy fits into the daily lives of people around the world." By the time you read this book, you may see a different campaign in action (or none at all).

FIGURE 3-8:
You may see links
to various
campaign
initiatives on
Etsy's home page.

#DifferenceMakesUs
We celebrate differences in everything - even the simplest coffee mug

Learn more ›

Say What? Discovering What Etsy Is

Want to get a better sense of what Etsy's all about? Click the Read All About It link in the What Is Etsy section of the home page (see Figure 3-9). This opens Etsy's Mission & Values page. It explains the "Etsy economy," provides a link to a progress report that tracks Etsy's "efforts to minimize the harm and maximize the benefit we create for people and the planet," and trumpets Etsy's status as a Certified B Corporation (meaning that an independent nonprofit organization, B Lab, has certified Etsy's "treatment of their workers, the benefit they provide to the community and the environment, and their overall governance and transparency").

What is Etsy?
We're more than a marketplace.
Read all about it ›

Get top trends and fresh editors' picks in your inbox with Etsy Finds.

Subscribe

FIGURE 3-9:
Find out more
about Etsy.

TIP

If you haven't signed up to receive Etsy Finds, Etsy's daily email that's chock-full of goodies for sale on the site, both the Etsy home page and the Mission & Values page feature a Subscribe link. Just click the link to subscribe. (You can even subscribe if you're not signed in to your account — you just have to type your email address in the provided field first.)

Playing Footsie: Exploring Footer Links

At the bottom of every Etsy Marketplace page, including the home page, you find a series of links to pretty much everything you may ever need to find on the site. As shown in Figure 3-10, these links are categorized as follows:

>> Sell on Etsy

>> Join the Community

>> Discover and Shop

>> Get to Know Us

>> Follow Etsy

Source: Etsy.com

You can also find a Help button in the bottom-right corner of the home page. Click it to search for help on the site. (For more on using Etsy's Help feature, see Chapter 23.)

Sell on Etsy

This category contains links to Etsy's Seller Handbook and to information about Etsy's credit card reader (used to accept credit card transactions with your tablet or smartphone). (Parts 3 and 4 of this book cover more about selling on Etsy and managing your shop.)

Join the community

For quick access to Etsy's community features — the teams and forums, as well as a list of upcoming events — check out the links in this section. You can also find links to info on becoming an Etsy affiliate and attending local events hosted by Etsy sellers. (Etsy affiliates are people who feature Etsy items on their own sites and earn commissions on items sold.)

Discover and shop

Attention, shoppers! This category has links to various shopping-related features:

>> **Gift Cards:** If you're in a giving mood, you'll love that Etsy offers gift cards. Available in denominations of $25, $50, $100, and $250, you can email these directly to the recipient or print them out for an in-person handoff. Whether you want to purchase a gift card or redeem one that someone else gave you (aren't you lucky?), start by clicking the Gift Card link under Discover and Shop.

>> **Blog:** The Etsy Blog is accessible from this link. When you click it, you see the same list of blog post headlines discussed earlier in this chapter.

>> **Mobile Apps:** If you have an Apple or Android device, you can enjoy Etsy on the go by downloading the Etsy Mobile app, accessible from this link. In addition to the Etsy Mobile app, there's also the Sell on Etsy app, which you can use to manage your Etsy store. If you're looking to unshackle yourself from your desk and venture out into the wide world, these apps are ideal. (We talk more about both of these apps throughout this book.)

>> **Gift Registries:** Etsy provides simple registry tools you can use to create a gift registry or to find someone else's. To access these tools, click the Gift Registries link.

>> **Wholesale:** Maybe you make things and you want those things to be available for purchase at real-world stores. Or maybe you own a real-world store and you want to sell things people make. Either way, this is the link for you. Click it to access all the information you need to sell or buy wholesale through Etsy.

>> **Search:** You'd think that clicking the Search link would open a page with tools to help you search for items on Etsy. But you'd be wrong. Instead, clicking Search opens Etsy's All Categories page, which you can use to drill down by category to the item you seek.

>> **Editors' Picks:** When you click this link, you open the same page that you do when you click the Browse Our Latest Collections link discussed earlier. Whoa, *déjà vu*!

Get to know us

Maybe you just want to find out a little bit more about Etsy. If so, you can use the links in this section. These links are as follows:

» **About:** For a general overview of Etsy, click this link. Etsy directs you to a page containing a brief history of the company, some key stats, the benefits of buying and selling on the site, and an FAQ.

» **Policies:** You can access Etsy's policies — what it calls its "House Rules" — from this link. (For more on Etsy's policies, check out Chapters 2 and 6.)

» **Careers:** We get it. Who *wouldn't* want to work for Etsy? Click this link if you're interested in exploring employment opportunities with the site.

» **Press:** This link directs you to a page tailor-made for journalists. It has press contact info, Etsy news, press releases, and reports. Or you can peruse recent stories about the site from outlets ranging from *Fortune* to the *Huffington Post*.

» **Developers:** Tons of tech-savvy types have built apps to improve your Etsy experience. For example, one app makes it easy to post your Etsy listings to your WordPress blog. Another helps you to streamline social media efforts for your store. If you're interested in contributing an app of your own, click this link to get started. It offers easy access to the Etsy API as well as to apps that are already available. (For more on Etsy apps, see Chapter 18.)

» **Investors:** In 2015, Etsy launched its initial public offering, making it a publicly traded company. If you've bought shares, click this link to stay in the loop.

Follow Etsy

Etsy maintains a strong presence on social media. To view its Facebook, Twitter, Pinterest, or Instagram page, click the corresponding link in this section. You can then choose to follow Etsy on those platforms (if you don't already).

'Appy Days: Exploring the Home Page on the Etsy App

Of course, you don't have to be tied to your computer to get the latest on Etsy. That's where the Etsy app comes in. If you have an Apple or Android device, you can download the Etsy app from the Apple App Store (iPhone and iPad) or Google Play (Android), install the app on your device, and access Etsy while you're on the go.

As shown in Figure 3-11, the home screen on the Etsy app looks a bit different from the one you see in your Internet browser, but it has many of the same features — personalized picks, Etsy editors' picks, recently viewed items, and so on. You'll quickly find that the Etsy app is remarkably easy to use!

FIGURE 3-11:
The Etsy app home screen looks different but offers many of the same features.

Source: Etsy.com

Chapter **4**

Account Trackula: Navigating Your Etsy Account and the Shop Manager

N ormally, when you create an account with a site, you manage it from one main set of screens. There, you update your password, change your privacy settings, update your credit card information, and so on. With Etsy, it's a little different. Instead of having one main set of screens to manage your account, you have two — one for you and one for your shop.

You access these two account-management tools from two separate links called — wait for it — You and Shop Manager. In this chapter, we show you the ins and outs of using several of the features accessible from these links to manage your account and your Etsy shop. (Other options are covered elsewhere in this book.)

Hey You! Exploring the You Menu

The You menu is your portal to all things . . . well, all things *you*. From this menu, shown in Figure 4-1, you can choose from the following options:

» **View Profile:** Select this option to populate your public profile. Your public profile is just what it sounds like: a page where other Etsy types can go to learn all about you. Maintaining a public profile is a big part of running a successful Etsy shop; after all, a big reason people shop on Etsy is to forge a personal connection with the people who make or design what they buy. For more on populating your public profile, check out Chapter 2.

» **Conversations:** When one Etsy user wants to communicate with another, she launches a conversation — *convo* for short — using Etsy's internal messaging system. To access and manage your convos or to start a new one, click the Conversations option in the You menu. We go into more about convos in Chapter 17.

» **Purchases and Reviews:** Etsy keeps track of everything you buy on the site. To view this information, open the You menu and choose Purchases and Reviews. For example, you might want to see your purchases to review the receipt for a particular item or to reconnect with the seller. See Chapter 5 for more about reviewing your purchases.

» **Account Settings:** On Etsy, viewing and changing your account settings is a breeze. Simply open the You menu and choose Account Settings. The page that appears includes several tabs, each with a series of settings and options to help you manage your account. We talk more about managing your account settings in the next section.

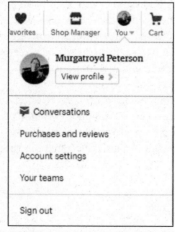

FIGURE 4-1:
The You menu is your starting point to manage your Etsy account.

Source: Etsy.com

>> **Your Teams:** Etsy enables its members to form or join teams. This helps them to connect with other members, share information, get advice, or just shoot the breeze. To explore Etsy teams, open the You menu and choose Your Teams. You can then search for teams that match your interests, access teams you've joined, or even start your own. Find out more about teams in Chapter 20.

Final Account-down: Managing Your Etsy Account

In the previous section, we mention that you access your Etsy account settings by opening the You menu and choosing Account Settings. This opens the Settings page shown in Figure 4-2.

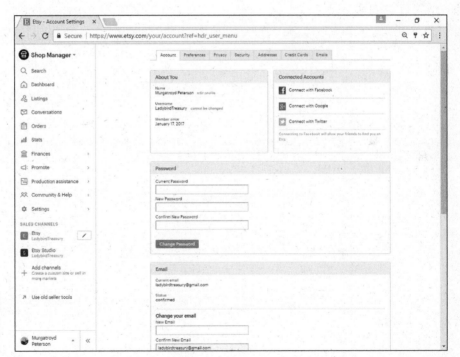

FIGURE 4-2:
You manage your Etsy account with the page shown here.

Source: Etsy.com

This page includes several tabs:

>> **Account:** This tab — the default — shown in Figure 4-2, is where you change your password and update your email account. You can also edit your public profile (click the Edit Profile link) and connect your Etsy account with your account on Facebook, Google, or Twitter so your friends can find you on the site (click Connect with Facebook, Connect with Google, or Connect with Twitter). For more on editing your public profile, see Chapter 2. Find out how to connect your Etsy account to Facebook, Google, and Twitter in Chapter 16.

>> **Preferences:** In the Preferences tab, shown in Figure 4-3, you establish your default language and currency. You also indicate your region (so Etsy can send you customized content) and whether you're open to receiving postal mail and/or phone calls from Etsy. If you change any settings in the Preferences tab, simply click the Update Preferences button at the bottom of the page to enact them.

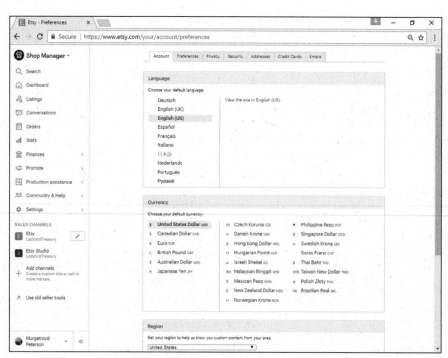

FIGURE 4-3:
The Preferences tab.

Source: Etsy.com

>> **Privacy:** Privacy is important! That's why Etsy includes a pair of settings to protect yours. One of these settings pertains to findability and the other to your Etsy browsing history. You can change them both from the Privacy tab, shown in Figure 4-4. For more on protecting your privacy on Etsy, see Chapter 6.

FIGURE 4-4:
The Privacy tab.

>> **Security:** Related to privacy is security. On Etsy, you can help ensure your security by enabling two-factor authentication, sign-in notifications, and the ability to view recent sign-ins and sign-outs. These settings appear in the Security tab, shown in Figure 4-5. Discover more about security on Etsy in Chapter 6.

FIGURE 4-5:
The Security tab.

>> **Addresses:** To add a new shipping address, edit an existing one, remove an old one, or change the default, visit the Addresses tab, shown in Figure 4-6.

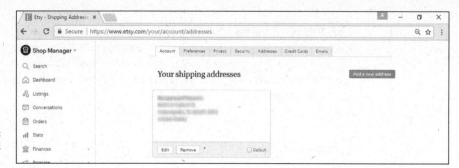

Source: Etsy.com

>> **Credit Cards:** This tab, shown in Figure 4-7, enables you to manage any credit cards you've used to purchase items on Etsy. Although you can't use this tab to enter a new credit card — that option is available only when you purchase an item on Etsy — you can use it to edit or remove any existing cards as well as set a default card.

Source: Etsy.com

>> **Emails:** When it comes to receiving emails, Etsy gives you lots of choices. Some relate to notifications. For example, you may choose to be notified when someone sends you a convo. Others are newsletters, including several that pertain to shopping. But there are lots of other options, too. You select which emails you want to receive from the Emails tab, shown in Figure 4-8. For more on receiving emails from Etsy, see Chapter 21.

If you've already set up your Etsy shop, you'll also see a Taxpayer ID tab. We touch on this tab in Chapter 18.

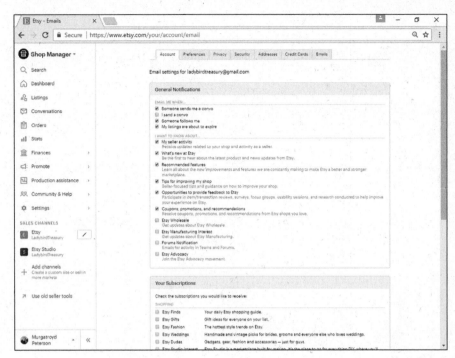

Source: Etsy.com

FIGURE 4-8:
The Emails tab.

Shop Talk: Familiarizing Yourself with the Shop Manager

The You menu is, well, all about you — your purchases, your account settings, and so on. In contrast, the Shop Manager is, you guessed it, all about your shop.

Figure 4-9 shows the main Shop Manager page, or *dashboard*. It offers an overview of your shop, including orders, conversations, stats, and recent activity. With the Shop Manager dashboard, you can easily see where you are with your shop and what you need to do next, whether it's ship an item that sold, reply to a convo, or take note to make more of a popular item.

The links on the left side of the Shop Manager page allow access to other shop-related tools. Using these tools, you can manage shop listings, engage in convos with buyers (and other Etsy users), track orders, check shop statistics, handle shop finances, promote your shop, find production assistance, engage in the Etsy seller community, change shop settings, and explore additional sales channels.

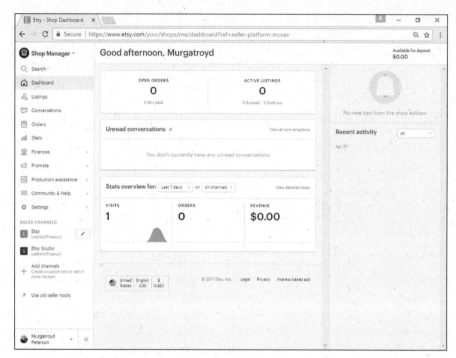

Source: Etsy.com

FIGURE 4-9:
The Shop
Manager
dashboard.

Managing your listings

Click the Listings link in the Shop Manager to open the Listings page. Here, you add new listings and manage existing ones. You find out how to create and manage listings in Chapter 13.

Accessing conversations

The You menu is one place to access, manage, and launch Etsy convos — but it's not the *only* place. You can also do this from within Shop Manager. We talk more about convos in Chapter 17.

Handling orders

When you want to view open, completed, or canceled orders, you click the Orders link in Shop Manager. (See Chapters 14 and 15 for details.)

Retrieving statistics

Etsy Shop Stats enable you to track all sorts of information about your shop, like shop traffic, which listings command the most attention for prospective buyers, and more. To retrieve these statistics, click the Stats link in Shop Manager.

Checking your Etsy finances

You know what they say: There's no such thing as a free lunch. In other words, if you opt to sell on Etsy, you have to pony up each month. To see how much you owe and settle your debt, click the Finances link in Shop Manager to open a menu of options and choose Your Bill.

In addition to options that relate to *spending* money, the Finances menu also contains choices that relate to *receiving* it. For example, you can choose Payment Account to see money you've received from customers via Etsy Payments and transfer that money to your bank account. Or you can select Payment Settings to specify what types of payments you're willing to accept, set your sales tax info, choose your currency, enter your credit card info, and set your mailing address (for payments sent via post).

Finally, if you want to get serious about accounting, you can choose the Quick-Books for Etsy option in the Finances menu to connect your Etsy shop to Quick-Books Self-Employed, which offers you a simple and straightforward way to become a bookkeeping boss.

REMEMBER

If you've set up your Etsy shop, you'll also see a Taxpayer ID option in the Finances menu. Select this option to enter or change your taxpayer ID.

For more on paying your Etsy bill and managing incoming cash, see Chapter 18.

Promoting your shop

With literally millions of Etsy shops for buyers to choose among, making yours stand out is imperative. The Promote link in Shop Manager provides easy access to tools to help you achieve just that. For example, you can use these tools to do the following:

» Create Etsy and Google ads.

» Generate coupon codes.

» Post shop updates.

These tools are major topics of conversation in Chapter 16.

Finding a production partner

Maybe your Etsy shop is going like gangbusters and you need a little help to stay on top of demand. Enter Etsy Manufacturing. Etsy Manufacturing matches designers with Etsy-approved manufacturers to produce their designs. To use Etsy Manufacturing, click the Production Assistance link and select Find a Partner from the menu that appears. The Production Assistance menu also includes a Manage Projects option (to manage any projects you launch with a production partner) and a Getting Started option (to step you through the manufacturing process and help you assess whether you're ready to expand with a partner). For more on Etsy Manufacturing, see Chapter 19.

Learning more

Look, we'll be honest: Starting and running an Etsy shop is not terribly difficult. But that doesn't mean you won't find yourself a bit lost every so often. Fortunately, Shop Manager can connect you to various resources, including Etsy teams and Etsy forums (covered in Chapter 20), Etsy's Help page (see Chapter 23), the Seller Handbook (also discussed in Chapter 23), shipping help (see Chapter 15), and site policies (major topics in Chapters 6 and 7). You can also review any cases reported by you (covered in Chapter 5) or about your shop (see Chapter 17), peruse special apps to help you manage your shop (discussed in Chapter 18), or contact Etsy. You access all these options from the Community & Help link in Shop Manager.

Changing shop settings

Shop Manager offers several tools for changing shop settings. To access these tools, click the Settings link in Shop Manager. A menu appears with the following options:

>> **Info and Appearance:** Choose this option to access settings that enable you to change the look and feel of your shop and to broadcast info about your shop and its policies (covered in Chapters 8 and 9).

>> **About Your Shop:** Select this choice to add shop members (that is, anyone who helps to make the things you sell or to run the shop — including you). You can also choose to share a "shop story" and list any manufacturers you partner with. For more on these settings, see Chapter 8.

- » **Options:** Pick this menu item to set certain shop-related settings, like how your shop is arranged, whether you accept custom orders, whether your listings are automatically translated into other languages, and whether your shop displays items that have been sold. (For more on these options, see Chapter 8.) It also gives you access to tools like shop data and web analytics, as well as options to shutter your shop either temporarily or permanently. These topics are covered in Chapter 18.

- » **Shipping Settings:** Choose this option to set your shipping policies—including creating new shipping profiles, indicating your package preferences, and specifying rates and upgrades. For more on shipping settings, see Chapter 15.

- » **Production Partners:** If you decide to enter into a relationship with a production partner, you must list them on your Etsy shop. To do so, select Production Partners from the Settings menu in Shop Manager. For more on working with production partners, see Chapter 19.

- » **Shopping Engine Ads:** A *shopping engine* is an online tool that enables consumers to find and compare products from different retailers. You can opt to list your own items in these shopping engines to pull in buyers from outside Etsy. To do so, choose the Shopping Engine Ads option in the Shop Manager Settings menu. For more on shopping engine ads, see Chapter 16.

Adding sales channels

Problem: You want to expand your brand beyond Etsy, but you don't want to give up your Etsy shop. Solution: Add a new sales channel by clicking Add Channels under Sales Channels in Shop Manager. From there, you can opt to use a tool called Pattern to build a website for your shop — one that's separate from Etsy. Or you can opt to expand your shop to sell on Etsy Studio — a sister site for craft supplies. For more on Pattern and Etsy Studio, see Chapter 19.

Chapter **5**

Buy and Buy: Finding and Purchasing Items on Etsy

Y ou've set up your Etsy account. You've gotten your bearings on the Etsy home page. You've explored your account and shop settings. After all that work, you deserve a break! You know as well as we do that there's no better way to recharge than to engage in a little retail therapy. And there's no better way to engage in a little retail therapy than to shop — you guessed it — on Etsy. In this chapter, you discover how and why to buy on Etsy.

Gimme One Reason: Understanding Why You Should Buy on Etsy

Why buy on Etsy? Simple: Where else are you going to find a handmade bracelet featuring images of *The Golden Girls* cast in resin? Of course, even if you don't maintain a shrine to Rue McClanahan in your foyer, you can find plenty of compelling reasons to buy on Etsy. Consider just a few:

» Etsy features loads of unique, one-of-a-kind handmade and vintage items — goodies you simply can't find anywhere else.

>> Etsy offers an incredible breadth of items for sale, from accessories to ceramics, from jewelry to quilts, and everything in between.

>> If you're in the market for craft supplies, Etsy is for you. At last count, Etsy's Supplies category listed more than 7.5 million items, including beads, buttons, fabric, yarn, paper, stamps, and more.

TIP

For even more craft supplies, visit Etsy Studio (www.etsystudio.com). In addition to offering every type of craft supply you could conceivably want, this new site also publishes boatloads of DIY projects with direct links to the supplies you need to complete them.

>> Many sellers on Etsy are artists and craftspeople. When you buy directly from them, you cut out the middleman — meaning prices on Etsy are generally reasonable. At the same time, your purchase helps these skilled artisans earn a living wage.

>> Buying on Etsy can make you a savvier seller. As a customer, you'll develop an eye for which selling practices work and which don't.

Go Fish: Using Etsy's Search Tool

If you've landed on Etsy with the idea of finding a specific item or certain pieces that relate to a particular theme — say, snowflakes — you'll be grateful for the site's robust Search tool. You can also use it to locate a particular shop. To use the Search tool, follow these steps:

1. **Type a keyword or phrase in the Search field that appears in the header bar of every Etsy Marketplace page.**

   As you type your keyword or phrase, Etsy displays links for items or shop names that may constitute a good match (see Figure 5-1).

FIGURE 5-1:
Type a keyword or phrase in the Search field.

2. **If one of the search suggestions matches what you're looking for, click it to view a list of relevant items. Or click the Search button or press the Enter or Return key on your keyboard.**

   Etsy returns a list of items that match your criteria. (See Figure 5-2.)

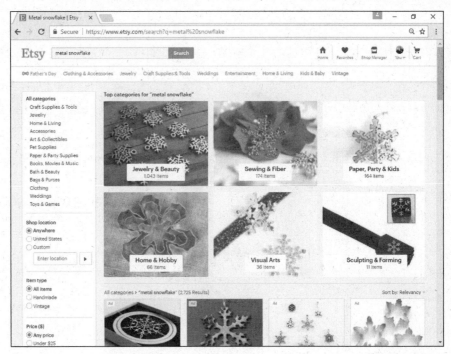

FIGURE 5-2:
Etsy displays your
search results.

3. **To refine your search, you can click a relevant category link on the left side of the page.**

Etsy displays only those items that match your search criteria and the category you chose.

4. **You can refine your search further by specifying a shop location, item type, price range, or color.**

You can also specify that the search results display only items that are in your Favorites, that are from shops that accept gift cards, or that are customizable, and you can also specify that search results show only those items that can be shipped to a specific country of your choosing.

5. **To sort the search results, click the Sort By down arrow and choose Most Recent, Relevancy, Highest Price, or Lowest Price.**

Etsy sorts your matches.

6. **Click an item in the list to view the item's listing.**

Etsy opens the listing, as shown in Figure 5-3.

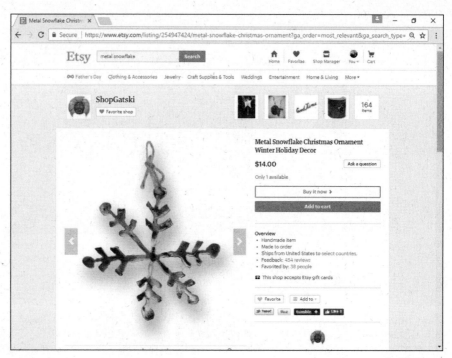

FIGURE 5-3:
Open the listing.

Source: Etsy.com

TIP

If your search efforts fail to yield useful results — for example, Etsy returns too many matches — try these techniques:

>> **To search for a specific phrase, surround it with quotation marks.** For example, say you want to find items related to the film *Roman Holiday.* Searching for the phrase *Roman Holiday,* without quotation marks, returns pages that contain the phrase *Roman Holiday.* However, it also returns pages that simply contain the individual words *Roman* and *holiday,* which likely have nothing whatsoever to do with Audrey Hepburn's romp across Roma. Enclosing the phrase in quotation marks ("Roman Holiday") limits the results to pages that contain that phrase only.

>> **To exclude pages with a certain word from your results, precede the word you want to exclude with a hyphen.** For example, suppose you want to find listings that pertain to mustangs (as in, the horses). To omit listings that relate to the Ford Mustang automobile, you could add *-Ford* to the search string. (***Note:*** There is no space between the hyphen and the word.)

REQUESTING A CUSTOM ITEM

Want a special, one-of-a-kind piece? Your favorite Etsy shopkeeper may be able to accommodate you. To find out, see whether the shop features a Request Custom Item link, located in the Shop Info section on the left side of the shop's main page. If so, click it to launch a convo with the seller about the item you'd like to commission. Don't see a Request Custom Item link? Then you can always launch a convo with the seller to inquire. Many shop owners on Etsy are open to special projects.

TIP

Searching is great when you know what you're looking for. But what if you just want to poke around the site? In that case, you'll enjoy Etsy's many browsing-related features on its home page. These include category links, Recently Viewed, Recently Favorited, Our Picks for [You], Browse Our Latest Collections, Shop for Gifts, New from Your Favorite Shops, Shops Worth Exploring, and From People You Know. (For more info on these features, see Chapter 3.) Or maybe you're fond of a particular shop. In that case, you can simply visit its main page to scroll through what's on offer.

Transaction Oriented: Delving into Transaction Details

As you browse or search the gazillion items available for sale on Etsy, you're bound to find a thing or two (or 7,968) that you simply can't live without. Fortunately, Etsy makes buying a breeze. As you find out in the following sections, all you do is add the item to your cart, check out, arrange for payment, and submit your order.

To add an item to your cart and commence checking out, follow these steps:

1. **Click the Add to Cart button found on the listing page for the item you want to buy (refer to Figure 5-3).**

Etsy displays your shopping cart (see Figure 5-4).

TIP

Suppose that you are absolutely positively sure you want the item. In that case, you can click Buy It Now instead of Add to Cart. This enables you to bypass the cart to speed up the purchase process. (This assumes that you've already set up your preferred payment method.)

CONFIRMING THAT A SELLER IS ON THE UP AND UP

You'll find that the vast majority of sellers on Etsy are stand-up people. Still, no one likes to get burned by a bad sale. You can avoid this by taking a moment to view the seller's reviews *before* you buy. To do so, click the stars on the tab next to Item Details in the product listing or on the shop's main page. (To access the shop's main page, click the shop's name in the upper-left corner of the product listing.) If the seller boasts positive feedback, you can feel confident buying from her. If not, you may want to reconsider your purchase. (You find out more about reviews later in this chapter.)

To gain even more confidence in the seller, check out her shop's About section and her public profile. To open the About section, click the About link above the shop announcement. To view the public profile, click the seller's name or photo in the upper-right corner of the shop.

Finally, it doesn't hurt to take a gander at the store's policies. To do so, click the Shipping & Policies tab in the product listing (to the right of the tab that contains reviews) or the Policies link above the shop announcement on the shop's main page.

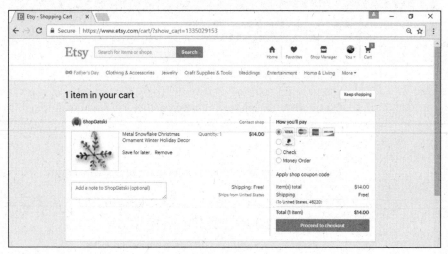

FIGURE 5-4:
The item appears in your shopping cart.

2. **If you want to continue shopping, click the Keep Shopping button.**

   You can return to your cart at any time by clicking the Cart link that appears in the header bar along the top of every Etsy Marketplace page.

Got cold feet? No worries. You can remove the item from your cart by clicking the Remove link in the shopping cart page. Or if you *think* you want the item but you're not 100 percent sure, click the Save for Later link. The next time you open your shopping cart, you'll have the option to move the item back into it. (Alternatively, you can move the items to your Favorites or remove it.) What if you're *pretty* sure you want the item, but you have some questions about it? In that case, click the Contact Shop link (above the item price) to launch a convo with the shop owner. (Flip to Chapter 17 for the scoop on convos.)

3. **Under How You'll Pay, indicate how you want to pay for the item.**

    Options include credit card, PayPal, check, money order, or Etsy gift card. (Note that the options you see may vary, depending on what forms of payment the shop owner accepts.)

Some Etsy sellers issue coupon codes for their shops. If you have a coupon code for the shop you're buying from (maybe you grabbed one from a blog, or it could be the seller posted it in her Etsy shop), click the Apply Shop Coupon Code link in the How You'll Pay section of the cart, enter the code in the Coupon Code field that appears, and click the Apply button. Etsy updates your order total.

4. **If you want, type a note to the seller in the Notes section.**

    Adding a note is important if you want to make a special request or you have a unique specification. In addition, some sellers request that you leave specifics about your order here — for example, personalization information.

    Note: When you purchase some items, you'll be prompted to supply additional information, such as size, quantity, or color.

5. **Click the Proceed to Checkout button.**

    Note that the exact verbiage on this button differs depending on which payment method you choose in Step 3. That is, it says *Proceed to Checkout* if you selected the credit card, check, or money order payment option. But if you chose PayPal, the button will change to read *Check Out with PayPal*.

What if your shopping cart contains items from multiple shops? As long as those shops accept Etsy Payments, then you can complete the checkout process just once. If, however, any of the shops don't accept Etsy Payments, you'll have to complete the checkout process for each of those shops separately.

What happens next depends on three things:

» **Whether this is your first purchase on Etsy:** If this is your maiden Etsy purchase, congratulations! You're one of us now! You'll be prompted to enter your shipping address and, if you selected a credit card as your payment method, your payment details. (You'll have to do this only once. The next time you buy something on Etsy, it'll apply this same info automatically.) After you do so, you'll land on the Review and Submit Your Order page (see Figure 5-5).

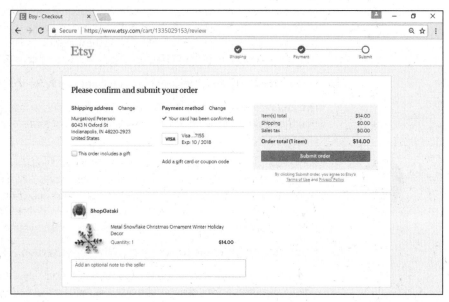

FIGURE 5-5:
Review your
order here.

PAYING WITH AN ETSY GIFT CARD

Did someone give you an Etsy gift card? They must really like you! To redeem it, click the Add a Gift Card or Coupon Code link in the Review and Submit Your Order page and enter the code in the field that appears. Alternatively, follow these steps:

1. **Scroll down to the footer area of any Etsy Marketplace page and click the Gift Cards link under Discover and Shop.**

2. **The Etsy Gift Cards page opens. Click the Redeem a Gift Card button at the top of the page.**

3. **Enter the 16-digit code on the gift card and click Apply Now.**

To check your gift card balance, open the You menu. Etsy automatically applies this balance to any future purchases you make at Etsy shops that accept Etsy gift cards. If the gift card balance doesn't cover the entire purchase, you can make up the difference by using another form of payment.

>> **Whether you plan to pay by credit card, gift card, check, or money order:** If this is *not* your first Etsy purchase and you opted to pay by credit card, gift card, check, or money order, you'll be sent right to the aforementioned Review and Submit Your Order page.

TIP

If you opted to pay via check or money order, launch a convo with the seller to make the appropriate arrangements after you complete the sale. (See Chapter 17 for the full scoop on convos.)

>> **Whether you want to pay using PayPal:** If this is not your first Etsy purchase and you opted to pay by using PayPal, you'll first be directed to the PayPal website. Enter your login info and review your info — your shipping address and the account you'll use to pay for the item — and change it if needed. Then click Continue. You, too, will be directed to the Review and Submit Your Order page.

TIP

Don't have a PayPal account? Don't worry. Setting one up is as easy as pie. You can even do it from Etsy during the checkout process. Simply choose PayPal as your payment method and click the Check Out with PayPal button. Then, when you're prompted to pay, follow the onscreen instructions to register for a PayPal account.

Before you submit your order, take a moment to review the order summary:

>> If the shipping address shown isn't correct, click the Change link next to the Shipping Address heading. Then choose the address you want to use or add a new one.

>> If you opted to pay by credit card and the credit card shown isn't the one you want to use, click the Change link next to the Payment Method heading, select the card you want to use, and click Use This Card. Or, add a new card.

>> If you want to choose a different payment method — for example, switch from credit card to check or whatever — click the Back button in your browser to return to your cart and choose the method you want to use.

If your order details check out, click the Submit Order button. In addition to displaying a confirmation screen, Etsy emails you to confirm your order. All you have left to do is install yourself in the proximity of your mailbox until your item arrives.

TIP

While you wait for your purchase to arrive, you may need to review your order information. To do so, open the You menu and choose Purchases and Reviews. As shown in Figure 5-6, your item will be listed among any other purchases you've made. This item listing includes some helpful info. For example, if the seller left you a note about the transaction — how long the order might take to reach you or other helpful info — you'll see it here. You can also see whether the item has been shipped. If so, you'll see a Track Package button; click it to check its status. Finally, you can click View Receipt to view transaction details, or click Contact the Shop to launch a convo.

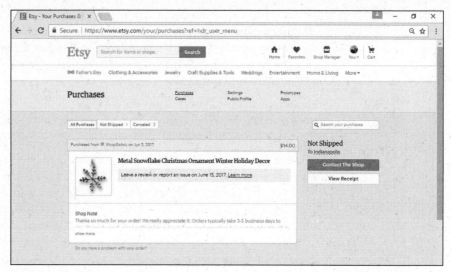

FIGURE 5-6:
This screen keeps you apprised of the status of your order.

A Review to a Kill: Leaving a Review After You Buy

After you receive your item, take a moment to leave a review about the transaction. It's easy! All you have to do is rate the sale on a scale of one to five stars (with five being fantastic and one being, like, the *worst*). You can also leave a comment about the transaction. Other Etsy users can view this feedback to determine whether a particular seller is reliable.

REMEMBER

Your review affects your seller's feedback score — and, by extension, her reputation on the site. It's super-important that you issue reviews consistently, fairly, and honestly.

Although leaving a review is purely optional, doing so is a good idea because it helps ensure that everyone feels safe shopping on Etsy. Note that you cannot leave a review until the estimated delivery date has passed. Once it does, you have 60 days to leave a review.

To leave a review, follow these steps:

1. **Open the You menu in the header bar and choose Purchases and Reviews.**

   The Purchases page opens.

2. **Locate the purchase you want to review and click the number of stars you want to leave as your rating.**

3. A Write a Review dialog box opens (see Figure 5-7). Type a comment about the item, transaction, or seller, and click Post Your Review.

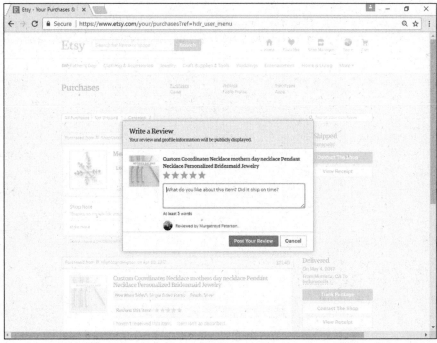

FIGURE 5-7:
Optionally, leave a comment about the item, transaction, or seller.

If you use the Etsy app, you can take a photo of the item to upload for the seller. Sellers often like to see their items in their new habitats!

TIP

If you've had a negative experience with a seller, see whether you can hammer out whatever issue is bothering you via email or a convo before you toss the bad-review grenade her way. Often, conflicts on Etsy are simply the result of a misunderstanding.

Case in Point: Filing a Case Against a Seller

Suppose that you ordered a Mr. T tea towel, but it never arrives! Or it arrives, but it does not match its description. What then?

First, you should launch a convo with the Etsy seller. Odds are, you've been on the pointy end of a simple mistake or misunderstanding — one that's easily rectified. But if that doesn't work, then you can file a case against the seller.

To file a case, follow these steps:

1. **Open the You menu in the header bar and choose Purchases and Reviews.**

2. **Find the transaction and click the I Haven't Received This Item or the Item Isn't As Described link, depending on your situation (see Figure 5-8).**

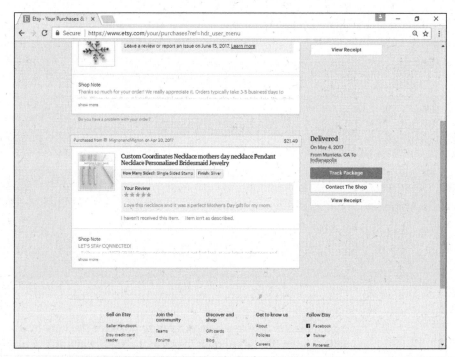

Source: Etsy.com

FIGURE 5-8:
Click the link that describes your situation.

REMEMBER

Don't see a link? It could be that it's too early — or too late — to file a case. Once you become eligible to file a case, you have up to 60 days to do so. To calculate eligibility, Etsy adds the seller's estimated processing time (as specified in the item listing) and the number of days it will likely take the item to reach its destination after it is shipped (two weekdays if the buyer and seller are in the same country or ten weekdays if they are not).

3. **Click the Report This to Etsy by Opening a Case link.**

The Open a Case screen appears (see Figure 5-9).

4. **Specify your reason for filing the case.**

5. **If you are reporting an item that is not as it was described, upload one or more photos of the item to show the difference between it and its description.**

Open a Case

If you are not able to resolve your issue with the seller, you can open a case with Etsy. This files a formal report with Etsy where we will assist you and the seller in reaching a resolution.

Metal Snowflake Christmas Ornament Winter Holiday Decor

Price $14.00

Quantity 1

Choose a resolution and add a note for ShopGatski:

How would you like the seller to help you?

I would still like to receive t ▾

Please provide any additional information that may help resolve this issue.

Thank you for resolving this problem.

Maximum 900 characters, 263 remaining

Submit   Cancel

FIGURE 5-9:
Open a case against the seller.

6. **Indicate what you would like to do to resolve the problem.**

   Optionally, you can add a note in the Choose a Resolution section to add more details either about the reported item or how you'd like to resolve the problem.

7. **Click Submit.**

To view the status of your case, follow these steps:

1. **Open Shop Manager, click Community & Help along the left side of the dashboard, and choose Cases.**

   The Your Cases page opens. By default, you'll see any open cases reported by you. (See Figure 5-10.)

2. **Click the link for the case to view details about the case (see Figure 5-11).**

3. **Use the Add Comment box to communicate directly with the seller about the case.**

If you and the seller come to an agreement that is amenable to you, you can close your case. To do so, simply click the Close Case button (see Figure 5-11). Etsy asks you to confirm that you want to close the case; simply click the Submit button to proceed. When you do, both you and the seller will receive an email confirming that the case is closed.

FIGURE 5-10:
View your cases here.

An item did not arrive

Case #104872675797 — Opened on February 15, 2017

Thanks for letting us know there was an issue with your order. The shop, ShopGatski, should be in touch soon. If your case hasn't been resolved by February 23, 2017, you can escalate it to Trust and Safety for review. If you feel your issue has been resolved, please close the case.

Learn more about Etsy's case system.

Your ideal resolution is receiving the item.
Thank you for resolving this problem.

Close Case

Reported Transactions

Feb 2, 2017
$14.00 View Receipt

Not Shipped

Metal Snowflake Christmas Ornament Winter Holiday Decor

Price	Quantity
$14.00	1

Shipped To
Murgatroyd Peterson
6043 N. Oxford St.
Indianapolis, IN 46220
United States

Case created   February 15, 2017

Murgatroyd Peterson from ☆ LadybirdTreasury says:

FIGURE 5-11:
View details about your case.

If, after seven days, the case remains unresolved, you can escalate it. When you escalate a case, you submit it to Etsy for review. At that point, Etsy will review the case and take what action it deems necessary. (Note that if you do not escalate your case, it may be closed automatically.)

Note: Although Etsy can refund your money if you paid using Etsy Payments, it can't if you paid via, say, PayPal. In that case, you may want to contact PayPal directly for help.

Chapter **6**

Safe Word: Maintaining Privacy and Safety on Etsy

On Etsy, as in life, safety is paramount. Just as you wear a seat belt when you drive, a helmet while on your bike, and knee pads during roller derby, you must take the appropriate steps to remain safe on Etsy. In this chapter, you discover the precautions you must take to ensure your security and maintain your privacy on Etsy.

Oh, Behave! Adhering to Etsy's House Rules

REMEMBER

Every Etsy member must make it a point to peruse the site's Our House Rules page (see Figure 6-1). This page links to everything you need to do to avoid committing a potentially embarrassing gaffe on the site. To view this page, click the Help button in the bottom-right corner of any Etsy Marketplace page to open the Help page, scroll down to the Still Have Questions? section, and click the Read Our Site

Policies link. Alternatively, scroll to the bottom of any Etsy Marketplace page and click the Policies link in the Get to Know Us section in the footer area.

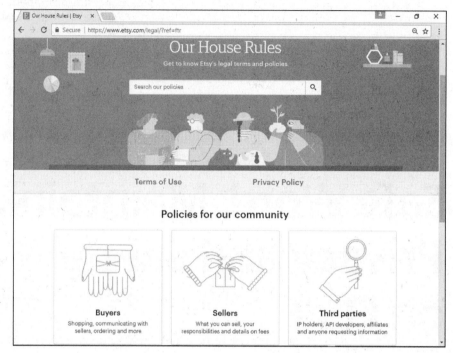

Source: Etsy.com

FIGURE 6-1:
The Our House
Rules page.

The Our House Rules page contains a link to the site's terms of use (discussed in Chapter 2) and its privacy policy (discussed in the next section). In addition, you'll see the following links:

» **Buyers:** Click the Buyers link on the Our House Rules page to access links to policies that pertain to shopping, communicating with sellers, ordering, and more. These include the Buyer Policy, Anti-Discrimination Policy, Community Policy, Etsy Gift Cards & Etsy Credits Policy, Etsy Payments Policy, Etsy Wholesale Buyer Policy, and Sanctions Policy.

» **Sellers:** For access to seller policies, click the Sellers link. Seller policies include the Seller Policy, Advertising Policy, Anti-Discrimination Policy, Community Policy, Etsy Gift Cards & Etsy Credits Policy, Etsy Payments Policy, Etsy Wholesale Seller Policy, Fees & Payments Policy, Handmade Policy, Intellectual Property Policy, Manufacturing Policy, Pattern Policy, Prohibited Items Policy, Sanctions Policy, Sell on Etsy App & Reader Policy, Seller Protection Policy, Seller Referrals Policy, and Shipping Policy.

>> **Third Parties:** These are policies for intellectual property (IP) holders, API developers, affiliates, and others. They include an Intellectual Property Policy, Affiliates Policy, Anti-Discrimination Policy, API Terms of Use, Requests for Information Policy, and Sanctions Policy.

Private Party: Guarding Your Privacy on Etsy

Just because you're on Etsy doesn't mean you want everyone there all up in your business. Fortunately, Etsy takes your privacy seriously.

TIP

If you're particularly concerned about maintaining your privacy, consider using a post office box as your address when conducting business on Etsy. That way, even when you buy or sell an item on the site, your home or work address remains private.

Understanding Etsy's Privacy Policy

Like all reputable websites, Etsy maintains rigorous standards with respect to privacy. Etsy outlines these standards in its privacy policy, which you access by clicking the Privacy Policy link on the Our House Rules page. In broad terms, these standards relate to the following:

>> **Information collected or received:** This portion of the privacy policy outlines what personal info you must provide to the site and what info will be visible to other users. It also notes the various tracking technologies used by the site to collect information about you and your activity on the site.

>> **Uses and sharing:** This section of the policy explains the various ways Etsy uses and shares your personal information — both the information you supply and the information it gathers about you. For example, if you buy something on Etsy, the site shares your shipping info with the seller. In addition, the site uses data analytics for targeted marketing.

>> **Choices:** In this part of the privacy policy, Etsy spells out what choices you have with respect to your personal information and how you receive communications from Etsy.

Changing your privacy settings

Etsy's all about DIY. That's why it gives you two key settings to enable you to take control of your privacy on the site:

>> **Findability:** You can limit your findability by hiding your info from other Etsy members who use Etsy's Find Your Friends feature to find real-world friends on the site.

>> **Recently viewed listings:** As we share in Chapter 3, Etsy displays recently viewed listings on the home page. If you want to clear those listings (maybe you were looking for a birthday present for a family member and you don't want to tip your hand, or maybe you'd rather not be reminded about that recent Barry Manilow–related search), you can easily do so. Your recently viewed listings will be removed, but listings you view in the future will be recorded.

To change these settings, follow these steps:

1. **Open the You menu in the header bar along the top of any Etsy Marketplace page and choose Account Settings.**

2. **Click the Privacy tab at the top of the page (see Figure 6-2).**

FIGURE 6-2:
Change your privacy settings.

3. **In the Findability section, select the No option button to prevent other Etsy members from finding you by entering your email address.**

4. **To clear recently viewed listings, click the Clear Recently Viewed Listings button.**

You can also keep your Favorites private. To find out how, see Chapter 22.

Choosing a strong password

When you set up your Etsy account, you're prompted to select a password to prevent others from accessing your account (see Chapter 2 for details). Unfortunately, many people opt for decidedly lame passwords — their birthdays, their kids' names, the word *password*, or something equally easy to guess.

To ensure that no one accesses your account without your authorization, you need to set a strong password. A strong password is at least eight characters long, doesn't contain your username or your real name, doesn't contain a complete word, differs from passwords you've used in the past, and contains a mixture of uppercase letters, lowercase letters, numbers, symbols, and spaces.

WARNING

Don't use the same password on multiple sites. Otherwise, if someone figures out your password for one site, that person will have access to all your online accounts. For an added layer of protection, you need to periodically change your password — ideally, every 30 to 90 days.

To change your password, follow these steps:

1. **Open the You menu in the header bar along the top of any Etsy Marketplace page and choose Account Settings.**

   The Settings page opens with the Account tab displayed (see Figure 6-3).

FIGURE 6-3:
Change your Etsy password on this page.

Source: Etsy.com

2. **In the Password section of the Account tab, type your current password in the Current Password field.**

3. **In the New Password field, type your new password.**

4. **Retype your new password in the Confirm New Password field.**

5. **Click the Change Password button.**

TIP

If you're worried about forgetting your password, you can write it down — but make sure you store it somewhere safe and private. If you forget your password *and* where you wrote it down, you can enter the email address you used to set up your account on this page: www.etsy.com/forgot_password.php. If you forget your password *and* where you wrote it down *and* the email address you used to set up your account, you'll have to contact Etsy at support@etsy.com to ask for help (after upping your daily dose of *Ginkgo biloba,* of course).

REMEMBER

If you've signed in to your Etsy account using a public computer — for example, one at your local library or in an Internet cafe — be sure you sign out when you're finished. Otherwise, the next person who uses that computer will be privy to your account information.

Safe Passage: Keeping Yourself Safe on Etsy

The good news is, since its inception in 2005, the Etsy community has grown like Shaquille O'Neal in the ninth grade — in other words, a lot. Unfortunately, that growth has made the site all the more attractive to scammers and flimflammers, not to mention just plain jerks. In this section, you find out how to keep yourself safe on the site.

Avoiding scams on Etsy

Etsy isn't just home to artists and crafters; it also features the occasional con artist and shafter. As you use Etsy, be on the lookout for scams.

On Etsy, most fraudulent activities involve the use of money orders. For example, if someone contacts you with a vague offer to buy something in your Etsy shop via money order but offers to pay more than is necessary to expedite the item or includes some other weird request or instructions, beware. This interaction is typically an attempt to relieve you of your merchandise.

Some of these scammers operate by purchasing an item — usually something expensive — and indicating that they'll pay by money order, but they tack on a substantial amount along with a request to, say, buy them a new notebook computer and ship it to them along with your valuable piece. The catch? The money order is really a forgery. The end result is that not only does the scammer effectively steal your item, but you reward her by buying her a computer!

REMEMBER

If anyone asks you to front him some cash or some other expensive item, pronto, your answer should be a polite but firm "N to the O, no."

Sometimes people do have gift emergencies. They need one of your kitten-soft hand-knit scarves, like, yesterday. But sometimes people will foster a sense of urgency in an attempt to prey on your kind nature — for example, begging you to ship an item right away, even though their money order hasn't cleared. Don't be reeled in by this tactic!

TIP

Given how many scams involve the use of money orders, you may reasonably choose not to accept those forms of payment for items in your Etsy shop. (We discuss forms of payment in Chapter 8.)

Beyond these very obvious examples, how do you determine whether the person you're dealing with on Etsy is on the up and up? If she has engaged in countless transactions and received reviews as glowing as Kate Winslet's skin, then you can probably proceed without fear. (For help checking a seller's reviews, see Chapter 5.) But trust your instincts. Assuming that you're not Billy Idol, those hairs on your neck are standing on end for a reason. Pay attention to them.

REMEMBER

So what do you do if you get taken on Etsy? First, contact your financial institution, on the double. Second, report the situation to Etsy. (See the section "Brooklyn, We Have a Problem: Reporting Issues to Etsy," later in this chapter, for details.) You may also opt to alert your local law enforcement.

Staying safe in Etsy's public places

REMEMBER

One of the great things about using Etsy is its robust community of interesting, arty folk. But as with any community — especially online — not everyone on Etsy is honest or sincere. For this reason, it's critical to take steps to keep yourself safe on Etsy's public places, such as its forums and teams (which we describe in detail in Chapter 20). Keep a few points in mind:

>> **Lurk before you leap.** Before jumping into a forum or team discussion, monitor it for a while. See whether the people engaged in the discussion are ones you want to interact with.

>> **Don't hesitate to exit left.** If a discussion goes south, simply disengage. Life's stressful enough — why embroil yourself in a conflict on a site that's supposed to be fun?

>> **Limit personal information.** Don't share your digits or other personal details, such as where you live or work, on Etsy's forums, teams, or other public spaces.

>> **Avoid oversharing.** Although participating in the Etsy community can foster a sense of closeness among members, avoid the temptation to overshare. If you wouldn't be comfortable sharing something with, say, your girlfriend's grandmother, then it probably doesn't belong on Etsy, either.

>> **Think before you connect in real life.** Although using Etsy is certainly a great way to pick up a new BFF and even fall in love, take care before you agree to connect with other Etsy users in real life. If you do decide to meet in person, pick a neutral public place — somewhere you'll feel comfortable. Make sure a friend or family member is hip to your plans, and be sure to bring your phone.

>> **Be nice.** If you're kind to others online, chances are others will be kind back. Not only is it bad karma to knowingly insult or harass another Etsy member, but it's against the site's rules. Abusive behavior can get you kicked off the site for good.

REMEMBER

Tons of people read Etsy's forums. If you're not on your best behavior, it can cast a long shadow on you, your shop, and your business!

Making your account more secure

In case you're extra concerned about security, Etsy offers a few optional features to make your account more secure:

>> **Two-Factor Authentication:** This security feature adds a layer of protection above and beyond your password. Here's how it works: You receive a text message or phone call with a super-secret code, which you must enter in addition to your password to log on to Etsy. You'll receive a new code every 30 days or when you attempt to log in using a different browser.

>> **Sign In Notifications:** When you enable this feature, Etsy sends you a notification anytime someone accesses your account from a new device or browser.

>> **Sign In History:** Enable this feature to track when and where you sign in on Etsy. This is handy if you're concerned that someone else may be logging on to your account. As an added bonus, it enables you to close any open sessions — for example, if you signed in on Etsy using a public computer (say, at the library or at an Internet cafe) and you forgot to log off when you were finished.

To access these features, follow these steps:

1. **Open the You menu in the header bar along the top of any Etsy Marketplace page and choose Account Settings.**

2. **Click the Security tab along the top of the Settings page.**

   The Security Settings page, shown in Figure 6-4, opens.

FIGURE 6-4:
The Security Settings page.

3. **To enable two-factor authentication, click the Enable button in the Two-Factor Authentication section.**

   Etsy prompts you to enter a mobile phone number and to indicate whether you want to receive your two-factor code via text or phone call. Do so, and click the Confirm Phone Number button. Then obtain your code from your phone and enter it in the field that appears.

4. **To enable sign-in notifications, click the Enable button in the Sign In Notifications section.**

5. **To enable the tracking of your sign-in history, click the Enable button in the Sign In History section.**

SOCKET TO ME: ETSY AND SECURE SOCKETS LAYER

All pages on Etsy use Secure Sockets Layer (SSL). SSL is a special security technology that establishes an encrypted link between a web server and a web browser. This encrypted link ensures that any sensitive information transferred between the server and browser remains private. (You can tell when pages are encrypted with SSL by their URL, which starts with https instead of http.)

Using Etsy's Seller Protection program

Try as you might, not every transaction will be as smooth as Mick Jagger with the ladies. Fortunately, Etsy offers Seller Protection, which guarantees that your account status will remain unaffected if a buyer reports a problem with a transaction with your shop.

To be eligible for Seller Protection, do the following:

>> Enroll in Etsy's payment platform, Etsy Payments.

>> Publish your policies with regard to returns, exchanges, and custom orders on your shop's Policies page.

>> Accurately photograph and describe the items you list. Descriptions should include such details as color, size, materials, condition, and the like. (We cover photographing your wares and writing good descriptions in Part 3.) In the case of custom orders, it's critical that you confirm the details of the order via convos.

>> Provide buyers with a "ships by" date — that is, the date by which the item(s) will ship or the amount of time you need to process the order — and ship the item(s) as promised.

>> Ship your item to the address listed on the Etsy receipt (or to a different address if the buyer requested you do so via a convo).

>> After the item is sent, mark it as such on Etsy.

>> Provide proof of shipping and, for items shipped within the United States, proof of delivery.

>> Respond to cases and to correspondence from the buyer involved in the case within seven calendar days, and respond to requests from Etsy for more information about the case within five calendar days.

We talk about how to do all these things throughout this book.

Note that Seller Protection doesn't apply across the board. For example, it isn't available for transactions that involve digital goods or other items delivered electronically. The same goes for items that aren't shipped — for example, items delivered in person or in workshops or classes.

TIP

It's a good idea to communicate with buyers via convos (rather than, say, email or carrier pigeon). That way, if a transaction takes a terrible turn, you'll have an accurate and accessible record of every relevant communication.

Brooklyn, We Have a Problem: Reporting Issues to Etsy

Suppose that you run across a problem while using Etsy. For example, maybe you stumble across an item that shouldn't be sold on the site. (Chapter 7 outlines prohibited items.) If so, you can report it.

To report an item listing or shop that appears to be in violation of Etsy's policies, click the Report This Item to Etsy link (at the bottom of the listing page) or the Report This Shop to Etsy link (on the left side of the shop's main page). A dialog box appears, asking you to specify why you're reporting the listing or shop; click the appropriate option button, add any pertinent comments, and click Submit Report.

To report something else — say, a sketchy or harassing convo — contact Etsy Support. To do so, follow these steps:

1. **Click the Shop Manager button that appears along the top of every Etsy Marketplace page.**

    The Shop Manager dashboard opens.

2. **Click the Community & Help link on the left side of the page and select Contact Us from the list of options that appears.**

    The Contact Etsy Support page opens (see Figure 6-5).

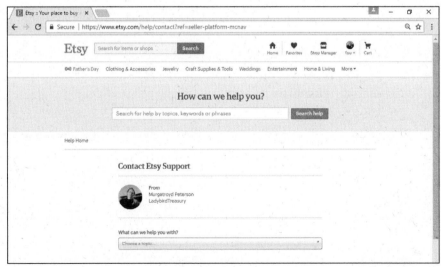

FIGURE 6-5: Reporting a problem on Etsy is easy.

3. Click the Choose a Topic drop-down list and choose the option that relates most closely to the issue you want to report.

4. Do the same for any Tell Us More drop-down lists that appear.

5. Click the Contact Us by Email button.

   In some cases, you may also have the option to contact Etsy by phone.

6. If prompted, provide additional information in any drop-down lists that appear.

7. Type a subject for your message in the Subject field.

8. Type your message in the Message field.

9. To attach a file to your message, click the Attach a File button and choose the file you want to attach.

   For example, you might attach a photo that helps you to describe your complaint.

10. Click Get in Touch.

    Etsy notifies you that your report has been submitted.

2

If You Build It, They Will Come: Setting Up Your Etsy Shop

Find out what you can — and can't — sell on Etsy.

Get tips on customizing your Etsy storefront and making it stand out in the crowd.

Explore the important yet often overlooked subject of shop policies.

Discover a foolproof method for pricing your work.

Chapter **7**

Sell Coverage: Understanding What You Can and Can't Sell on Etsy

Many people think of Etsy as a sort of eBay for arts and crafts. Indeed, Etsy and eBay *are* similar — people use both sites to buy stuff from other individuals; the sites' business models, which involve charging listing fees and taking a small commission on every sale, are clearly related; and members use feedback to rate sellers.

But the differences are hard to ignore. For starters, unlike eBay, Etsy doesn't use an auction format. Furthermore, although Etsy is certainly growing, it's significantly smaller than eBehemoth. But the biggest and most obvious difference is that, unlike eBay, where sellers can list pretty much anything (anyone need a ghost in a jar?), sellers on Etsy are limited to selling items that meet Etsy's strict criteria. In this chapter, we fill you in on what you can — and can't — sell on Etsy.

TIP

For more information about what you can and can't sell on Etsy, see the site's Prohibited Items Policy (www.etsy.com/legal/prohibited/?ref=list).

Yes, We Can! Figuring Out What You Can Sell on Etsy

In a nutshell, you can sell three types of items on Etsy:

>> Items you made or designed yourself

>> Vintage goods (20 years or older)

>> Supplies for crafting

The following sections describe these three categories in detail and address questions you may have about them.

TIP

Some items transcend these categories. For example, maybe you have vintage or handmade items that also qualify as a supply. If your inventory includes items like these, you need to decide which category applies best.

Selling items you made or designed yourself

Etsy's primary *raison d'être* is to serve as a marketplace for makers and designers to sell their goods. According to Etsy, a *maker* is a seller who personally makes the items she sells in her shop. A *designer*, in contrast, "is a seller who has come up with an original design, pattern, sketch, template, prototype, or plan to be produced by in-house shop members or a production partner."

REMEMBER

If you're more "designer" than "maker," you'll need to adhere to Etsy's Manufacturing Policy. It's spelled out here: www.etsy.com/legal/manufacturing/?ref=list.

Whether you're a maker or a designer (or you sell vintage goods or craft supplies, as discussed in the next sections), transparency is key. You *must* honestly and accurately represent yourself, your items, and your business. That means telling the story of your business in your shop's About page — including listing the names and roles of anyone who helps produce your products. (For more info about adding this information to your shop's About page, see Chapters 8 and 19.) It also means using your own words and photos (read: *no* stock photos) to describe your items. Finally, it means responding to inquiries from Etsy regarding how your items are made; what workspace, tools, and equipment you use; and how you communicate and collaborate with your production partners in a timely manner.

REMEMBER

The whole point of Etsy is to enable makers and designers to connect with buyers. Etsy is more than an online craft fair, though. It's an attempt to build an alternative, artisanal economy of sorts — one with high ethical standards that eschews mass production. If your inventory isn't in line with this philosophy, Etsy may not be the marketplace for you.

Offering vintage items

Although Etsy was originally conceived as a marketplace for handmade goods, it also serves as an excellent venue for vintage goods and collectibles. Items can include bags, books, clothing, electronics, furniture, jewelry, toys, and more.

So how old does something have to be in order to be considered vintage? It depends on who you ask. But if you ask Etsy, the answer is 20 years old. Unless your item was manufactured prior to Puff Daddy/P. Diddy/Sean Combs's musical career, you need to find another venue for it.

Selling supplies

To support its crafty community, Etsy allows the sale of commercial crafting supplies on the site, including beads, buttons, fabric, findings, paper, patterns, tools, trim, wire, wool, and whatnot. Shipping and packaging supplies are also acceptable.

What's not allowed: items that, although perhaps considered commercial crafting supplies, are ready for use as is — think dollhouse furniture and the like. Ditto mass-produced goods that may be used in conjunction with handmade items but aren't crafting supplies themselves. In other words, although your handmade eye shadow is a totally legitimate item on Etsy, selling the mass-produced brush you use to apply it as a separate item isn't kosher.

TIP

Do you have a closet full of crafting supplies? If so, consider culling your collection and listing your leftovers on Etsy. Not only will you pull in a little extra cash, but you'll give those goodies a new lease on life.

Just Say No! Understanding What's Not Allowed on Etsy

You know what you can sell (thanks to the previous section): handmade items (that you've designed and/or made yourself), vintage goods, and supplies. You may assume, then, that as long as your item fits into one of those categories, it's acceptable for sale on Etsy. But you know what happens when you assume! In the following sections, we describe the products that Etsy *doesn't* allow.

Knowing what items are prohibited

WARNING

Any number of items may meet the aforementioned criteria but aren't permitted on Etsy. One obvious example is items that are illegal. (Every Etsy seller is responsible for following all local laws.) Other prohibited items include the following:

» Alcohol, tobacco, drugs, drug paraphernalia, and medical drugs

» Animal products and human remains

» Dangerous items (hazardous materials, recalled items, and weapons)

» Hate items (items that promote, support, or glorify hatred)

» Violent items (items that promote, support, or glorify violence)

» Illegal items, items promoting illegal activity, and highly regulated items

» Internationally regulated items

» Pornography and mature content

Selling only certain services

In general, you can't sell your services on Etsy. The site is designed as a marketplace for goods. So even if you're the best dog-walking, house-sitting masseuse this side of the Mississippi, you can't advertise your business on Etsy. You're not even allowed to avail yourself to members seeking your skills in the realm of tailoring, restoring antiques, retouching old photos, and the like.

TIP

If, however, your service results in a new, tangible item, you may offer it for sale on the site. For example, you may sell your services as a graphic designer, offering custom logos for clients, delivered via a digital file. Or maybe you give workshops; in that case, as long as participants leave your class with an actual physical object — an instructional booklet, a finished project, or what have you — it counts.

Off with Their Heads! Knowing What Happens If You Break a Rule

If you list a prohibited item or service on Etsy, vigilant staffers or other site members may flag it for review. (Note that you're not privy to information about who flagged your item.)

In extreme cases, Etsy may delist your item immediately. More typically, however, Etsy will contact you to attempt to remedy the problem. In some cases, you may be asked to remove the prohibited item from your shop. If you fail to do so, Etsy will remove it for you.

In egregious cases, Etsy may opt to suspend or even terminate your selling privileges. (Note that, as a seller, you'll still be responsible for any outstanding fees if Etsy removes an item or suspends or terminates your account.)

AN APPEAL A DAY: FILING AN APPEAL

If you find yourself in the unfortunate position of having your account suspended or terminated, you may be able to file an appeal. Follow these steps:

1. **Click the Shop Manager button that appears along the top of every Etsy Marketplace page.**

2. **Click the Community & Help link on the left side of the Shop Manager dashboard and select Contact Us from the list of options that appears.**

3. **Click the Choose a Topic drop-down list and choose More Options.**

4. **Click the Tell Us More drop-down list and choose Some of My Account Privileges Have Been Suspended.**

5. **Click the Contact Us by Email button.**

6. **Type a subject for your message in the Subject field.**

7. **Type a detailed message in the Message field — including what changes you'll make to adhere to Etsy's policies from here on out.**

8. **To attach a file to your message, click the Attach a File button and choose the file you want to attach.**

9. **Click Get in Touch.**

After you submit your appeal, an Etsy Member Appeals agent will review it. You will receive the agent's final decision regarding your account via email.

Chapter **8**

Come on In! Creating an Eye-Catching Storefront

I f you want to join the ranks of people who supplement their income or earn their living on Etsy, you need to take one important step: Set up your Etsy shop. Fortunately, doing so is a snap, as you discover in this chapter.

You can personalize your Etsy shop in a few different ways: adding a cover photo, selecting a shop icon, and including a shop title and a shop announcement. You can also personalize your shop by populating your public profile (discussed in Chapter 2) and your shop's About section.

REMEMBER

One major reason people shop on Etsy is to feel connected to the creative types who design and/or make what they buy. To make sure people buy from *you*, you want your Etsy shop — and the items you list there — to reflect your personality. Whether you're serious or whimsical, modern or traditional, edgy or frilly, let your individuality shine through in your choice of images, colors, fonts, and other visual elements. Your choice of words in your bio and other text-based elements should also reflect your personality. By revealing your true self in your Etsy shop, not only are you likely to increase your sales, but you may just make some friends along the way!

Shop to It: Setting Up Your Etsy Shop

Becoming an Etsy seller is easy. Simply create your shop on the site, choose a shop name, list your first item, and set up your billing information.

Creating your shop

At the risk of sounding like Mr. Obvious, the first step to setting up your Etsy shop is to create the shop in the first place. Follow these steps:

1. **While signed in to your Etsy account, click the Sell on Etsy link in the upper-right corner of the main page.**

The page that appears (shown in Figure 8-1) offers links to tools, information, and support just for sellers. There's also an Open Your Etsy Shop button, which you click to begin setting up your shop.

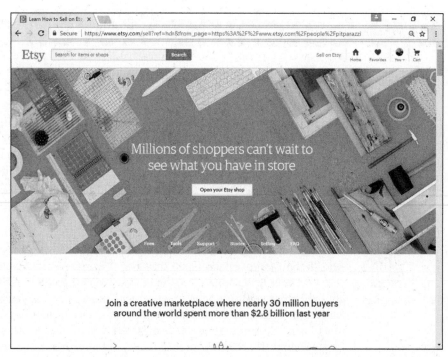

Source: Etsy.com

FIGURE 8-1:
Click the Sell on Etsy link to access this page, which contains links to tools, information, and support just for sellers.

2. **Click the Open Your Etsy Shop button.**

Etsy prompts you to choose a language, country, and currency for your shop. (See Figure 8-2.)

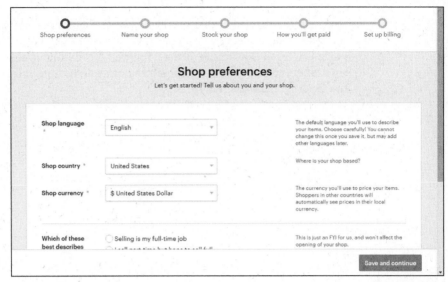

FIGURE 8-2:
Choose a shop language, country, and currency.

TIP

Although most Etsy sellers hail from the ol' U.S. of A. — which is one reason the site's default currency is the U.S. dollar — plenty of Etsy sellers call other countries home. If you're in that latter group, or if you find that your buyers tend to be clustered in a particular region abroad, you can list items and receive payments in a different currency (assuming it's one of the other 20-plus currencies supported, including those of Australia, Canada, the European Union, Great Britain, Hong Kong, Israel, Japan, Mexico, New Zealand, Singapore, and Thailand).

3. **If your shop language is English, your shop currency is the U.S. dollar, and your shop country is United States, you don't need to do anything. You can simply accept the default selections. If not, choose the desired options in the Shop Language, Shop Country, and Shop Currency fields.**

   In addition to asking you to select your shop language, country, and currency, Etsy also asks you to indicate what type of seller you plan to be: full-time, part-time with the hope of eventually selling full-time, or part-time, period. In case none of these choices describe you, Etsy also includes an option for Other.

4. **Choose the option that best describes you. Then click the Save and Continue button.**

   Etsy saves your changes.

Picking a name

After you click the Save and Continue button (refer to Step 4 in the preceding section), Etsy prompts you to select a shop name, as shown in Figure 8-3. Simply type the name you want to use for your shop. If no other seller has beaten you to the punch and selected your shop name already, Etsy will inform you that the name you typed is available. If the name you typed is *not* available, you'll have to try a different one. Keep entering names until you find one you can use. Then click the Save and Continue button.

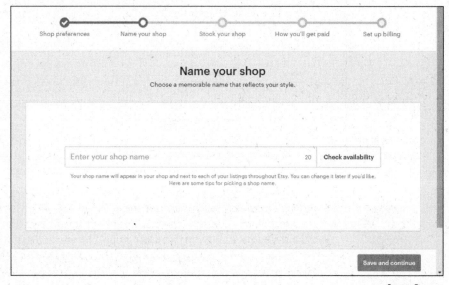

Source: Etsy.com

FIGURE 8-3:
Etsy prompts you to choose your shop name.

REMEMBER

Your shop name must contain only unaccented Roman letters and numbers, without spaces or punctuation, and must consist of fewer than 20 characters. If the name you choose consists of multiple words, consider capitalizing each one to make it easier to read.

Creating your first listing

With your shop name set, Etsy prompts you to create your first listing(s). Click the Add a Listing link in the Stock Your Shop page (see Figure 8-4). When you're finished creating the listing(s), click Save and Continue.

TIP

We cover the ins and outs of building a solid listing in Chapter 13. We recommend you flip ahead to discover how to create a listing that's sure to turn heads. Then return to this chapter to proceed.

CHOOSING A SOLID SHOP NAME

When choosing your shop name, keep these points in mind:

- **Opt for a name that's easy to remember, that's easy to spell, and that contains no more than a few words that flow well together.**

- **If you already have a following elsewhere — for example, at craft fairs, in art galleries, or somewhere else — consider using your own name as your shop.** Using your own name may make it more difficult to maintain your privacy on the site, but it can help you capitalize on your real-world successes.

- **Consider choosing a name that reflects what you sell.** For example, if you specialize in selling refrigerator magnets, you may want to include the word *magnet* in your shop. Keep in mind, though, that this leaves little room for growth if you decide to expand your selection beyond the magnetic.

  Note that you can create multiple accounts to run more than one Etsy storefront — say, one for your thriving refrigerator magnet business and another for your hand-knit fingerless gloves enterprise. Doing so creates its own set of problems, though, most stemming from the challenges of keeping up with more than one shop.

- **Alternatively, choose a name that *doesn't* reflect what you sell.** That way, you give yourself room to grow. Double points if the name you choose is an uncommon word or one you made up, like *Dillytante* or *Farmtastic*. (Etsy calls these "abstract names" and notes that a major advantage of these types of names is that "they will likely be totally unique to your business, making them easier for customers to search online.")

- **Select a name that reflects your style.** You don't want to select an elegant, refined name if you plan to sell wacky hand-knit beard balaclavas.

- **For legal reasons, steer clear of trademarked words (including the word *Etsy*).**

- **Don't be a copycat.** Do some research across the Internet, not just on Etsy, to make sure you aren't infringing on someone else's brand name or shop name.

Note: You can change your shop name, but if you do so more than once, you may have to run it by Etsy first.

Setting up Etsy Payments

At the risk of sounding crass, odds are that you've set up your Etsy shop in the hopes of pulling in some coinage. To aid in that, Etsy provides a service called Etsy Payments. Using Etsy Payments, you can seamlessly accept payment via credit card (Visa, MasterCard, American Express, and Discover); Etsy gift card; Apple Pay; Android Pay; and PayPal, which is integrated into the service. (Etsy offers an additional payment option, iDEAL, for people who live in the Netherlands. And if you live in Austria or Germany, you can accept Sofort.) Etsy automatically transfers funds you receive via Etsy Payments into your bank account. As an added bonus, Etsy also offers fraud protection for any transactions involving Etsy Payments.

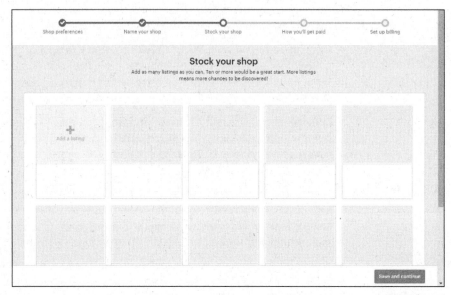

FIGURE 8-4:
Create your first listing.

REMEMBER

Etsy charges a processing fee for each Etsy Payments transaction. This fee varies by country. In the U.S., the fee equals 3 percent of the total sale (including shipping and sales tax) plus 25¢. This is on top of your Etsy listing fee.

When you first set up your shop, Etsy prompts you to sign up for Etsy Payments, as shown in Figure 8-5. To start, select the country where your bank is located from the drop-down list at the top of the page. Then enter the requested information — your bank's routing number, your account number, and some personal details to verify your info. When you're finished, click Save and Continue.

REMEMBER

At the time of this writing, the Etsy Payments option is available in more than 30 countries around the world. If this option is not supported in your country, however, you can accept electronic payments directly through PayPal.

In addition to Etsy Payments, Etsy also permits sellers to accept the following forms of payment:

FIGURE 8-5:
Set up Etsy
Payments.

>> **Money order:** Some people are old school. They prefer the time-honored system of paying by money order over using newfangled digital solutions like Etsy Payments. Fortunately, Etsy allows you to accommodate these buyers. The downside? Unlike with Etsy Payments, payment isn't rendered on the double. You have to wait for the buyer to snail mail you the money order (or send it via some other type of delivery service).

>> **Personal check:** Allowing payment by personal check offers the same basic advantages and disadvantages as permitting payment via money order: You indulge the Luddites, but you have to wait for delivery of payment. *And* you have to wait for that payment to clear.

>> **Other:** If you want, you can accept additional payment methods — say, cashier's checks, gold doubloons, shiny beads, or what have you.

WARNING

If you choose to accept personal checks, money orders, cashier's checks, or gold doubloons as payment, do so with care. These forms offer less protection from fraud (in part because they're not covered by Etsy's fraud protection program, the way Etsy Payments sales are). Oh, and never, never, *ever* ship an item to a buyer until her personal check, money order, or cashier's check clears, no matter how nicely she asks!

Etsy does not give you the opportunity to accept these alternative forms of payment during the shop-setup process. Instead, you'll have to follow these steps after you finish setting up your shop:

1. **Open Shop Manager, choose Finances, and select Accepted Payments.**

   The Payment Settings page opens.

2. **Click the Enable Manual Payment Methods link.**

   The page displays two additional payment settings: Payment by Mail and Other. (See Figure 8-6.)

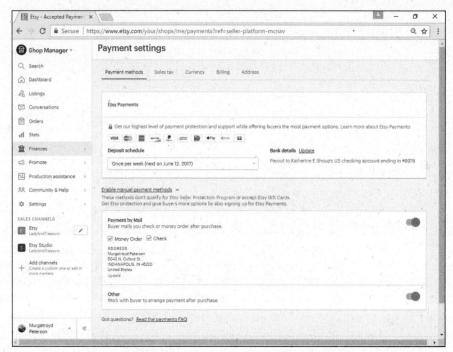

Source: Etsy.com

FIGURE 8-6:
Set up additional payment methods.

3. **To accept checks or money orders, click the Payment by Mail toggle button.**

   The Enter an Address dialog box appears.

4. **Enter your mailing address and click Save.**

5. **Click the Money Order and/or the Check check box to accept these forms of payment.**

6. **To accept other forms of payment, click the Other toggle button.**

   Etsy automatically saves your changes.

REMEMBER

This is a global shop setting. Any items that you list in your shop will offer these payment options.

Setting up your credit card

Of course, you're not the only person here trying to make a buck. Etsy deserves a bit of compensation for helping you to sell your item, wouldn't you agree? As mentioned in Chapter 1, Etsy stays afloat by charging sellers a listing fee (currently, 20¢) for each item listed on the site. In addition, Etsy collects a commission from the seller for each item sold — currently, 3.5 percent of the total price of the item, not counting shipping or tax. (Note that this is on top of any fees Etsy collects for your use of Etsy Payments.)

Instead of relying on muscle and intimidation to obtain payment for these fees, Etsy requires you to register a credit card number with the site. (Indeed, you can't open your shop until you do.) Then, each month, Etsy automatically charges the appropriate amount to the credit card to cover your listing and Etsy Payments fees. Etsy also charges your card anytime you exceed a predefined fee threshold. (The fee threshold for new sellers is $25 by default; as you sell more on Etsy, you may see this threshold rise.)

As shown in Figure 8-7, Etsy prompts you to enter this information as the final step of the shop-setup process. (If you've already entered a credit card — for example, to purchase something on Etsy — then Etsy automatically uses that card for billing.) To add a new card, click the Add a Credit or Debit Card option button and enter the requested information in the dialog box that appears.

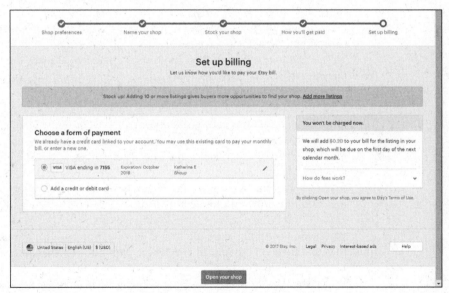

FIGURE 8-7:
Enter your credit card information.

Source: Etsy.com

Opening your shop

After you set up your billing, you're ready to open your shop. Simply click the Open Your Shop button at the bottom of the Set Up Billing page (refer to Figure 8-7) to go live!

Picture This: Adding a Cover Photo and Shop Icon to Your Shop

To spruce up your Etsy shop, you can add a cover photo and shop icon. A cover photo is a graphic that runs across the top of your page, while a shop icon serves as an avatar for your shop. Don't just choose a cover photo and shop icon willy-nilly. These visual elements should reflect the aesthetic of the items you sell and tie in with your overall branding. (You find out more about branding in Chapter 16.)

WARNING

It's not a bad idea to include your shop's name in your cover photo, but apart from that, you should use text sparingly. Otherwise, anyone viewing it on a mobile device will develop instant eyestrain when trying to read it.

You can create your cover photo and shop icon from scratch using just about any image-editing software you like — even free stuff online. Unfortunately, we can't cover the ins and outs of actually *creating* a cover photo and shop icon. If you're new to image-editing software, you'll have to delve into your program's Help info for guidance. But we can give you this pointer: Whatever tool you use, the key to creating a cover photo for your Etsy shop is ensuring that it's cropped to fit properly on your Etsy shop page. Specifically, all cover photos should be 3,360 pixels wide and 840 pixels high. And shop icons should be at least 500 × 500 pixels (but smaller than 10 megabytes).

TIP

If you're no Rembrandt, why not let the pros take over and invest in a professionally designed custom cover photo and/or shop icon? Many talented designers offer this service from their own Etsy shops. Try searching Etsy for "Etsy shop cover photo" or "Etsy shop icon" and see what comes up. Just be sure you go the "custom" route instead of opting for a ready-made version. Otherwise, buyers may well stumble upon other shops using the same cover photo as yours. Not the best way to build your unique brand!

When you have your cover photo and shop icon in hand, it's time to upload them to your Etsy shop. To upload your cover photo, follow these steps:

1. **If the Edit Shop page isn't open already, open Shop Manager and, under Sales Channels, click the pencil icon next to your shop name.**

   The Edit Shop page opens (see Figure 8-8).

2. **Click the Add a Cover Photo to Highlight Your Brand link.**

   Etsy prompts you to select a branding option. Your choices are Small Banner (which is smaller than a cover photo and does not appear on mobile devices), Cover Photo, and None.

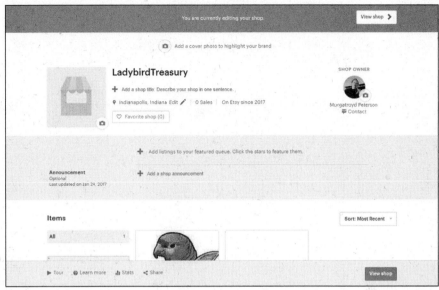

FIGURE 8-8:
You edit your shop's appearance from this page.

3. **Choose Cover Photo and click Add Cover Photo.**

   A standard file-selection dialog box appears.

4. **Locate and select the image you want to use as your cover photo.**

   Etsy shows you a preview of the cover photo (see Figure 8-9).

5. **If needed, drag the cover photo to position it. Then click Save.**

   Etsy uploads your cover photo to your shop.

The process for uploading your shop icon is similar. Follow these steps:

1. **In the Edit Shop page, click the small camera icon on the graphic to the left of your shop name. (If the Edit Shop page isn't open already, open Shop Manager and, under Sales Channels, click the pencil icon next to your shop name.)**

   Etsy displays the Add a Shop Icon dialog box.

2. **Click Choose a File.**

   A standard file-selection dialog box appears.

3. **Locate and select the image you want to use as your shop icon.**

   Etsy gives you a chance to reposition and/or crop your shop icon.

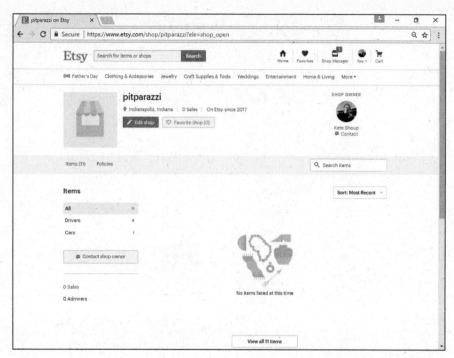

FIGURE 8-9:
Preview your
cover photo here.

4. **If needed, reposition and/or crop the shop icon. Then click Save.**

   Etsy displays a preview of the shop icon (see Figure 8-10).

FIGURE 8-10:
Preview your
shop icon here.

5. **Click Looks Good.**

   Etsy uploads your shop icon to your shop (see Figure 8-11).

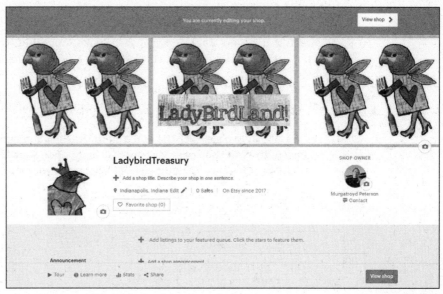

Source: Etsy.com

FIGURE 8-11:
What a difference
a cover photo
and shop icon
make!

TIP

If you have commitment issues, fear not. You can change your cover photo and shop icon any time you want. For example, you may change these visual elements to reflect promotions that you're running or update them seasonally to keep your shop looking fresh.

Title Wave: Adding a Shop Title and Announcement

Looking for a way to tell visitors what your shop's about? Look no further. Etsy enables you to include a shop title and shop announcement on your shop's main page.

Think of your shop title as a tagline of sorts. It needs to briefly sum up what your shop is about. For example, if you sell belt buckles, your shop title — which appears just below your username on your Etsy shop page — may be "Keep Your Pants On . . . with Becky's Belt Buckles." If customers are likely to search for you by your full name or your business name, consider including that in your shop title, too.

The shop announcement, in contrast, is a great way to, well, announce things about your shop. For example, you may use it to trumpet the types of items you sell or your artistic philosophy. Or it could broadcast when your next sale will be or that you're away on vacation. Either way, Etsy suggests that you keep it short and sweet. If it's more *Anna Karenina* than haiku, not all of it will be visible by default. To read it in its entirety, click the Read More link that appears after the first few lines.

To add a shop title and shop announcement to your shop, follow these steps:

1. **In the Edit Shop page, click the Add a Shop Title link beneath your shop name. (If the Edit Shop page isn't open already, open Shop Manager and, under Sales Channels, click the pencil icon next to your shop name.)**

    Etsy displays the Shop Title dialog box (see Figure 8-12).

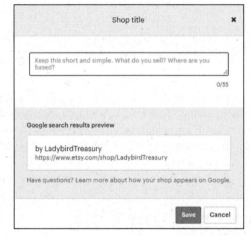

FIGURE 8-12:
Type your shop title in this dialog box.

Source: Etsy.com

2. **Type your shop title and click Save.**

    Etsy adds your shop title to your shop.

3. **Click the Add a Shop Announcement link in the Announcement section of the Edit Shop page.**

    A text box appears.

4. **Type your shop announcement in the Shop Announcement text box (see Figure 8-13).**

5. **Click the Save button.**

    Etsy adds your shop title and shop announcement to your shop (see Figure 8-14).

FIGURE 8-13:
Type your shop announcement in this text box.

FIGURE 8-14:
Etsy adds your shop title and shop announcement to your shop.

All about Me: Adding an About Section

Part of the reason people shop on Etsy is that they want to feel a personal connection with the living, breathing artists, craftspeople, and other creative types who design and/or make what they buy. Enter the About section on your shop's main page. This section is a bit like the bio in your public profile, only expanded. It can include the following page elements:

>> **Video:** Maybe you have a video that shows you, your process, your workspace, or maybe a partly finished project. If so, you can upload it to your shop's About section. (Obviously, you must own the rights to any video you share on Etsy.) You upload a video by clicking the Add Video link on the About section of the Edit Shop page (see Figure 8-15). (You'll need to scroll down a bit to see this section.) This launches a standard file-selection dialog box, where you can specify the video you want to upload.

>> **Photos:** These may be similar in nature to a video — that is, depicting you, your process, and so on. You can add as many as five photos, which will be presented in slide show form in the About section on your shop's main page, and you can enter your own captions for each one. To do so, click the Add Up

to 5 Photos with Captions link and choose the first photo you want to add. Then click the Add Caption button that appears and type your caption in the text box that opens (see Figure 8-16).

FIGURE 8-15:
You can add a video and photos to your shop's About section.

FIGURE 8-16:
Add photos to your shop.

>> **Shop story and story headline:** Your shop story may be similar to the bio you wrote for your public profile, but it doesn't have to be. Lots of Etsy sellers use the Story section to get into the nitty-gritty of what they do and why. Alternatively, it may discuss who sellers are on a more personal level, what their studio is like, or what a normal day is like. Oh, and if you've gotten some good press lately, your shop story could toot that horn. As for your story headline, that may be something akin to your shop title. To enter your shop story and story headline, click the Add Your Story and Add a Story Headline links, respectively (see Figure 8-17). Then type in the text boxes that appear and click Save.

TIP

Many Etsy sellers donate a portion of their take to charity. If you're one such seller, you can indicate that in your bio. (Note that charitable listings and shops are subject to a few rules, outlined here: www.etsy.com/help/article/4528.)

FIGURE 8-17:
Share your
shop story.

>> **Links to other sites:** You can add links to other sites you maintain for your craft business to the About section on your shop's main page. This may be a Facebook page, a Twitter feed, an Instagram account, a Pinterest site, a company website, or a blog. To do so, click the Add Links to your Website and Social Media link (see Figure 8-18). Then choose the type of link you want to add (Facebook, Twitter, and so on) from the drop-down list that appears and enter its URL in the text box to the right. Finally, click Save.

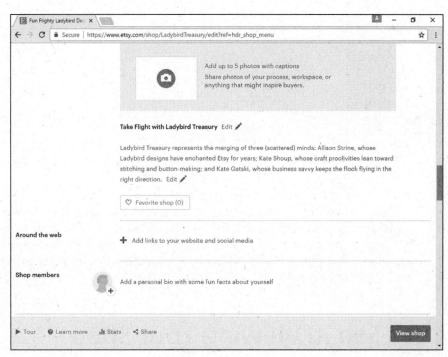

FIGURE 8-18:
Connect your
customers to
your other sites.

» **Shop members:** To add a few personal details to the About section, click the Add a Personal Bio . . . link (refer to Figure 8-18) to open the Add Shop Member dialog box (see Figure 8-19). Type the shop member's name, open the Add a Role drop-down list and select the appropriate role(s) (options include Owner, Assistant, Creator, Customer Service, Designer, Marketer, Photographer, and Shipper, or you can choose a custom role), and type a brief bio. (This may be similar to what appears in your public profile, but it doesn't have to be.) Finally, click Choose File to select a photo and then click Save. Note that if you run your shop with someone else — say, your grandma — you'll need to add her bio here, too. (Find out more about adding shop members in Chapter 19.)

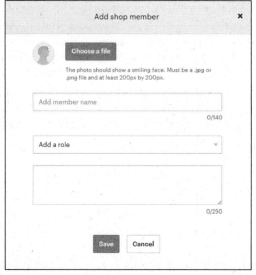

FIGURE 8-19:
Add your own bio as well as bios for each shop member.

Source: Etsy.com

REMEMBER

Don't forget to proofread all the text in your Etsy shop — your shop title, shop announcement, section titles, bio, and so on. Running a shop that's riddled with spelling and grammatical errors sends shoppers the wrong message — namely, that you're sloppy, lazy, and/or incompetent. That image isn't likely to win you any buyers!

Let's See It! Viewing Your Shop

You've done it! You've set up your Etsy shop! Now it's time to review your handiwork. To do so, click the View Shop button at the bottom of the Edit Shop page. Etsy displays your shop, the way your customers will see it. (See Figure 8-20.)

FIGURE 8-20:
Your shop — as it
appears to your
customers!

Source: Etsy.com

REMEMBER

Your shop will look different on the Etsy Mobile app (which you can use on a smartphone or tablet) but will offer many of the same features.

Team Edit-ward: Editing Your Shop Settings

Inspiration may strike after you set up your shop. Maybe you'll want to update your cover photo, revise your shop announcement, or change some other aspect of your storefront. Fortunately, doing so is easy. Simply open the Your Shop menu and choose Edit Shop. You'll find the exact same Edit Shop page that we discuss in this chapter.

Chapter 9

Policy Academy: Setting Your Shop's Policies

Rules. Who needs 'em? In a word, you. Or, to be more precise, your Etsy shop. As you set up your Etsy shop, it's critical that you lay some ground rules for buyers. You want to establish clear store policies, especially with respect to shipping, payment, returns and exchanges, and privacy. That way, your customers know what to expect if they buy from you, and they'll feel more confident and at ease. Setting clear policies also enables you to head off problems down the road.

To help you set and communicate your policies, Etsy offers an easy-to-use Shop Policies template. This template contains boilerplate text that you can use for your own shop policies as well as a series of policy-related settings you can select (or not). When you finish entering your policy info into the Shop Policies template, you simply publish your policies to your shop. Your policies appear on your shop's main page in the Shop Policies section. They also appear in emails sent to buyers when they make a purchase.

In case you want to implement policies above and beyond those that appear in the Shop Policies template, you can create a Frequently Asked Questions (FAQ) section for your shop to cover your bases. This FAQ section appears below your shop policies.

You can avert a lot of crises by establishing clear store policies. However, you'll still face the occasional conflict with customers. When that happens, you need to take three actions: Communicate, communicate, and communicate. Oh, and one more thing: Communicate. For more on dealing with disagreements and other customer service issues, see Chapter 17.

Fair and Square: General Policy Tips

Before we get into policy specifics in the rest of this chapter, we want to talk in general terms about what, apart from honesty, constitutes a good policy. A good policy has two key characteristics:

>> **It's fair.** Yes, you put policies in place to protect your business. But a good policy also protects your customers. Your shop policy should be one for which you would be grateful if, through some amazing breach in the space-time continuum, *you* were your customer.

>> **It's simple.** Although it's important to use your words, you don't want to use too many of them when crafting your shop policies. Keep your policies simple, clear, and concise.

When it comes to setting your shop's policies, you have a lot of leeway. Different shops' policies are often as unique as the items they sell. That being said, you do need to adhere to Etsy's terms of use and respect the site's House Rules. And of course, you must comply with all local and federal laws.

Policy Wonk: Using Etsy's Shop Policies Template

As mentioned, Etsy offers a handy Shop Policies template to help you set and communicate your shop policies. The following sections comprise this template:

>> Shipping

>> Payment options

>> Returns and exchanges

>> Privacy policy

In addition, an FAQ section enables you to customize your shop policies.

The Shop Policies template appears on the Edit Shop page. To access this page, follow these steps:

1. **Click the Shop Manager link in the header bar that appears along the top of every Etsy Marketplace page.**

   The Shop Manager opens.

2. **In the bottom-left area of the Shop Manager screen, under Sales Channels, click the pencil icon next to your shop name.**

   The Edit Shop page appears.

3. **Scroll down to the Shop Policies section and click the Edit button to access the Shop Policies template.**

REMEMBER

You can't publish your shop's policies until you've opened your shop. (See Chapter 8 for more info.)

Shipping

The Shipping section of the Shop Policies template (see Figure 9-1) covers the following topics:

>> **Processing Time:** This part of the Shipping section contains the following boilerplate text: "The time I need to prepare an order for shipping varies. For details, see individual items." This text can't be changed.

>> **Estimated Shipping Times:** This section reads, "I'll do my best to meet these shipping estimates, but cannot guarantee them. Actual delivery time will depend on the shipping method you choose." However, this section also enables you to display an estimated shipping time. To do so, click the Add Estimated Shipping Time link. Then choose the continent or country to which the estimate applies, enter a numeric range, and specify whether the range refers to business days or weeks. (Note that you can add estimated shipping times for as many different continents and countries as you like.)

>> **Customs and Import Taxes:** Like the other sections, this section contains boilerplate text that can't be changed. It reads as follows: "Buyers are responsible for any customs and import taxes that may apply. I'm not responsible for delays due to customs."

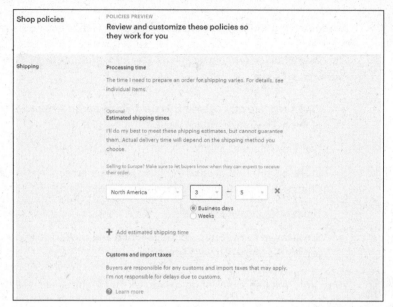

Source: Etsy.com

FIGURE 9-1:
The Shipping
section of the
Etsy Shop Policies
template.

As noted, the boilerplate text in the Processing Time section indicates that additional shipping policy info can be found in individual item listings. You discover how to set these policies — including policies related to shipping costs, processing time, which countries you'll ship to, which shipping services you'll use, whether you offer free shipping, and whether a handling fee applies (and if so, how much) — in Chapter 13, when you build your first listing. For more on shipping in general, see Chapter 15.

Payment options

The Payment Options section of the Shop Policies template, shown in Figure 9-2, reflects the payment options you selected when you set up your shop. (See Chapter 8.) It also contains some boilerplate text, which can't be changed. It reads as follows: "Etsy keeps your payment information secure. Etsy shops never receive your credit card information."

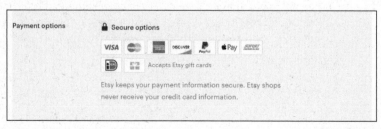

FIGURE 9-2:
The Payment
Options section
of the Etsy Shop
Policies template.

Source: Etsy.com

REMEMBER

The payment options can't be changed from within the Shop Policies template. To change them, you must edit your payment settings. See Chapter 8 for help editing shop settings such as the payment settings.

Returns and exchanges

Obviously, you want all your customers to love your items. But — no disrespect — sometimes they won't. (What? We said "no disrespect"!) When that happens, you need to refer buyers to your policy on returns and exchanges.

You can set this policy in the Returns and Exchanges section of the Shop Policies template (see Figure 9-3). This section is broken down into the following parts:

» **I Accept the Following:** In this part of the Returns and Exchanges section, you specify whether you accept returns, exchanges, and/or cancellations by selecting the appropriate check box. (Some sellers do; other sellers don't.) Selecting any or all of these check boxes reveals an additional pair of settings: Just Contact Me Within *X* Days of Delivery and Ship Items Back to Me Within *X* Days of Delivery. Each of these settings has a drop-down list from which you can select a numeral to represent the number of days.

» **The Following Items Can't Be Returned or Exchanged:** Some categories of items just aren't conducive to being returned — think custom or personalized orders, perishable items (like food or flowers), digital downloads, and intimate items (for health/hygiene reasons). By default, all four of these categories appear in this area of the Returns and Exchanges section of the Shop Policies template. In addition, a fifth category, items on sale, is available from the Select an Item Category drop-down list. To remove a category from your shop policies, simply click the X to its right.

» **Conditions of Return:** This part of the Returns and Exchanges section contains boilerplate text, which can't be changed. It reads as follows: "Buyers are responsible for return shipping costs. If the item is not returned in its original condition, the buyer is responsible for any loss in value."

Privacy policy

The Privacy Policy section of the Shop Policies template is where you reassure buyers that you'll use their shipping address, billing address, and other contact information only for very specific purposes: to communicate with them about their order, to fulfill their order, and for legal reasons (like paying taxes). (See Figure 9-4.) There is also an Other option. If you select this option, a text box appears, where you can specify exactly how the buyer's information will be used.

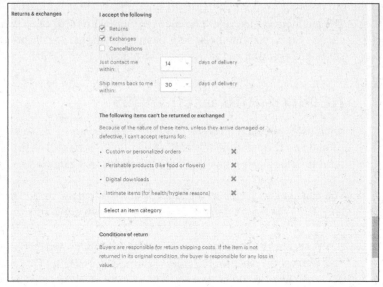

FIGURE 9-3:
The Returns and
Exchanges
section of the
Etsy Shop Policies
template.

Source: Etsy.com

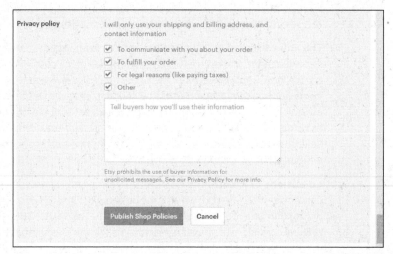

FIGURE 9-4:
The Privacy Policy
section of the
Etsy Shop Policies
template.

Source: Etsy.com

REMEMBER

If, in the Other text box, you indicate that you intend to use the buyer's contact info to "send unsolicited messages," be prepared to face the wrath of Etsy. These types of unwanted communications are like bread in a low-carb diet: forbidden.

Publishing your shop policies

When you've finished entering the necessary information into the various sections of the Shop Policy template, you're ready to publish your policies to the Shop Policies section, found on your shop's main page. To do so, simply click the Publish Shop Policies button at the bottom of the template. (Refer to Figure 9-4.) Etsy publishes your shop policies. To see them, click the View Shop button. Figure 9-5 shows the published policies.

You can edit your shop policies anytime you like using the Shop Policies template. You edit these policies the exact same way you created them the first time around.

Source: Etsy.com

FIGURE 9-5:
Etsy publishes
your shop
policies.

That's a FAQ, Jack! Fielding frequently asked questions

The Shop Policies template is great, but it doesn't cover everything. Fortunately, Etsy provides yet another way for you to pin down your policies: by including a frequently asked questions (FAQ) section on your shop's main page. You may use the FAQ section to indicate whether you accept custom or personalized items, whether you offer gift-wrapping services, and whether you offer items wholesale. You could also use the FAQ section to convey information such as sizing details or care instructions, or copyright and/or licensing information. Or if potential buyers often ask the same question ("Are your sweaters really knit from kitten hair?"), you can choose the Custom option to provide your answer ("Yes").

To add a FAQ section to your shop, follow these steps:

1. **Scroll down to the Frequently Asked Questions section of the Edit Shop page.**

   This section is located just below the Shop Policies template.

2. **Click the Add an FAQ link.**

   The section expands to display a Question drop-down list and an Answer text box (see Figure 9-6).

FIGURE 9-6:
Create a FAQ.

Source: Etsy.com

3. **Click the Question drop-down list and select from the available options.**

   Options include Custom and Personalized Orders, Sizing Details, Care Instructions, Gift Wrapping and Packaging, Wholesale Availability, and Custom. (If you select Custom, a new text box appears under the Question drop-down list, where you can type a custom question.)

4. **Type your answer to the question in the Answer field.**

5. **Click Save.**

As shown in Figure 9-7, Etsy adds the question and answer to the main page of your Etsy shop, just below your shop policies. (You must click the View Shop button to see it.)

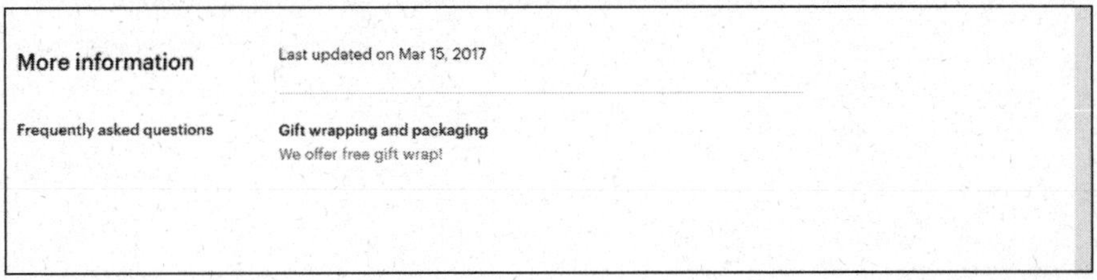

FIGURE 9-7:
The question and
answer in an FAQ
section in your
shop's main page.

More information

Last updated on Mar 15, 2017

Frequently asked questions   **Gift wrapping and packaging**
We offer free gift wrap!

Source: Etsy.com

6. **To add more questions and answers, simply repeat Steps 1 through 5.**

Chapter **10**

The Price Is Right! Pricing Your Pieces

Years ago, a close friend developed a keen business idea: the million-dollar hot dog. The million-dollar hot dog would be just like any other hot dog, except that it would cost a million dollars. Yes, demand for the million-dollar hot dog may be low. But as our friend rightly points out, "You really only ever need to sell *one!*"

Ironically, most Etsy sellers err on the other end of the spectrum, underpricing the pieces they sell. Often, they're so thrilled someone wants to buy something they made, it doesn't occur to them that they could've sold it for more. But just as overpricing your pieces has its problems (you never sell anything), so does underpricing them. Specifically, it results in lost profits and, perhaps worse, the perception that your pieces are cheap, meaning low quality. Particularly with one-of-a-kind items like yours, customers use the piece's price to assess its value.

The trick, then, is to strike a balance with your pricing. You want to price your pieces high enough to cover your costs and turn a healthy profit. (After all, you're running a business.) But you need to price your items low enough that you can sell a reasonable volume of goods. Finding that sweet spot is the focus of this chapter.

As you become more adept and efficient at crafting your pieces and running your business, your profit margin will naturally improve.

Formulaic Plot: Breaking Down Your Pricing Formulas

One of our favorite *Saturday Night Live* sketches is the one with Chevy Chase as President Gerald R. Ford, taking part in a presidential debate. After being asked an extremely complicated question involving numerous dollar figures and percentages, Chase, sweating profusely, stammered, "It was my understanding that there would be no math during the debates. . . ."

No doubt, many Etsy sellers feel exactly the same way. After all, don't most of us become creative types specifically to avoid ever having to do arithmetic? Unfortunately, if you hope to run a profitable Etsy shop, you need to get comfortable with doing a little math, especially when it comes to pricing your pieces. But don't freak out! We're not talking calculus here or even trigonometry. All you have to learn are two very simple formulas:

Wholesale Price = (Materials + Labor + Overhead) × 2

Retail Price = Wholesale Price × 2

In the following sections, we break down each item in the preceding formulas and show you how to put the formulas to work.

Calculating the cost of materials

When calculating your cost for materials, include the price of every little component in your piece. For example, suppose that you sell handmade puppy plush toys for babies. Your material cost for each pup may include the cost of fabric, a label, rickrack, stuffing, and thread.

Note that what matters here is the cost of what you used to produce one piece. For example, suppose that you spent $125 on materials to produce 50 plush pups. To calculate the price of materials per piece, you divide $125 by 50, for a total of $2.50 per piece.

Figuring labor costs

What if, while perusing the want ads in your local newspaper, you happened upon this listing:

> **Wanted:** Skilled professional to expertly fabricate product by hand. Must also run every aspect of business, including sourcing supplies, maintaining and marketing shop, interacting with customers, and ensuring that items sold are artfully packaged and shipped to buyers. Pay: Nil.

Odds are, that's a job you'd pass up. Why, then, do so many Etsy sellers seem to pay themselves *nada* to run their shops? Don't fall into this trap! Like anyone, you deserve to be compensated for your work; your pricing formula must include the cost of your labor.

Calculating your labor costs requires you to first set an hourly rate for your time. Be sure to pay yourself a fair wage — one that accounts for the skill required to craft your piece. Also, think about how much you want or need to earn for your time. (This consideration is especially important if you're looking to quit your day job.)

If you're just starting out, you may opt for a lower hourly rate. You can give yourself periodic raises as your skills improve.

Another approach to figuring your hourly rate is to work backward. That is, figure out how much you need to be able to "bill" for each day and divide that by the number of hours you intend to work. For example, if you need to earn $160 a day to survive, and you plan to work eight hours per day crafting the items you plan to sell, then you can simply divide $160 by 8, for an hourly rate of $20.

Armed with your hourly rate, you're ready to work out your labor costs. These costs must take into account the time it takes to design a piece, shop for supplies for the piece, construct the piece, photograph the piece, create the item listing for the piece (including composing the item title and description), correspond with the buyer, and package and ship the item.

As with materials costs (described in the previous section), you can *amortize* some of the labor costs — that is, you can spread them out. For example, if it took you four hours to develop the design for a piece, but you plan to make 50 of them, you have to amortize those four hours over the 50 finished pieces. Similarly, you likely shop for supplies for several pieces at once, meaning that you can spread the time that you spend shopping across all the projects that you plan to craft using those supplies. Oh, and if you're collaborating with others, you'll want to make sure that you include the cost of *their* labor as well!

Let's use those plush toy pups as an example. Suppose that you spend four hours designing your toy and another hour shopping for enough supplies to construct 50 units. Your labor cost — assuming your hourly rate is $20 — is $100, or, spread out over 50 toys, $2 per toy. Suppose further that each toy takes 30 minutes to make, photograph, and package ($10 in labor). (Yes, we know. Thirty minutes is on the low end. Humor us. It makes the math easier.) Your labor cost per toy is then $12.

Adding up overhead

In addition to calculating your costs for materials and labor, you want to account for your overhead. Your overhead may encompass tools and equipment used in the manufacture of your products, office supplies, packaging supplies, utilities (for example, your Internet connection, electricity used to power your sewing machine, and so on), and Etsy fees. (*Note:* These costs don't include shipping. You generally calculate those costs separately and pass them along to the buyer. Chapter 15 has more details on calculating shipping costs.)

As with your labor costs, you need to amortize your overhead costs. That is, you total your overhead and then spread out that cost over all the items you make. As a simple example, if you calculate your monthly overhead at $50, and you produce 50 pieces a month (like with those plush pups), your overhead is $1 per piece. Of course, this calculation gets tricky when your overhead involves purchases of such things as tools and equipment used in the manufacture of your products. In those cases, you want to amortize the items over their life span. For example, suppose that you buy a $250 sewing machine that you plan to use for five years. In that time, you anticipate that you'll sew 500 pieces. Your overhead for the machine is then 50¢ per piece.

TIP

If you simply can't face calculating all these overhead costs, add up your materials cost and your labor cost for each piece you make, multiply the sum by 10 or 15 percent, and call that your overhead. It won't exactly reflect your actual overhead, but it'll be in the ballpark.

Understanding the "times 2"

In the formula we provide earlier in this chapter, you may have noticed that after adding together your costs for materials, labor, and overhead, you multiply the sum by 2. What's up with that? Simple. That "times 2" is your profit. It's what you invest back in your business. If your sewing machine breaks, the "times 2" is what you use to buy a new one. If you decide to expand your product line, that "times 2" is where you find the capital you need to grow. Or you may just use your "times 2" revenue to build a nice nest egg for your business or a fund to fall back on if times get tough.

Although some sellers may feel uncomfortable with all this two-timing, thinking that their labor costs are their "profit," don't make the mistake of omitting this part of the formula. Yes, you may be paying yourself to make your products, but if your business grows, that may not always be the case. Multiplying your costs by 2 enables you to ensure that your business is profitable, regardless of how it's structured.

Pricing for wholesale and retail

As the proprietor of your own small manufacturing business, you need to establish two prices for your goods: the wholesale price and the retail price. The wholesale price is for customers who buy large quantities of your item to resell it. That customer then sells your piece to someone else at the retail price, which is usually (though not always) double the wholesale price. To review, you obtain your wholesale price by using the following formula:

Wholesale Price = (Materials + Labor + Overhead) × 2

TIP

As mentioned, to determine the retail price, we typically multiply the wholesale price by 2. Some sellers, however, may choose a higher number, multiplying the wholesale price by 2.5 or even 3 to determine the retail price (assuming the market will bear it).

We know what you're thinking: "I'm going to sell my stuff only through my Etsy store, so I'll just charge everyone my wholesale price." Wrong! Even if you plan to sell your items exclusively through your Etsy shop, you need to establish both a wholesale price and a retail price, and you need to sell your pieces on Etsy at the retail rate. Why? A couple of reasons. First, even if you have no plans to expand beyond your Etsy shop, you don't want to cheat yourself of the chance to offer wholesale prices to bulk buyers if the opportunity arises. And second, you'll almost certainly want to run the occasional sale in your Etsy shop. Pricing your goods for retail gives you some leeway to discount them as needed and still turn a profit.

WARNING

If you do develop a wholesale business, it's especially important that you sell the pieces in your Etsy shop at the retail price. Otherwise, you're undercutting your wholesale customers! Unless it's your stated goal to alienate these customers, avoid this practice.

TIP

Etsy supports a special marketplace for connecting sellers like you with wholesale buyers, called Etsy Wholesale. See Chapter 19 for more information about using Etsy Wholesale to take your business to the next level by selling wholesale to bricks-and-mortar outlets.

Putting it all together

To help you get comfortable with pricing your pieces, we run through a couple of examples here. Let's start with the puppy plush toys mentioned earlier. To recap, the cost of materials for each toy is $2.50; your total labor rate is $12 per item; and your overhead for each piece is $1. Your pricing equation, then, looks something like this:

Wholesale Price = (Materials + Labor + Overhead) × 2 = ($2.50 + $12 + $1) × 2 = $31

Retail Price = Wholesale Price × 2 = $31 × 2 = $62

Here's another example. Suppose that you've designed a new bracelet for your jewelry line, and you need to determine how much to charge for it. The beads, findings, and thread you used to construct the bracelet put you back $12. Your labor rate is $14 per hour, and it takes you 45 minutes to make each bracelet (including amortized values for time spent on other business-related activities). Your labor cost, then, is $14 × 0.75 = $10.50. Finally, suppose that your overhead for each bracelet is $1.75. Here's what your pricing equation looks like:

Wholesale Price = (Materials + Labor + Overhead) × 2 = ($12 + $10.50 + $1.75) × 2 = $48.50

Retail Price = Wholesale Price × 2 = $48.50 × 2 = $97

TIP

Offering products at different price points is a great way to increase your customer base. For example, say that you specialize in ceramics. In that case, you may make ceramic mugs to sell at a lower price point; simple, medium-sized bowls to sell at a slightly higher price point; and ornate platters to sell at a premium price point. This structure enables you to reach a larger range of potential buyers, which may help you increase your overall sales. As a bonus, if you're just starting out on Etsy, this strategy is a great way to nose out your niche in the market. You'll soon see which products your buyers respond to best.

Eyes on the Price: Evaluating Your Prices

You've used the pricing formulas in the preceding section to determine your wholesale and retail prices. You're finished, right? Wrong. These formulas simply deliver the price you need to charge for your piece to turn a healthy profit. To ensure that the price you've hit on is, in the immortal words of Goldilocks, "just right," you need to do a little research.

Many creative types underestimate their worth. They lack confidence in their work and their vision. Hence, they inevitably underprice their pieces. Underestimating the value of your work doesn't just hurt you; it hurts everyone who's trying to earn a living by selling their handmade goods. Deflated prices are bad all the way around! If you suffer from this malaise, channel your inner Stuart Smalley and repeat after us: "You're good enough, you're smart enough, and, gosh darn it, people like you!"

Assessing your competition's pricing

Your first order of business is to scope out your competition, both on and off Etsy. If their prices are roughly in line with yours, you're probably in good shape. If they're significantly higher or lower, put yourself in your prospective buyer's shoes and ask these questions:

>> Would I buy my product or a competitor's product? Why?

>> Is my product made of better materials than my competitors' products?

>> Did crafting my product or my competitors' products require more skill?

>> Is my product different or special in any way?

>> What do I think my product is worth?

Your answers to these questions help you determine whether you need to adjust your price upward or downward. For example, if your product is better made than your competitor's, you may be able to adjust your price upward. Ditto if it required more skill to build. Of course, if the opposite is true, you may need to lower your price.

Your competition doesn't consist just of people who make items like yours. It's anyone targeting the same market as you. Using the puppy plush example, your competition wouldn't be just shops that sell puppy plush toys; it would be any shop that sells handmade toys or gifts for babies.

Studying your target market

In gauging your price, you need to consider your target market. Who, in your estimation, will buy your piece? How much disposable income does that person have? If your target market is 20-something hipsters, chances are they're not quite as flush as, say, the 40-something set, so you may need to keep your prices lower. On the flip side, if that 40-something set is the market you're after, you may be able to command a higher price.

BUNDLE UP: BUNDLING YOUR ITEMS

You may be able to increase sales by *bundling* your items — that is, selling multiple items together, as a package deal. For example, suppose that you specialize in making jewelry. Instead of selling a $20 pair of earrings and a $30 necklace separately, you could bundle them into a single listing for $45. Offering value bundles — say, buy two, get one free — is another tactic. Yes, you'll make less than you would if you sold them separately, but you'll move more merchandise, you'll save time on shipping, and your customer will feel like she's gotten a super deal.

TIP

People often shop for gifts with a certain price point in mind — say, $25 for a friend or $50 for a family member. If your product is aimed at this market, ask yourself, who's the ultimate recipient for this gift? A best friend? An acquaintance? Someone's nephew? Then think about what most people would spend on a gift for that person and price your piece accordingly.

Figuring out how to lower your prices

If your research has revealed that your prices will likely give your market sticker shock, you may need to lower them. The best way to do this is to lower your own costs. Can you purchase your materials more cheaply from a different supplier? Can you spend less time making each piece? Can you redesign your product to require less in the way of supplies or labor — for example, omitting the decorative rickrack piping on your plush pup? After you manage to lower your costs, apply the formulas we talk about earlier in the chapter to determine the new price.

REMEMBER

Don't lower your prices to compete with machine-made or imported items. Handmade items inherently have more value and need to be priced accordingly.

Knowing when to raise your prices

In some circumstances, you need to lower your price. But other times you can charge — wait for it — *more.* See, people perceive some products to be more valuable than others — even if, from a practical standpoint, they're not.

Consider how some painters command stratospheric prices for their paintings. It's not because their raw materials were substantially more expensive — paint and canvas cost pretty much the same for everybody. And it's not that their paintings took longer to create. No, these paintings are insanely expensive because the public *perceives* them to be valuable.

When pricing your items, try taking advantage of this notion of "perceived value" and position your pieces as "premium" products. Maybe you employ exceptional materials in crafting your piece. Or maybe you use a unique technique that makes your piece especially durable. Buyers will also perceive your work as more valuable if you've developed a reputation as an artist — perhaps by showing your pieces at galleries or gaining publicity in some other way.

TIP

Talk up your work in your shop, sharing *why* your pieces are valuable. For example, if you not only craft necklaces but also make your own beads, say so. If you use only the best organic cotton to sew your baby clothes, include words to that effect. If you use a particularly difficult technique that only a few other people have mastered, spell that out, too.

Sometimes just tagging your piece with a higher price can make buyers perceive it as more valuable. Of course, that doesn't mean you should offer some useless doodad or otherwise unremarkable item at an outrageous price. (Remember the million-dollar hot dog we mention earlier in this chapter?) People will see right through that ploy. But if you offer an item that's beautifully crafted and truly unique, you may be able to capitalize on this phenomenon.

If demand for an item that you sell is so high that you simply can't keep up, it may be an indication that you've priced it too low. On the flip side, when items don't sell, many shop owners assume it's because they're priced too high. However, it may be the case that your price may be too *low.* Before you start slashing prices in your store, try raising them. You may be pleasantly surprised by the result!

TIP

Evaluate and adjust your prices on an annual basis. The beginning of the new year is a good time to bump up prices.

Something Old: Pricing Vintage Items

If your Etsy shop specializes in the sale of vintage goodies rather than handmade items, you can forget about everything that we discuss earlier in this chapter. No "formula" exists for pricing these types of items. Instead, you must rely on your knowledge of the piece. Specifically, you want to be armed with the following information:

>> **What is the piece?** Obviously, you want to know what, exactly, you have for sale.

>> **How old is the piece?** Older pieces tend to be more valuable than newer ones.

>> **What company manufactured the piece?** Certain manufacturers are held in higher esteem than others. That's why a Tiffany lamp is a lot more valuable than one made by another company and can command a much higher price.

>> **What condition is the piece in?** Clearly, an item in good condition can command a higher price than one that appears to have passed through a farm thresher.

>> **How desirable is the piece?** Items that are rare or highly collectible generate much more interest than run-of-the-mill pieces.

>> **How much time did you invest in the piece?** Consider how much time you spent researching it and in finding it in the first place.

>> **How much did it set you back?** Assuming that you bought the item (instead of, say, unearthing it in your Aunt Mildred's attic), take into account how much you paid for it, as well as any costs you incurred to clean it up, fix any broken bits, and so on.

If you're still not sure where to start, try scoping out the competition. Search Etsy or, dare we say it, eBay to see whether any other sellers have listed something similar, and if so, how much they are charging. This can give you a good starting point (assuming that your piece is in the same condition as theirs).

How Low Can You Go? Pricing for Sales

Many businesses use any excuse to run a sale ("It's Arbor Day! Take 20 Percent Off!") in an attempt to draw in loads of customers and move more merchandise. Although this may be an effective strategy for large, mass-market stores, it's not the best model for your Etsy shop. Running frequent sales not only devalues your work, but it trains your customers to buy from you only when you're running some type of promotion.

That's not to say, however, that you should *never* run a sale. For example, you might run a once-a-year sale to celebrate your store's anniversary or a twice-a-year sale to let go of seasonal inventory. Another idea is to create a permanent "sale" section in your Etsy shop for discontinued, seasonal, or experimental pieces. Or you could generate coupon codes for valuable customers. (Etsy makes this easy, as you see in Chapter 16.)

When you do run a sale, you want to ensure that you still turn a profit on your items — or at least break even. Fortunately, you can easily do so if you use the formula outlined earlier in this chapter to price your goods and list them at the retail price. You can then discount them and still make money.

TIP

Anytime you run a sale, you'll want to spread the word through your marketing efforts. For more information, see Chapter 16.

3

She Sells Seashells (And More): Understanding the Etsy Selling Process

Chapter **11**

Say Cheese! Photographing Your Wares

E ver heard the saying "It's a vision thing"? Nowhere is this more true than on Etsy. Because shoppers on Etsy can't touch, smell, lick, or otherwise handle the goodies in your Etsy shop, they must evaluate each item based on sight.

If you plan to sell on Etsy, it's up to you to supply potential buyers with excellent images of your products — beautiful photos that not only convey the shape, size, color, and texture of your pieces but also reflect you and your broader brand identity. Your photos must elicit in potential buyers a deep, abiding thirst for your items that they can quench only with their purchase.

To make that happen, you need to be handy with a camera. Unfortunately, we can't tell you everything there is to know about photography in just one chapter; after all, books on becoming an expert photographer could fill entire libraries (like the latest edition of *Digital Photography For Dummies*, by Julie Adair King [Wiley]). But by reading this chapter, you can at least master the basics.

TIP

You can find lots of photography resources on Etsy. A good place to start is here: www.etsy.com/seller-handbook/category/photography.

I'll Take That-a-One! Choosing a Camera

When it comes to photographing your wares for Etsy, you don't need some fancy camera that can do everything for you *and* draw you a bubble bath afterward. A trusty digital point-and-shoot in the 8-megapixel range will do the trick, especially if it offers a couple of key features:

>> **A macro setting:** The macro setting, typically represented by a flower icon, enables you to shoot extreme close-ups — critical when photographing smaller pieces, such as jewelry, or when you want to reveal the texture of an item. (If your camera does not have this setting, a simple zoom feature is a decent — though not ideal — substitute.)

>> **Autofocus:** These days, pretty much all cameras offer autofocus. In most cases, you use it by pointing your camera at your subject and pressing the camera's shutter button halfway down; the camera automatically focuses on the subject. To capture the image, simply press the shutter button the rest of the way.

TIP

If you want the area of focus to be off center, just move your camera to the left or right while keeping the shutter button pressed halfway down; then, when you've achieved the desired composition, press the shutter button the rest of the way. (We talk about focusing your photos later in this chapter.)

In addition, here are some "nice to have" features. (Note that these are typically found on digital SLR cameras rather than point-and-shoot models.)

>> **A white balance setting:** With this setting, usually represented with a light bulb icon, you can help your camera identify pure white. The idea here is that if the camera can capture pure white correctly, it can correctly capture (and render) all other colors as well. Setting your camera's white balance before you shoot can save you a bushel of time later trying to correct the color in image-editing programs. (You find out more about image-editing programs later in this chapter.)

>> **A manual mode:** Although you can certainly use the automatic settings on your digital camera, switching to manual mode gives you scads more control over your image's exposure. (*Exposure* refers to the amount of light that strikes a digital camera's sensor.) With manual mode, you can set the camera's

aperture size (that is, the size of the hole through which light passes *en route* from the camera's lens to the digital sensor), shutter speed (the speed at which the aperture opens and closes to capture a photograph), and ISO (which measures the sensor's sensitivity to light). In this way, you prevent the image from being underexposed (too dark) or overexposed (Justin Bieber).

» **An aperture-priority mode:** Like we said, the camera's aperture is the hole through which light passes through the camera's lens to the sensor. You change the size of the aperture by changing the camera's f-stop setting. (Somewhat counterintuitively, the smaller the f-stop value, the larger the aperture.) The size of the aperture affects the image's depth of field. *Depth of field* describes how much of the area in front of and behind the subject appears in focus. In an image with a shallow depth of field, the subject is in focus but the background is blurred. (It's like the photo equivalent of a mullet — clear in the front and blurry in the back.) You achieve a shallow depth of field by using a low f-stop setting. In images with a deep depth of field, the background, subject, and foreground are all in focus. A high f-stop setting yields a deep depth of field. When you use aperture-priority mode, you set the aperture, and the camera adjusts the shutter speed and ISO settings as needed to ensure a proper exposure. (More on that in a minute.) To use aperture-priority mode, simply engage aperture-priority mode on your camera, set your camera's f-stop as low as it goes, press the shutter button halfway down to autofocus on your item, and then snap your photo. (You can read more about the benefits of blurry backgrounds later in this chapter, in the section "Focus, People! Focusing Your Image.")

PHONE HOME: USING THE CAMERA ON YOUR SMARTPHONE

According to research by the Pew Research Center, released in January 2017, 77 percent of Americans own smartphones. That means that more than three-quarters of us have easy access to a digital camera — and a pretty good one, too. True, the camera in your smartphone can't match a good dedicated camera in terms of quality, speed, or control, but that doesn't mean it's not up to the task of capturing clear and compelling product images for your Etsy shop. Indeed, the latest smartphone cameras boast high-resolution sensors (12 megapixels or more — more than enough for use on the web), image-stabilization features, zooming capabilities, and more. Besides, using the camera on your smartphone offers one key benefit: it's a ginormous timesaver. After snapping your shot, you can use your phone's photo-editing tools to clean it up, and then upload it straight to your shop from the Sell on Etsy app. Voilà!

REMEMBER

The aperture size, shutter speed, and ISO work in concert to achieve an optimal exposure. Therefore, if you change one of these settings, you have to adjust the other two as well. For example, if you make the aperture larger, you need to increase the shutter speed and/or choose a less sensitive ISO to ensure that the resulting image isn't overexposed. The key is to strike a balance. (If all this information is freaking you out, simmer down. Just use your camera's automatic setting.)

REMEMBER

If you're in the market for a new camera, get the best model you can afford. And don't be turned off by gently used models — they can be just the ticket for an Etsy seller, at a much lower price!

In Style: Styling Your Photos

Photographers who specialize in product shoots are no strangers to *stylists* — people who work closely with the photographer and other professionals to ensure that the shot contains all the necessary elements. Indeed, high-profile shoots — for example, shoots for magazine advertisements, brochures, and the like — may well have multiple stylists on set, including prop stylists, food stylists, and wardrobe stylists, not to mention full-blown set designers.

Chances are the shoots you conduct for your Etsy shop won't look anything like these affairs. Still, you can adopt some of the practices of these style pros when you're setting up your shoot. These extras include backgrounds, props, and live models to both complement and emphasize the pieces you photograph.

REMEMBER

Your item listing can feature as many as five photo slots, and you should use them all. Etsy suggests that you include one studio shot (that is, a shot of your product with a plain background), a macro shot (a close-up to bring out fine details), a snap for scale (here, you place your product next to a recognizable object or on a model to show its size), and a lifestyle shot (to show your product in its "natural habitat").

Using backgrounds

Although white is the background color of choice for many Etsy sellers — it's crisp, simple, and neutral — it's not your only option. When choosing a background for your photo shoot, keep these points in mind:

>> **Scout your environment for "everyday" backgrounds.** Do you have a garden? If so, consider using a plant or flower as your background (see

Figure 11-1 for an example). Or maybe your living room wall is exposed brick, another excellent background. Really, just about anything works — wooden tables, stone walkways, whitewashed fences . . . the list goes on. These types of backgrounds can serve as excellent complements to your piece.

FIGURE 11-1: Sometimes everyday backgrounds are best.

Photo courtesy of Angela Mahoney (www.etsy.com/shop/swede13)

>> **Reflective surfaces can really shine.** This advice is especially true if your items are delicate or finely made. Placing them on a mildly reflective surface, such as a sterling platter or a white ceramic plate, enables you to add interest as well as improve lighting.

>> **Avoid basic black.** Although black is indisputably the color of choice if you're attempting to hide those ten extra pounds, it's not so great as a background color when you're photographing goodies destined for your Etsy shop. Why? Because darker pieces get lost. Instead, opt for an *almost*-black background — charcoal works well — preferably with a bit of texture to add visual interest.

>> **Add pop with color.** Pieces can really pop with a contrasting color paper or fabric background. Subtle patterns that complement your piece also work well as backgrounds.

TIP

For inexpensive colorful backgrounds, check out your local craft store's scrapbook section. There, you'll find 12-x-12-inch sheets of paper in more colors and patterns than you ever dreamed possible. These papers make perfect backgrounds for smaller pieces. Just steer clear of patterns that are super busy.

>> **Create a seamless background.** Tape one end of a long sheet of thick paper — the kind you cut from a roll — to your wall. Then let it drape down onto a table, where you can clamp the other end. You'll get a seamless "runway" effect that's especially useful for extreme close-ups or times when you don't want anything to distract from your piece (see Figure 11-2).

FIGURE 11-2:
Call attention to your item with a seamless background.

Photo courtesy of Mark Poulin

WARNING

>> **Avoid the "accidental" background.** Heavens to Etsy! The last thing you want potential buyers to see is all your dirty dishes or that pile of newspapers you keep forgetting to recycle! Don't taint your item by photographing it amid all your daily detritus. Make sure that any background you include in your product shots is there *on purpose*.

REMEMBER

>> **Don't give your background star billing.** If your background is more noticeable than the piece you slaved over for days, don't use it.

Working with props

REMEMBER

Props are a great way to add interest to your shot or convey something about the item you're selling. The trick to using them is to make sure they don't detract from the piece you want to sell or otherwise confuse potential buyers. A prop must enhance your piece, conveying to buyers its possibilities. Props also must reflect your brand (see Chapter 16). That is, if your brand is elegant, you want to steer clear of props that scream "Behold my quirkiness!" (and vice versa).

The swell thing about props is that they're everywhere! You can find potential props in your garden shed, your craft closet, your grandmother's attic, your nephew's toy chest, or your uncle's garage. Experiment with lots of different props to see what works best. For example, you can use props as follows:

» **To convey the scale of your piece:** Using a universal prop — something everyone recognizes, like a coin, a book, a pencil, a chair, a toy, food (like in Figure 11-3, which shows a necklace on a pile of beans), or whatnot — is a great way to show potential buyers the size of your piece.

FIGURE 11-3:
Using a universal prop can convey the scale of your piece.

» **To show how your piece can be used:** By putting your piece in its "natural environment," you give potential buyers an idea of how they can use it. For example, if you make USB drives shaped like R2-D2, you could insert one into your laptop's USB port. Or maybe you craft gorgeous place cards; in that case, you might position one atop a lovely vintage plate, to reinforce what your item is and does. (Figure 11-4 shows a colorful handmade pillow on a little girl's bed.)

» **To reflect how your piece was made:** Do you use special tools to construct your item? If so, consider using those implements as props. Knitting needles, embroidery hoops, pliers, cutters, paintbrushes, pencils, scissors, blowtorches — all these constitute excellent props; they add interest by conveying how the piece was made.

» **To suggest what inspired your piece:** Did the idea for your piece come to you while you were walking in the woods? Then a leaf, branch, or pine cone may make an excellent prop. Or if you had the epiphany for your piece while strolling along the seashore, a bit of sand or a seashell may serve as a prop. As another example, Figure 11-5 shows an orange soap set with a group of oranges.

FIGURE 11-4:
You can feature a prop that suggests how to use your piece.

Photo courtesy of Elizabeth Wallberg, e photography

FIGURE 11-5:
Try using a prop that suggests what inspired your piece.

Photo courtesy of Whispering Willow (www.etsy.com/shop/WhisperingWillowSoap)

>> **To complement your piece:** A great way to create interest in your product shots is to place your piece alongside an object that complements it visually. Maybe the object you use as a prop is a complementary color — for example, the object is violet, and your piece is yellow. Or maybe the object reflects the genre of your piece in some way — say, the object is a vintage bowling pin, and your piece is a hand-sewn bowling shirt.

Using live models

Yes, models can be terrible divas. But the fact is, when they're not busy pouting or flinging cellphones at your head, models — whether they're babies, kids, adults, or your pet hamster — can do wonders for your product photos. Why? For two reasons:

>> **Using a live model helps you convey the scale or fit of your piece.** If you shoot your gorgeous necklace with a simple white background, potential buyers may not be able to get a handle on its length. Photographing that same necklace on a model, however, enables buyers to deduce at a glance how long it is, as well as how it rests on the décolletage (see Figure 11-6). Likewise, if you sell hand-sewn clothes in your Etsy shop, photographing your pieces on a live model shows potential buyers how they'll fit.

FIGURE 11-6:
Using a live model can really bring your piece to, er, life.

Photo courtesy of Rae Aldrich-Keisling

>> **Using a live model makes your piece more relatable.** Models humanize your piece. When potential buyers see a model wearing your item, they inevitably imagine it looking just as fantastic on themselves. The same is true when you show a model using your item: Potential buyers naturally imagine themselves using it in the same way.

Of course, you can't use just any model. You want to choose models who enhance, not detract from, your piece. Be sure to select models who reflect your brand and your target audience. For example, if your brand and target audience are on the edgy or punk end of the spectrum, your models need to be, too (think tattoos, piercings, mohawks, and so on). However, if your aesthetic is more romantic, your models need to look that way as well.

TIP

Who should you enlist to model your pieces? Friends and family are obvious (and inexpensive) choices — assuming that they're appropriate for your brand and aesthetic. If you're selling a premium item, consider investing in a pro.

Lighting Bug: Lighting Your Shot

If you've ever seen Cybill Shepherd in *Moonlighting*, you know the importance of flattering lighting! No doubt about it, whether you're photographing an aging actress or a tea towel on which you've embroidered the periodic table, good lighting is essential. Without it, your camera simply can't capture the color and texture of your piece.

REMEMBER

The good news is, you don't need to start selling your plasma to afford to buy an expensive lighting rig. When it comes to photographing the goodies you've made for your Etsy shop, natural lighting — say, from a north-facing window or outside on an overcast day — is best. It's by far the most flattering light source. In addition, it enables you to capture the colors and texture of your piece.

On the topic of shooting outdoors, a word of advice: Avoid direct sunlight. Direct sunlight — the kind you get midday, when the sun is high in the sky, and when there are no clouds — can overexpose your photo, washing it out. It also causes the image to appear harsher to the eye. Instead, try to capture your photos during the "golden hours." No, we're not recommending that you shoot during reruns of *The Golden Girls*. We're encouraging you to use the natural light available in the early morning, right after the sun rises, or near sunset, when the sun is low in the sky. You'll find the natural light during these periods to be as flattering as 4-inch heels.

If you can't avoid shooting in direct sunlight, try diffusing the light — for example, positioning a sheer curtain between the sun and the piece you're photographing. Figures 11-7 and 11-8 show the difference between an object photographed in full sun and one photographed in diffused light. Notice how the diffused light in the second image softens the whole shot.

FIGURE 11-7:
Notice how shooting in full sun results in a harsh image.

TIP

For the love of all that's holy, if you can avoid it, don't use your flash when photographing items for your Etsy shop — unless harsh shadows, glare, reflections, and a generally flat appearance will somehow enhance your item's salability.

If you simply can't achieve the necessary exposure without using your flash, consider covering the flash with tracing paper, white tissue paper, or some other sheer material to diffuse it. Even better, you can put reflectors to work. Use white walls or other homegrown reflective surfaces (think white poster board, a hanging bed sheet, or, for a brighter reflection, a mirror) to "bounce" light onto your piece. Figures 11-9 and 11-10 show two images from the same shoot — the first without reflectors and the second with reflectors. Notice that the first image is darker and a wee bit muddy. In contrast, the face of the angel in the second image pops a bit more, for an overall brighter, happier look.

Photo courtesy of Rebecca Lang

Photograph courtesy of Allison Strine

TIP

Especially if you craft wee things — jewelry, personalized guitar picks, pet por-
traits on grains of rice — you may want to consider using a light tent. A *light tent*,
sometimes called a *light box*, is a small structure made of transparent white fabric or plastic in which you place your item to photograph it. Light tents, which
can be used with natural light or a simple lighting kit, come in a variety of

shapes and sizes. Alternatively, you can build your own light tent for a song. For help, visit www.etsy.com/seller-handbook/article/how-to-make-your-own-photography/22926118925.

FIGURE 11-10:
Notice how using a reflector really lights up the piece.

Compose Yourself: Composing Your Shot

Suppose that you found yourself at the Statue of Liberty with Annie Leibovitz. And suppose further that both of you were photographing Lady Liberty. No offense, but her pictures would probably be way better than yours — more captivating, more vital, more powerful, more interesting. Why? Well, lots of reasons. One, Leibovitz probably has a camera that's so good, it practically has super powers. But more than that, Leibovitz has a keen eye for *composition* — the arrangement of visual elements in an image. Take heart, though. Just because you're no Annie Leibovitz doesn't mean you can't compose some really swell photos of your own for your Etsy shop. The pointers in the following sections can help.

Trying basic composition principles

As you shoot your pieces, keep these basic compositional points in mind. These will make your photographs truly stand apart.

>> **Angle the camera.** Angling, or tilting, the camera puts the subject slightly off center and creates movement and flow. The result: a more dynamic, intriguing image, as you can see in Figure 11-11.

FIGURE 11-11:
Angling the
camera produces
interesting
results.

Photo courtesy of Colette Urquhart

>> **Shoot tight.** Filling the frame with your subject not only adds visual impact but also enables potential buyers to see how well made your piece is (see for yourself in Figure 11-12).

FIGURE 11-12:
Shoot tight, for
added impact.

Photo courtesy of Kristen Timmers

>> **Blur the background.** Remember that photographic mullet we mentioned earlier? It's such a good idea, we're bringing it up again. By using a shallow depth of field (read: a low f-stop setting), you can blur the background to dramatically highlight your piece, as shown in Figure 11-13.

Photo courtesy of Betsy and Bess (Christopher and Adrienne Scott; www.etsy.com/shop/betsyandbess)

TIP

When the background is blurred, you can shoot in almost any setting; just make sure that the background colors don't clash with your subject. (For more on depth of field, see the later section "Focus, People! Focusing Your Image.")

>> **Less is more.** Don't crowd the scene with extraneous objects. Otherwise, potential buyers may not understand exactly which item in your photo is for sale.

>> **Frame your subject.** One way to highlight your piece is to frame it — that is, place some darker element in the perimeter. This technique helps prevent the viewer's eye from straying from your item.

>> **Group pieces.** Especially if you make itsy-bitsy goodies, you can try grouping them to catch a buyer's eye. Not only does this strategy make for a more eye-catching photograph, but it also shows potential buyers how pieces in your collection work together. Just be sure to note in your listing description which one of the items in the group is actually up for grabs. Also, avoid groups that are too large; three to five pieces does the trick.

Applying the rule of thirds

TIP

To be perfectly honest, we're not big on rules. (This may explain why we're both self-employed.) But one rule we can absolutely get behind is the rule of thirds. In addition to conveying a sense of tension and energy, the rule of thirds helps pique the viewer's interest.

According to this rule, you should use two horizontal lines and two vertical lines to divide the scene you're photographing into nine equal parts (think of a tic-tac-toe grid, like in Figure 11-14). Then place key elements at any of the four points where the vertical and horizontal lines intersect (see Figure 11-15), or use the lines themselves as guides as you compose your image.

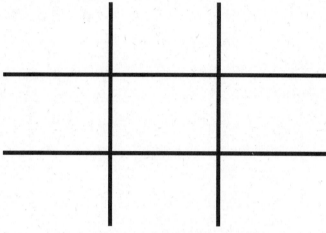

FIGURE 11-14:
Imagine a three-by-three grid.

Illustration by Wiley, Composition Services Graphics

FIGURE 11-15:
Use the grid to compose your image.

Photo courtesy of Heather Torre (www.etsy.com/shop/myselvagedlife)

With some digital cameras and even cameras in smartphones, you can display a grid on the screen, enabling you to organize your image around the lines and cross points.

TIP

Focus, People! Focusing Your Image

A surefire way to turn off buyers is to include blurry images in your Etsy shop, especially if they're close-ups. How's a potential buyer supposed to view your piece in all its detailed splendor if your photos are as hazy as a bootlegger's alibi? It's imperative that your product photos be crisp and clear, as in Figure 11-16.

FIGURE 11-16: Notice how crisp and clear this in-focus photo is.

Photo courtesy of Becca Balistreri

To ensure excellent focus if you're shooting a close-up, use your camera's macro setting. This setting (which, as mentioned, is usually indicated with a flower icon) ensures that your focus is sharp. This setting works better than simply zooming in. If you're using the camera on your smartphone, you may not have access to a macro setting. In that case, look into buying a macro phone lens.

TIP

If you're using a slower shutter speed or you just drank a quadruple espresso, you need to take special care to keep your camera still as you photograph your piece. Using a tripod is one way to go; alternatively, you can rest your camera on a table or a stack of books.

Shoot, Shoot, and Shoot Some More: Taking Lots of Pictures

Back when film — not to mention the cost of developing it — put you back a pretty penny, you may have been justified in being stingy with your shots. But these days, it's all digital, dawg! You can — and should — shoot lots of shots. And by lots, we mean *lots*. Like, a whole bunch. A gazillion should do the trick.

TIP

If you end up with more photos than you need, you can always add them to your Shop Updates feed. That way, your followers can see more of your photo shoot. For more on the Shop Updates feed, see Chapter 16.

The point is, your product photos have to be *great* — like, Muhammad Ali, Audrey Hepburn, Paul Newman great. Like we said earlier, they need to convey the shape, size, color, and texture of your piece as well as reflect you and your broader brand identity. On top of all of that, they need to be easy on the eyes. Unless you're Helmut Newton (which would be amazing, given that he's dead), you're just not going to capture all of that with a single click of the shutter button.

One more tip: As you shoot, make it a point to experiment. Swap out props and backgrounds. Try different angles, lighting, and depths of field. It's the only way to ensure that you wind up with a winning picture.

TIP

Whatever your approach, you should try to designate a place for taking pictures and establish a routine. At the very least, write down your methods. All sellers, but particularly vintage sellers, will find themselves spending a lot of time taking pictures. Developing a specific method to follow each time will help keep labor costs down.

Clean-Up on Image Five: Tidying Up Your Photos with Image-Editing Software

Even the best photos can use a little tidying up. For example, you may want to adjust the image's brightness or contrast, tweak the color in an image to make it really pop, or crop the image to make your subject stand out.

REMEMBER

Please, we beg you: Don't use image-editing software to try to "fix" a bad photo. Some photos — photos that are dark, blurry, or otherwise foul — are simply beyond repair. Image-editing programs are for enhancement purposes only.

Fortunately, any number of image-editing programs are available to you, ranging in price from free to the cost of your arm and your leg. Unfortunately, we can't cover the ins and outs of using all these programs. But to give you a basic idea of how it's done, in the following sections, we step you through the process using Pic Monkey (www.picmonkey.com), a free online photo-editing service, to fix your photos.

Starting with Pic Monkey and opening a photo

Before you begin, copy the images you want to clean up from your camera to your computer. Then direct your web browser to www.picmonkey.com. On the site's main page, click Edit a Photo. Then, in the screen that appears, click the Open button, and choose Computer from the menu that appears. Pic Monkey launches a standard File Open dialog box. Navigate to the folder that contains the photo you want to edit, click the photo file, and click Open. The photo opens in Pic Monkey, as shown in Figure 11-17.

FIGURE 11-17:
Open your photo in Pic Monkey.

Source: picmonkey.com

Editing your photo in Pic Monkey

One way to edit your photo using Pic Monkey is to use the site's Auto Adjust feature. Simply click the Auto Adjust button in the top-left area of the screen, under Basic Edits. Pic Monkey automatically adjusts the photo's exposure, color, and clarity settings.

If you don't like the results of an edit, click the Undo button. It's in the toolbar just below the photograph. (It features a curved arrow pointing to the left.)

If you still want to tweak the photo, you can use the various Basic Edits settings below the Auto Adjust button. For example, if you've captured some extraneous items in your image, or you simply want to focus it more tightly on your piece, you can crop it. To crop the image using Pic Monkey, click the Crop option. The Crop section expands to reveal various cropping settings, as shown in Figure 11-18. These include a proportion setting, a size setting, an option to scale the photo, and an option to rotate the crop box, which appears over the photo on the right to indicate which portion of the image will be cropped. Adjust these settings as needed; then click on an edge or corner of the crop box and drag inward or outward to shrink or expand the box, respectively. To adjust the placement of the box over the photo, click inside the box and then drag it in the desired direction.

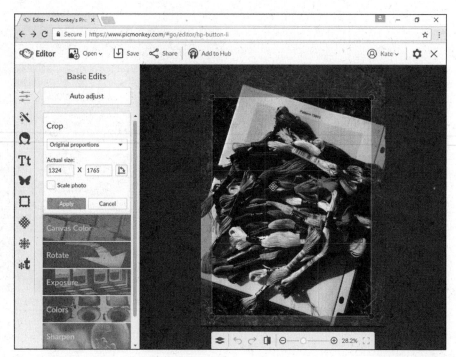

FIGURE 11-18: Crop your photo.

Source: picmonkey.com

REMEMBER

Etsy recommends that product images bound for your Etsy shop be at least 1,000 pixels wide. That way, shoppers will be able to use the site's Zoom button to zoom in on your image.

Earlier, we talked about how tilting your camera can create a more interesting photo. You can mimic this effect by using Pic Monkey's Rotate tool. You can use this tool to rotate the photo by 90 degrees counterclockwise or clockwise; flip the photo horizontally or vertically; or drag the Straighten slider left or right for more incremental adjustments.

Other useful Basic Edits settings include Exposure, Colors, and Sharpen. With the Exposure settings, you can tweak the image's brightness, highlights, shadows, and contrast. The Color settings allow you to adjust the image's white balance, color saturation, and color temperature. And the Sharpen tools enable you to boost the sharpness and clarity of the image. Or, for finer control, you can use the unsharp mask. All these tools are remarkably easy to use! (Figure 11-19 shows the Rotate, Exposure, Colors, and Sharpen settings.)

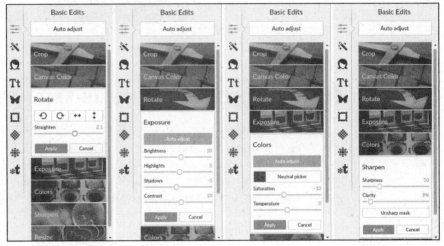

FIGURE 11-19:
Pic Monkey's
Rotate, Exposure,
Colors, and
Sharpen settings.

Source: picmonkey.com

Saving your changes

To ensure that all your hard work doesn't go to waste, you must save your edited photo. To do so, click the Save button at the top of the Pic Monkey screen. The Save My Masterpiece screen opens (see Figure 11-20). Choose a name for the photo, a quality level (named Roger, Pierce, and Sean in a clever homage to James Bond; naturally, Sean is best), and, optionally, the dimensions. Then click Save to My Computer. Pic Monkey launches a standard Save As dialog box; navigate to the folder where you want to save the file and click Save.

FIGURE 11-20:
Save your
changes.

Source: picmonkey.com

EDITING PHOTOS ON YOUR SMARTPHONE

If you captured your images using your smartphone camera, you can edit them right on your phone. Most phones include built-in editing tools, which work well. If you're looking for something a little more robust, you can download any number of suitable apps. Snapseed is a good one, and, like many of these apps, it's free for both iOS and Android users. Or use the photo-editing tools that are baked in to the Sell on Etsy app.

Chapter **12**

Word Up: Composing Engaging Titles and Descriptions

True, a gorgeous photo of your piece may catch a buyer's eye. But the way you write about your piece in your listing title and description can keep your buyer's attention. With these textual elements, you have an opportunity to engage buyers with a story about you and your piece. You can also answer questions about your piece, such as what it's made of, what it does, and why someone should buy it. Indeed, well-written and interesting titles and descriptions may just persuade a buyer to add your piece to her cart.

If your talents lie more in crafting and less in writing ("I'm a candy-wrapper handbag maker, not a writer!"), don't freak out. As you discover in this chapter, writing engaging listing titles and descriptions is plenty doable. You also find out how to optimize your listing titles, descriptions, and tags for searching, making it easier for prospective buyers to find your piece.

This chapter is about the nuts and bolts of writing engaging titles and descriptions, choosing good keywords, and what constitutes a good tag. In Chapter 13, you find out how to apply all this knowledge to an actual listing in Etsy.

Headline Muse: Writing Titillating Listing Titles

Your listing title acts like a good headline. It's designed to grab a buyer's attention. It also factors into Etsy's search system. So, although you want to come up with a title that will pique a buyer's interest, you also want to make sure it's optimized for search. Otherwise, that buyer may not ever find your listing! (You find out more about search engine optimization later in this chapter.)

Here are some things to keep in mind when composing listing titles:

- » **Keep it short.** Your listing title must be brief — no more than 140 characters (including spaces).

- » **Clearly describe your item at the beginning of the listing title.** This helps improve the chances that others will find your item when searching on Etsy.

- » **Use a mix of uppercase and lowercase letters.** Too many all-uppercase words and it seems like you're shouting. Too many lowercase words and it seems like you're e. e. cummings.

REMEMBER

Your listing title needs to broadcast key information about your piece — most notably, what it is, what it's made of, and perhaps a few choice details about the piece, such as its color, size, who it's for, or where you might put it.

Story Time: Telling a Story with Your Listing Description

People who buy on Etsy aren't interested in meaningless, mass-produced goods. They want pieces with a past — something that has a story. Etsy allows sellers to enter a listing description so they can tell the story behind their product. In the following sections, we explain how to uncover an item's story, answer questions about the item, and compose a thoughtful description.

TIP

If your product merits a disclaimer, you can include it in the listing. For example, if it's a vintage item, you may want to include a disclaimer indicating that it's old and used. If it's copper jewelry, you can mention in a disclaimer that the piece might turn people's skin green. Or if it's a hand-crafted toy that's suitable only for children above a certain age, you can include a disclaimer to that effect.

Uncovering your item's story

Not sure what your piece's story is — or whether it even has one? Fear not. Start spinning your yarn (figuratively speaking) by answering a few questions:

>> **What inspired you to create the piece?** Mentioning your source of inspiration is a great way to get the ball rolling. If you're a candy-wrapper handbag maker, maybe you got the idea to make candy-wrapper handbags while traveling in Mexico, where artisans craft all manner of items out of candy wrappers, including clutches, totes, and placemats.

>> **How was the piece made?** Indicating the skills involved in making an item can be an excellent way to forge a connection with buyers. Was it woven? Sewn? Assembled by magical hamsters?

>> **Who taught you the skills you use to create your piece?** Sharing how you learned the techniques you use to craft your pieces can be a great way to bond with prospective buyers. Maybe your great-grandmother learned the fine art of candy-wrapper handbag making and passed her skills down to you. Or maybe your uncle was a Mayan studies scholar and taught you their paper-weaving techniques — techniques that you then put to use making candy-wrapper handbags to justify your prodigious candy-eating habit.

TIP

Even if you choose not to focus on the story behind your item, don't hesitate to let your own personality and the "personality" of your brand shine through in your listing description. If you and your brand tend toward quirky, then your listing descriptions should, too. Ditto if you and your brand have a more formal bent.

Describing your item

It probably goes without saying that, in addition to including the "story" behind you and your piece, your listing description must contain, well, a description of your item. But we believe in being thorough, so we're saying it. Think about what questions buyers are likely to have about your piece. Then answer all those questions in your listing description. The description may cover the following points:

>> **What is your piece?** Although it may seem obvious to you that your item is a handbag made of Snickers wrappers, to others, it may be less apparent.

>> **What does your piece do?** Does your piece have a function? Or is it for decoration only? Be sure to note this info in your listing description.

>> **Who is your piece for?** Dogs? Babies? Men? On the flip side, who is it *not* for? For example, if it is a toy for older children that contains pieces on which an infant might choke, you should definitely note that in your listing description.

>> **How does your piece work?** Does it have a clasp? Buttons? A zipper? Do you tie it? Does it need batteries, or do you power it by driving a DeLorean equipped with a lightning rod past the town clock tower during a thunderstorm?

>> **What color is your piece?** Colors may translate differently on different computer monitors. Including detailed color information in your listing description is a good way to bridge that gap.

TIP

Be specific here. Don't say that your piece is red when it's actually scarlet, brick, ruby, cherry, crimson, or burgundy.

>> **How big is your piece?** Remember in *This Is Spinal Tap* when Nigel Tufnel sketches out specs for a Stonehenge stage set but accidentally uses a double-prime mark (for inches) instead of a prime mark (for feet)? The result is an 18-inch Stonehenge monument that is, as David St. Hubbins observes, "in danger of being crushed by a dwarf." To save your buyer from experiencing similar disappointment, include detailed and accurate sizing information about your piece. Avoid vague terms like *small* or *large*. Instead, opt for precise measurements, especially if you sell clothing. By the way, it doesn't hurt to include both systems of measurement — metric and old-school — in your listing descriptions.

>> **What materials did you use?** Do you use organic cotton? Hand-dyed wool? Swarovski crystals? Wrappers from Reese's Peanut Butter Cups? Whatever materials you use, they need to appear in your listing description. (Note that you can also add as many as 13 materials during the listing process, which will appear in the listing's overview. For more on that, see Chapter 13.)

>> **What techniques did you use to construct your piece?** Did you knit it? Weave it? Sew it? This info helps tell the story of your piece and reinforces to buyers that you made it by hand. It also helps attract buyers who are partial to a particular crafting technique.

TIP

If you've priced your item on the higher side, be sure to indicate why in your listing description. Whether it's because you used high-end materials or because you crafted it using a particularly difficult technique, you need to share this info with your buyer. What is it that makes it special or valuable or unique? (Flip to Chapter 10 for more information on pricing your items.)

>> **What does your piece feel like?** Is it soft? Smooth? Slick? Rough? Nubby? Scaly? Prickly? Stubbly? Indicate your item's tactile qualities in your listing description.

>> **What does your piece smell like?** Does it have a scent, such as lavender or ylang-ylang? If it's a vintage piece, does it have a musty odor? Does it come from a smoker's home?

Composing your listing description

You have a handle on the story behind your item, and you know what information your listing needs to contain. Now it's time to put the proverbial pen to paper and write your listing description.

REMEMBER

To make your listing description as effective as possible, put the most important information about your item first. This not only makes it easier for shoppers to quickly get the information they need about your piece, but it also enables you to optimize your shop for search. (We talk more about search engine optimization later in this chapter.) It's also more mobile-friendly, enabling shoppers with smaller screens to access the info they need right away.

Of course, what constitutes "the most important information" may differ from piece to piece; in general, however, this info likely includes what your item is, what it does, what it looks like, and what it's made of. From there, you can get into more "nice to know" information, such as what your item smells like (unless, of course, the whole point of your item is its smell, as is the case with soap, perfume, and the like) as well as the story behind your item or your work.

TIP

To keep your prospective buyer reading, use short paragraphs and bullet points. That construction is easier on the eyes than a gigantic block of text. Another way to break things up is to use subtitles — for example, one above the listing description, one on top of any measurements information, and so on. You can set these subtitles apart from regular text by using all caps or boldface font.

Consider this example of a listing description that falls short:

> Bag made of candy wrappers
>
> Size: Medium

We don't know about you, but nothing in this description makes us want to buy the bag. Yes, the seller was brief — score one for her. But this description almost completely lacks any useful information! Worse, it's as though the seller just can't be bothered to tell anyone about her item.

Following is an example of a much more effective listing description:

> Bonkers for bonbons? Then this candy-wrapper handbag is for you. This colorful, eco-friendly handbag, carefully hand-woven using Kit Kat, Nestlé Crunch, and Snickers candy wrappers, is just the right size to carry a phone, wallet, and candy bar (of course).

I crafted this handbag, which can double as a makeup bag, using a technique I learned from my candy-crazy aunt. The handbag, which measures 22 centimeters (8.7 inches) across and 14 centimeters (5.5 inches) high, features a zipper along the top as well as a color-coordinated wristlet for easy carrying. The use of candy wrappers gives the handbag a slightly shiny, reflective quality, and a mild, chocolaty aroma.

This candy-wrapper handbag is perfect for anyone with a sweet tooth!

Now, *this* description makes us want to buy this handbag, pronto. (And also pound a Kit Kat.)

SEO Speedwagon: Using Search Engine Optimization to Drive Traffic

Remember *Field of Dreams*? Spoiler alert: It told the story of a failing Iowa farmer, Ray Kinsella, who hears a mysterious voice in his cornfield that whispers, "If you build it, he will come." Soon thereafter, he has a vision of a baseball diamond in his field. He builds the diamond, which then attracts the ghost of Ray's favorite baseball player, Shoeless Joe Jackson, and the rest of the roster for the 1919 Chicago Black Sox. Subsequently, a large enough crowd of tourists arrives to save Ray's family farm. Don't get us wrong — it's a nice story and all. But unless you specialize in hand-crafting redemption for disgraced baseball players from another dimension, the odds of the same thing happening with your Etsy shop are slim to none.

You have to do more than just build your Etsy shop to entice people to visit it. As you find out in this book, you need to supply gorgeous photos and intriguing descriptions of your wares. In addition, you need to engage in a little something called *search engine optimization (SEO)*. By using SEO, you can increase the likelihood that people who use search engines such as Google, Yahoo!, or Bing to search for certain keywords will see — and click — a link to your Etsy shop or one of your listings in their list of results. SEO is also critical to ensuring that shoppers already on Etsy's site can find your items.

How can you harness the power of SEO for your Etsy shop? One way is to plant relevant keywords in your shop title and shop sections (see Chapter 8 for details). That way, people searching for those keywords will see your Etsy shop in their search results. Another way is to include these keywords in your shop listing titles, descriptions, and tags, which is the focus of this section.

Choosing the best keywords

First, what keywords should you use? Suppose that you hand-craft bracelets out of bottle caps. Sure, you can use keywords like *bracelet* or even *jewelry* in your item listings — in fact, you should. The problem is, you're not the only one using those terms. A recent Google search for the term *jewelry* yielded over a billion — that's *billion*, with a *B* — hits. Adding *bracelet* to the search string narrowed the list somewhat, but it still yielded roughly 92 million hits. Including *bottle cap* got us down to about 3 million matches.

No doubt about it, 3 million is less than a billion — but not if your shop is buried in the bottom 2,999,999 matches. Why? Because when most people use a search engine, they don't dig deeper than the first few pages of search results (if they even go that far) to find what they're looking for. To increase traffic to your Etsy storefront, you must ensure that links to your items or shop appear in those first few pages — preferably on page one.

REMEMBER

Now, you may think that you need to focus on the higher-volume keywords or phrases — that is, keywords like *jewelry* rather than phrases such as *bottle cap bracelet*. After all, more people are searching for those. But given how many matches are in that category, the chances of your shop or item ranking near the top are essentially nil. You have a much better chance of appearing near the top of the results for a narrow search, like *bottle cap bracelet*.

Etsy offers some handy tools to help you identify what keywords will drive traffic to your shop. One is Shop Stats. This tool lists the keywords people use most often to find your shop. If you're not currently using any of the top keywords in your shop title and shop sections, you can add them. Or you can look up synonyms for those keywords and add them, too. (For more about Shop Stats, see Chapter 18.)

Another way to identify top keywords is to use Etsy's Search feature. Just start typing what you sell into the Search bar and see what words and phrases pop up. These reflect popular search terms. You can incorporate these terms into your SEO strategy.

You can also employ third-party tools for help with SEO. One is EtsyRank (www.etsyrank.com). This free online service includes a keyword tool, which generates killer ideas for listing keywords and tags. Another is Marmalead (www.marmalead.com), which offers similar functionality.

IN-BOUND AND DETERMINED: GARNERING IN-BOUND LINKS

In addition to the keywords and phrases you plant in your listing title and listing description (as well as in your shop title and shop sections), you can optimize your Etsy shop and listings for search through in-bound links. An *in-bound link* is a link from another page to your Etsy shop or listing. Google and other search engines rate pages on how interesting they are, which they gauge in part by determining how many in-bound links a page has, as well as how credible the pages containing those links are. So the more pages that link to your Etsy shop or item listing and the more credible those pages are, the higher your shop or listing appears in search results.

How can you garner more in-bound links? One way is to ask friends and family members who maintain blogs or social media accounts (for example, on Facebook or Twitter) to link to your shop. You can also use your own blog and social media accounts for the same purpose. In addition, you can build in-bound links by participating in the Etsy forums (see Chapter 20) and commenting on Etsy Blog articles (see Chapter 21). You can even include links to pages in your shop *within your shop* to build in-bound links, even though that may seem kind of like cheating. And, of course, you can encourage others to link to your Etsy shop and items by linking to their Etsy shops and items. What goes around comes around!

Using SEO with your listing title and description

Like we said, it's not enough to write catchy listing titles. You also need to perform a little SEO magic to ensure that those titles are optimized for search. As you do, keep a few points in mind:

» **Include keywords but not too many.** Every listing title that you write needs to contain at least one keyword or phrase (more, if possible). But stuffing your title with too many keywords may render it completely unreadable. Ideally, try to write titles that are catchy for both people *and* PCs.

» **Put keywords first.** Place keywords at or near the beginning of your listing title. Although search engines search your entire title for keyword matches, they display only the first 66 characters (including spaces) of it in the list of results. To increase the chances that anyone searching for that keyword will visit your shop, you want to make sure that the keyword shows up in that results list.

The same points apply to your listing description — except one: Search engines display more characters from your listing description in search results (160 in all, including spaces). But again, even though you have a little more wiggle room, you want to make sure that your keywords appear toward the beginning. You also want to repeat any keywords at least once (but preferably two or three times) in your listing description, to boost your Etsy shop in the search rankings.

Here's an example of an item listing that makes good use of keywords:

Nehi Grape Bottle Cap Bracelet: Grape Expectations

Quench your thirst for handmade jewelry with this bottle cap bracelet! This eco-friendly bracelet represents the finest in bottle cap crafts. Constructed from vintage Nehi Grape bottle caps from my grandfather's attic, sterling silver findings, and purple Swarovski crystal beads, the bracelet measures 7 inches (17.7 centimeters) across but can be adjusted to accommodate a more diminutive wrist.

As you type your description in Etsy, you can view how it will appear in Google search results, as shown in Figure 12-1. Simply click the Show Preview link under the Description text box. (For more on entering titles and descriptions as you list items, see Chapter 13.)

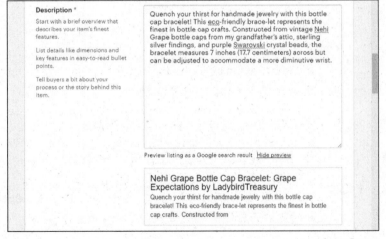

FIGURE 12-1:
Preview how your listing will appear in Google search results.

Source: Etsy.com

Understanding tags and attributes

In addition to incorporating keywords into your Etsy item listings, you should add tags. A *tag* is a word or short phrase, called *metadata*, that is attached to your item. Etsy uses these tags to help shoppers locate your item. Think of a tag as being the salt to a keyword's pepper . . . the Captain to its Tennille, if you will. In other words, tags and keywords often work together. For example, suppose that you've tagged your item with the term *bottle cap.* If someone types the keyword *bottle cap* when performing an Etsy search, your item will be among the results. (Adding tags to an item listing is covered in Chapter 13.)

Because tagging is so critical to Etsy's search functionality, it's crucial for you to apply strong tags to your listing. When deciding what tags to apply, ask yourself what keywords you would enter if you were searching for your item. Also, keep an eye on your Shop Stats to find out what search terms people are using to find your items. You can add as many as 13 tags per listing.

As you add tags, consider these tips:

>> **Start with the most obvious terms first.** For example, suppose that you're selling a hand-sewn handbag. You might apply tags such as *purse* and *handbag.*

>> **Apply tags that indicate the style of the handbag.** This could be *formal, casual, Goth, hippie, frilly,* or whatever.

>> **Select tags to convey the item's physical qualities.** For example, you could add a tag to convey the bag's size (for example, *large*) or texture (such as *quilted, shiny, matte,* or what have you).

>> **Add tags to indicate any motifs used in the purse.** Think *Betty Boop, owls,* or *race car.*

>> **Add tags that indicate who the item is for.** Maybe it's for men. Maybe it's for dogs. Maybe it's for men *and* dogs.

>> **Include phrases as tags.** People often enter phrases in the Search bar — think *Goth handbag* or *quilted purse.* If they type one of the ones you've selected as a tag, your listing will leapfrog to the top of their search results. (Note that tags can contain only 20 characters, though, so tags like *supercalifragilisticexpialidocious T-shirt* are a no-go.)

>> **Reuse keywords.** It doesn't hurt to use some of the keywords from the listing title and description as tags.

Etsy also leaves room for you to apply material–specific tags. These don't count toward the 13 tags. Examples of these types of tags might include *twill, satin, wool, leather,* and so on.

REMEMBER

If your piece is for a mature audience, you must tag it with the word *mature.*

In addition to any tags you choose to apply to your listing, Etsy includes a few more, based on item attributes you select in the item listing. These attributes include the item's primary color, its secondary color, and whether it's suitable for a particular holiday or occasion. Depending on what type of item it is, you may also be able to set other attributes, such as size, volume, and more. Check out more about attributes in Chapter 13.

Proofread, Please! Proofreading Your Listing

Years ago, a neighborhood garden store posted a lovely yellow sign. It had been painted with care, its green letters tidy and even. The problem? Those green letters spelled out the following word: SHURBS. Presumably, the nursery, known for its fine selection of plants, had intended to advertise its lovely collection of shrubs. Instead, it broadcasted its carelessness and lack of attention to detail.

As an Etsy shop owner, it's imperative that you (or someone you trust) proofread everything you post in your shop — listing titles and descriptions included. Failing to do so may well lead potential buyers to conclude that you're sloppy, that you don't take pride in your work, or that you're incompetent. And *that* will likely prompt them to shop elsewhere!

TIP

Use a word-processing program (like Microsoft Word) to compose your listing titles and descriptions instead of typing them directly into Etsy. That way, you can take advantage of word-processing tools like spell check. You can then copy and paste the listing title and description from your word-processing document to Etsy. As a bonus, this approach makes it easier to reuse listing descriptions either in part or in full for new items down the road.

In addition to proofreading for spelling and grammatical errors, peruse your posts for other problems, such as redundant information. Big, pretentious words and fancy, genre-specific terms are other no-nos. For best results, stick with the common vernacular. Finally, keep in mind that not everyone on Etsy speaks English as a first language. Don't include words or phrases in your listings that are likely to cause problems for these shoppers.

Chapter **13**

Selling Like Hotcakes: Listing Your Items

Fish gotta swim. Birds gotta fly. Camels gotta spit. And Etsy sellers . . . well, Etsy sellers gotta sell. The first step to selling on Etsy — after setting up your Etsy store (and crafting or curating the piece you want to sell) — is to create an item listing.

Simply put, an item listing is a page in your Etsy store that contains information about an item you have for sale. This item listing contains an item title and description, a list of materials you used to create your piece, a category and tags to help buyers find your item, images of your piece (you can include as many as five), pricing information, shipping details, and more.

In Chapter 11, you discover how to photograph your items. Chapter 12 is devoted to the ins and outs of composing item titles and descriptions. In this chapter, you put it all together and create your first Etsy listing!

Lister, Lister: Listing a New Item

Listing a piece in your Etsy shop is surprisingly painless — provided you've done all the necessary legwork first. That is, you've composed your item title and description, captured a few gorgeous pictures of your piece, set its price, established your shop policies, and so on. Etsy walks you through the whole process, which we cover in the following sections.

Starting the listing process

After you log in to your Etsy account, follow these steps to begin the listing process:

1. **Click the Shop Manager button along the top of any Etsy Marketplace page.**

   As shown in Figure 13-1, the Shop Manager page appears.

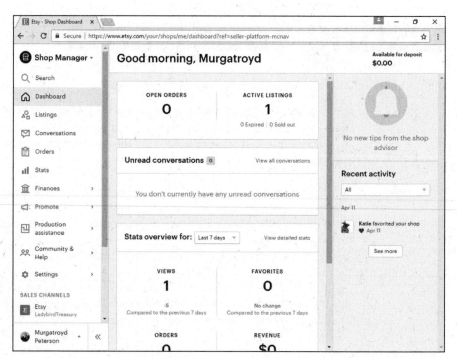

Source: Etsy.com

FIGURE 13-1:
The Shop Manager page.

2. **On the left side of the Shop Manager page, click the Listings link.**

   The Listings page opens (see Figure 13-2).

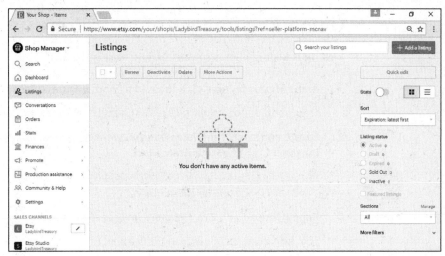

FIGURE 13-2:
The Listings
Manager.

Source: Etsy.com

3. **Click the Add a Listing button in the upper-right corner of the page.**

The Add a New Listing page opens (see Figure 13-3).

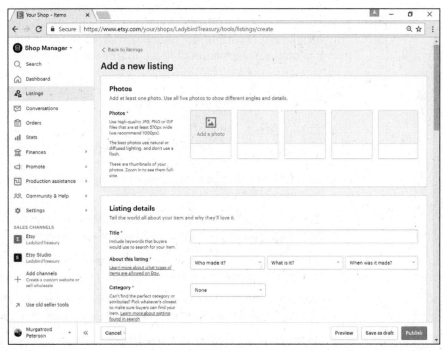

FIGURE 13-3:
Use this page to
create a listing.

Source: Etsy.com

Uploading images of your item

Next up is adding photos to your listing. Here's the drill:

1. **In the Photos section, click the Add a Photo button (refer to Figure 13-3).**

   The Choose File to Upload (PC) or File Upload (Mac) dialog box opens.

2. **Locate and select the first image you want to upload, and click the Open button (PC) or Choose button (Mac).**

   Per Etsy, images you upload should be JPGs, GIFs, or PNGs and be at least 1,000 pixels wide (the height can vary).

   REMEMBER

3. **Repeat Steps 1 and 2 to add more images to your listing.**

   Your listing can feature as many as five images — and that's how many you should add!

4. **To change the order in which the images appear in your listing, click the image that you want to move and drag it either left to move it up in the order or right to move it down in the order.**

   The first image in the list will be the thumbnail image that appears in search results and as the main, featured image in the item listing, so make it a good one! Ideally, this first image should be square. That way, the image won't get cut off in thumbnail view. (To adjust the thumbnail, click the Adjust Thumbnail button and zoom in on the image and/or drag it until the focal point is centered just right.)

   TIP

Describing your item

The Listing Details section of the Add a New Listing page (see Figure 13-4) is where you convey all the important details about your item. Follow these steps:

1. **In the Title field, type a title for your listing. (See Chapter 12 for help writing a solid listing title.)**

2. **Next to About This Listing, click the Who Made It? drop-down list and select the option that best reflects who made the item.**

3. **Click the What Is It? drop-down list that appears and indicate whether the item is a finished product or a supply or tool to make things.**

4. **Click the When Was It Made? drop-down list that appears and choose the option that best describes when the item was made.**

5. **In the Category section, click the drop-down list and choose a category for your item.**

Listing details

Tell the world all about your item and why they'll love it.

Title *

Include keywords that buyers would use to search for your item.

About this listing *

Learn more about what types of items are allowed on Etsy.

| Who made it? ▾ | What is it? ▾ | When was it mː ▾ |

Category *

Can't find the perfect category or attributes? Pick whatever's closest to make sure buyers can find your item. Learn more about getting found in search

None ▾

Renewal options *

Each renewal lasts for four months or until the listing sells out. Get more details on auto-renewing here.

◉ Automatic
This listing will renew as it expires for $0.20 USD each time.

◯ Manual
I'll renew expired listings myself.

Type *

◉ Physical
A tangible item that you will ship to buyers.

◯ Digital
A digital file that buyers will download.

Description *

Start with a brief overview that describes your item's finest features.

List details like dimensions and key features in easy-to-read bullet points.

Tell buyers a bit about your process or the story behind this item.

Preview listing as a Google search result Show preview

Section Optional

Group related listings into Sections to help shoppers browse (e.g., Bracelets, Father's Day Gifts, Yarn).

Add your first section

Tags Optional

What words might someone use to search for your listings? Use all 13 tags to get found. Get ideas for tags.

| Shape, color, style, function, etc. | Add | 13 left

Materials Optional

| Ingredients, components, etc. | Add | 13 left

FIGURE 13-4:
Enter listing details.

Source: Etsy.com

6. **Click the second and third Category drop-down lists that appear and choose any relevant subcategories.**

    After you select the item's categories and subcategories, Etsy displays a series of settings called *attributes*. Attributes work with tags to help make it easier for buyers to find your item. (See Figure 13-5.) Examples of attributes include primary color, secondary color, occasion, and more. Exactly which attributes appear depends on which categories and subcategories you selected in Steps 5 and 6.

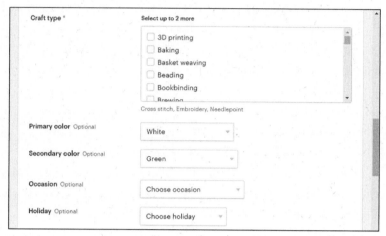

FIGURE 13-5:
Add attributes.

7. **Select attributes that describe your item.**

8. **Next to Renewal Options, click Automatic (to have Etsy renew the listing automatically; the default) or Manual (to renew the listing yourself if it expires).**

9. **In the Description field, enter a description of your item. (See Chapter 12 for details on writing a compelling description.)**

TIP

To see how your description will look in Google search results, click the Show Preview link below the Description field.

10. **If your shop sells different types of items, you can create a section for each type. To create a section, click the Add Your First Section link.**

A New Section dialog box opens.

11. **Type a name for the new section and click Save.**

A drop-down list appears with the section you created pre-selected.

To create more sections, click the Section drop-down list and choose Add a Section. Then repeat Step 11.

12. **Type a tag for your item in the Tags field and click the Add button. Repeat this step until you've added all appropriate tags. Or type all your tags at once, separating them with a comma.**

You can apply 13 tags to your listing. To maximize the chances of buyers finding your item, you want to use as many tags as you're allowed. Tags may describe what type of item you're selling (say, *tiara* or *vintage tire iron*), who the item is for (say, *babies* or *dogs*), or a style (maybe *Goth* or *kitsch* or *tribal*). If you run out of ideas for tags, use Etsy's search bar for help. Also, it's okay to use phrases. (Chapter 12 has the full scoop on tagging.)

13. **To indicate the materials used in your piece, type a material in the Materials field and click the Add button. Repeat this step until you've added all appropriate materials. Or type all your materials at once, separating them with a comma.**

You can apply 13 materials to your listing. Enter as many materials as you can.

Adding the price, quantity, and SKU

Next, you add the item's price, quantity, and SKU (stock keeping unit; optional). (See Figure 13-6.) Here's how:

1. **Enter the item's price in the Price field. (For help pricing your items, see Chapter 10.)**

2. **If you have more than one of these items available, type the quantity in — you guessed it — the Quantity field.**

If you enter a number higher than 1, Etsy will create one listing but will automatically generate a new listing as soon as the first listing results in a sale. Etsy will continue generating new listings until you sell all your items.

3. **Some sellers use SKUs to keep track of their inventory. If you're one of these sellers, you can type the item's SKU in the SKU field.**

Buyers won't be able to see the SKU. It's for your use only.

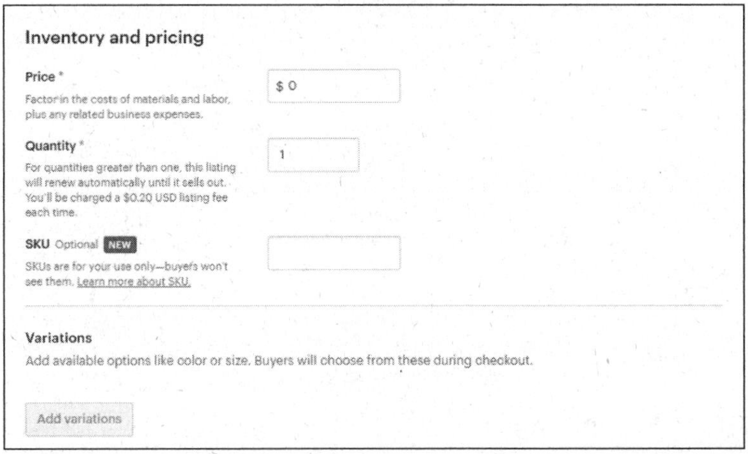

Inventory and pricing

Price *
Factor in the costs of materials and labor, plus any related business expenses.

$ 0

Quantity *
For quantities greater than one, this listing will renew automatically until it sells out. You'll be charged a $0.20 USD listing fee each time.

1

SKU Optional [NEW]
SKUs are for your use only—buyers won't see them. Learn more about SKU.

Variations
Add available options like color or size. Buyers will choose from these during checkout.

Add variations

FIGURE 13-6:
Enter the price, quantity, and SKU.

Source: Etsy.com

Adding variations

If your item comes in different sizes, materials, colors, finishes, or what have you, you can indicate these variations. First, you must define the variations. (You can choose two per item.) Then you can apply them. Here's how:

1. **Click the Add Variations button.**

   The Add Variations dialog box opens.

2. **Click the Add a Variation drop-down list and choose the variation type.**

   If the variation type is not listed, choose Create a New Variation, type a name for the variation, and click Add.

   Options for the variation type appear.

3. **Type a name for the first variation option and click Add. Repeat this step for each option.**

4. **Specify whether the price, quantity, or SKU will be different for each option.**

5. **Click Save and Continue.**

   The variation options appear in the Variations section under Inventory and Pricing (see Figure 13-7).

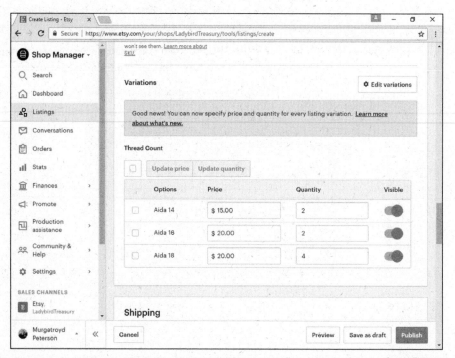

FIGURE 13-7: Setting variations.

Source: Etsy.com

6. **Configure the variation options. (In this example, we set option-specific pricing and quantities.) Then select the check box next to each variation you want to apply to this listing.**

TIP

It doesn't hurt to tag customizable item listings as "custom," "personalized," or "made to order." That way, buyers who use those terms in their search phrases are more likely to find your item.

CUSTOM MOVE: OFFERING CUSTOM ITEMS

In addition to using variations, you can accept requests for custom items. To let buyers know that you're open to their ideas, add a Request Custom Order link to your shop's main page. When a buyer clicks this link, Etsy launches a convo between the two of you.

To add a Request Custom Item link to your shop's main page, follow these steps:

1. **Click the Shop Manager link along the top of any Etsy Marketplace page.**

2. **On the left side of the Shop Manager page, click the Settings link and choose Options.**

The Shop Options page appears.

3. **Under Request Custom Order, click the Enabled option button.**

4. **Click the Save button.**

The Request Custom Item link will appear on your shop's main page.

If you decide to go the custom route, here are a few tips:

- **Charge a little more for custom items.** After all, they tend to involve more work.

- **Obtain payment upfront.** Otherwise, you may find yourself with a personalized item you can't sell or use.

- **Communicate with your buyer.** Let him know how your order process works and what he needs to do to keep things moving. Send this info to your buyer in a convo and post it on your shop's FAQ section.

- **Give buyers a time frame.** Custom items will take a bit of time to prepare. Be sure your buyer knows what to expect.

- **Send the buyer a photo of the item before you ship it.** That way, he knows he's getting what he asked for.

Setting shipping options

Your next task is to select shipping options. We go into these options in excruciating detail in Chapter 15. Flip to that chapter for guidance with this section of the Add a New Listing page.

Previewing and publishing your listing

Your last step is to publish your listing. When you do, it will appear in your Etsy shop. Before you publish your listing, however, take a moment to preview it. That way, you'll be able to see how it will look to potential buyers. Follow these steps:

1. **Click the Preview button at the bottom of the Add a New Listing page.**

    Etsy displays a preview of your listing (see Figure 13-8).

FIGURE 13-8:
Review your
listing.

Source: Etsy.com

2. **Review your listing.**

3. **If you notice something that you need to change, click the Continue Editing button at the bottom of the page, make your change, and click the Preview button again.**

4. **When you're satisfied with your listing, click the Publish button at the bottom of the page to publish it.**

A dialog box appears that reads, "This will cost a non-refundable fee of $0.20. By clicking 'Publish' you agree to pay this fee." This is a one-time listing fee, for which Etsy will bill you. Click Publish. The listing is submitted to Etsy and appears in the Listings Manager page in Shop Manager (see Figure 13-9).

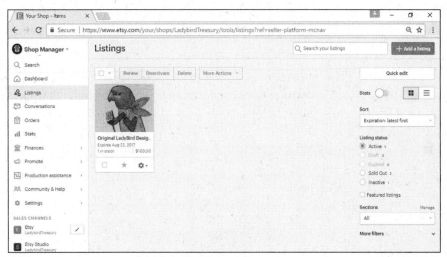

FIGURE 13-9:
Your listing is
posted.

Source: Etsy.com

REMEMBER

In addition to this one-time listing fee, you'll be charged a transaction fee when your item sells (not *if* — let's be optimistic!). This transaction fee amounts to 3.5 percent of your total sale price (not including shipping). These fees are assessed at the end of each month. For more info on paying your Etsy bill, see Chapter 18.

Ch-Ch-Ch-Ch-Changes: Editing a Listing

Look, nobody's perfect (although, obviously, you're pretty close). You may make a mistake when creating your listing and need to change it. Or maybe a potential buyer asks a question about the item you have for sale, and you want to update the item's listing to reflect your answer. Or you may want to add or change a listing photo.

Fortunately, regardless of why you need to change a listing, editing Etsy listings is a breeze (and free). You can edit any part of your item listing — the title, description, price, images, tags, materials, shipping information, you name it. Here's how:

1. **Click the Shop Manager button along the top of any Etsy Marketplace page.**

   The Shop Manager page opens.

2. **On the left side of the Shop Manager page, click the Listings link.**

   The Listings page opens.

3. **Click the Manage This Listing button (it looks like a gear) on the listing you want to edit and choose Edit from the menu that appears (see Figure 13-10).**

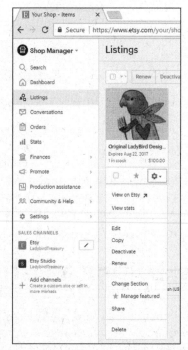

FIGURE 13-10:
Choose Edit from
the Manage This
Listing menu.

Source: Etsy.com

As shown in Figure 13-11, a page similar to the Add a New Listing page opens (but with all the settings filled in). Here, you can edit your listing.

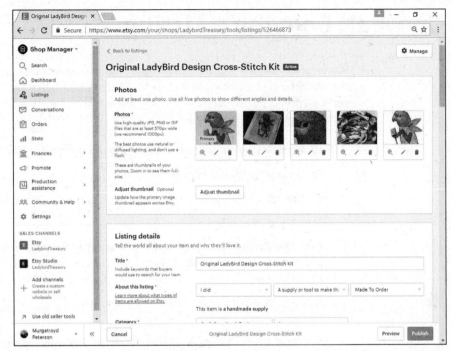

Source: Etsy.com

FIGURE 13-11:
The Edit Listing
page.

4. **Edit the listing using the same techniques you employed to create it.**

5. **Click the Preview button to preview the listing.**

6. **Click the Publish button to publish the edited listing.**

TIP

To hide the listing while you edit it, you can deactivate it. For more on deactivating a listing, see the section "Pull the Plug: Deactivating a Listing," later in this chapter.

USING QUICK EDIT TO EDIT YOUR LISTINGS

Maybe your listing just needs one wee tweak. If so, you may be able to use the Quick Edit feature to update it on the double. To do so, click the Quick Edit button in the upper-right corner of the Listings Manager page. Etsy displays key listing settings for all active listings, including settings for the description, price, quantity, section, weight, size, tags, and more. Just adjust the settings on the listing in question as needed and, when you're finished, click Exit Quick Edit to update it.

Copycat: Copying a Listing

Maybe you have two similar items to sell, but you've already created a listing for one of them. Instead of creating a new listing from scratch for the second item, you can just copy the first listing and then make any adjustments to the new listing as needed. Here's how:

1. **Click the Shop Manager button along the top of any Etsy Marketplace page.**

   The Shop Manager page opens.

2. **On the left side of the Shop Manager page, click the Listings link.**

   The Listings page opens.

3. **Click the Manage This Listing button (it looks like a gear) on the listing you want to copy and choose Copy from the menu that appears (refer to Figure 13-10).**

   A page similar to the Add a New Listing page opens but with all the settings filled in.

4. **Step through the listing-creation process, as described earlier in this chapter.**

   As you do, notice that the information in each section is entered for you, based on the listing you copied. You can change this information as needed.

5. **Click the Preview button to review your listing.**

6. **To post the listing, click the Publish Copy button.**

   A new listing based on the one you copied is posted.

Renewable Resources: Renewing a Listing

In addition to copying listings, you can renew them. For example, you can renew a listing if it has expired, or if the item has sold and you want to restock your shop by offering a new, identical item. You can also renew an active listing. When you do, the listing gets a new listing date and a new expiration date (four months from the date of renewal). A renewal can breathe new life into the listing, placing it closer to the top of item searches and in the New from Your Favorite Shops section (if others have favorited your shop).

REMEMBER

When you renew a listing, even an active listing, you're assessed a 20¢ listing fee.

Renewing a sold listing

To restock your shop by renewing a listing for a sold item, log in to your Etsy account and follow these steps:

1. **Click the Shop Manager button along the top of any Etsy Marketplace page.**

   The Shop Manager page opens.

2. **On the left side of the Shop Manager page, click the Orders link.**

   The Orders page opens.

3. **Click the tab that contains the listing you want to renew.**

4. **Click the check box in the lower-left corner of the listing you want to renew.**

   You can select multiple listings if you want to renew several at once.

5. **Click the Renew button at the top of the page.**

   Etsy displays a dialog box informing you that you are about to renew the listing and will be charged a new listing fee.

6. **Click Renew.**

   Etsy renews the listing.

TIP

An even faster way to renew the listing is to click the listing's Manage This Listing button (it looks like a gear) and choose Renew from the menu that appears.

Renewing active and expired listings

Renewing an active listing is just as easy as renewing a listing for an item that's been sold. Here's how:

1. **Click the Shop Manager button along the top of any Etsy Marketplace page.**

   The Shop Manager page opens.

2. **On the left side of the Shop Manager page, click the Listings link.**

   The Listings page opens.

3. **Repeat Steps 4 through 6 in the preceding section.**

   Etsy renews the listing.

To renew an expired listing, you follow these same steps. The only difference is that after you open the Listings page, you click the Expired option button under Listing Status on the right side of the page to access the expired listing.

TIP

You can set up a listing to renew automatically. One way is to select this option when you create the listing. Another is to select the listing in the Listings page, click the More Actions button, and choose Manage Renewal Options from the menu that appears. Then choose Automatic and click OK in the dialog box that appears.

Pull the Plug: Deactivating a Listing

Suppose that, after you crafted an item and listed it in your Etsy shop, your dog ate it. While you construct a replacement, you can deactivate the listing. Like we said earlier, you may also deactivate a listing while you edit it. When you deactivate a listing, it disappears from your Etsy shop. (Note, however, that deactivating a listing doesn't change its expiration date.) To deactivate a listing, follow these steps:

1. **Click the Shop Manager button along the top of any Etsy Marketplace page.**

   The Shop Manager page opens.

2. **On the left side of the Shop Manager page, click the Listings link.**

   The Listings page opens.

3. **Click the Manage This Listing button (it looks like a gear) on the listing you want to deactivate and choose Deactivate from the menu that appears.**

   Etsy prompts you to confirm the deactivation.

4. **Click the Deactivate button.**

When you're ready to reactivate the listing, again making it visible to people who visit your Etsy shop, here's what you do:

1. **On the right side of the Listings Manager page, click the Inactive option button under Listing Status.**

   Etsy displays your inactive listings.

MANAGING LISTINGS WITH THE SELL ON ETSY APP

You can also add, edit, copy, renew, and deactivate listings using the Sell on Etsy app on your mobile phone. To do so, you tap the Listings button on the bottom of the screen. Then do one of the following in the screen that appears.

- To add a new listing, tap Add Item and follow the on-screen prompts.

- To edit an existing listing, tap it to open it. Then tap on any of the fields in the listing screen to change the contents of that field.

- To copy, deactivate, or renew a listing, open the listing, tap Manage, and choose Copy Item, Deactivate Item, or Renew Item. (To access listings that are expired, inactive, or sold out, tap the Filter button and choose the appropriate option.)

Using the Sell on Etsy app is super-efficient — especially If you used your mobile phone to photograph your item, because you can access your photos from within the app. Talk about big time-savers!

2. **Click the Manage This Listing button (it looks like a gear) on the listing you want to reactivate and choose Activate from the menu that appears.**

   Etsy prompts you to confirm the activation.

3. **Click the Activate button.**

Rearrange Your Face: Rearranging the Listings in Your Etsy Shop

As you add more listings to your Etsy shop, you may decide that you want to rearrange the order in which they appear. For example, instead of having your items listed in the order you added them to your shop, with older items appearing farther down in the list (the default), maybe you want to group together all items of a certain color. Or put all items of a single type on one page. Or move all the most expensive items to the top of your store's main page. Or move an older listing to the top of your list. Fortunately, rearranging the listings in your shop is simple. Here's how it's done:

1. **Click the Shop Manager button along the top of any Etsy Marketplace page.**

   The Shop Manager page opens.

2. **On the left side of the Shop Manager page, under Sales Channels, click the pencil icon next to your Etsy shop.**

The Edit Shop page appears (see Figure 13-12).

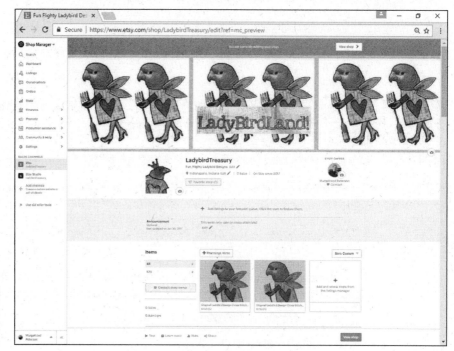

Source: Etsy.com

FIGURE 13-12:
You can rearrange your listings from this page.

3. **In the Items section, click the Rearrange Items button.**

4. **Click an item you want to move and drag it to the desired slot in the order.**

5. **When you're finished rearranging your items, click the Exit Rearrange Mode button.**

6. **To change the sort order of your items (for example, to put expensive items first), click the Sort button and choose the desired option from the list that appears.**

Your changes are saved automatically.

You can also sort your shop listings using the Sell on Etsy app. To do so, tap the More button, then Your Shop, and then the Sort link above your item listings. Then choose the desired sort option.

TIP

If you want to move a listing to a different section in your Etsy shop, click the listing's Manage This Listing button (it looks like a gear) and choose Change Section from the menu that appears. A dialog box opens. Open the drop-down list in the dialog box, choose the section you want to move the listing to, and click Apply.

Feature Comforts: Featuring an Item in Your Etsy Shop

Maybe you have one listing you *really* want people to see. In that case, you can feature it. When you feature a listing in your Etsy shop, it appears in the Featured section on your shop's main page, just above your shop announcement. You can feature as many as four item listings at a time. Here's how:

1. **Click the Shop Manager button along the top of any Etsy Marketplace page.**

   The Shop Manager page opens.

2. **On the left side of the Shop Manager page, click the Listings link.**

   The Listings Manager page opens.

3. **Click the Feature This Listing icon (it looks like a star) on the listing you want to feature.**

   Voilà! The listing appears as a featured item.

Chapter **14**

Wrap It Up: Closing the Deal

Hallelujah! You've made a sale! It's time for some rejoicing — and maybe some invoicing. In this chapter, you get the scoop on how to deal with such end-of-sale matters as finding out when you've sold something, tracking your sales, invoicing, and receiving payments.

You've Got Sale: Finding Out You Have a Sale

When you sell an item in your Etsy shop, Etsy notifies you via email straightaway. (You'll also be notified on the Sell on Etsy app if you've installed it on your mobile phone.) As you can see in Figure 14-1, this email contains loads of important information, including the following:

» Which item sold

» The price and quantity of the item that sold

>> The payment method used

>> The buyer's details, including his shipping address and email address

>> Any notes the buyer left

>> A link to the sales invoice (We discuss invoices in detail later in this chapter.)

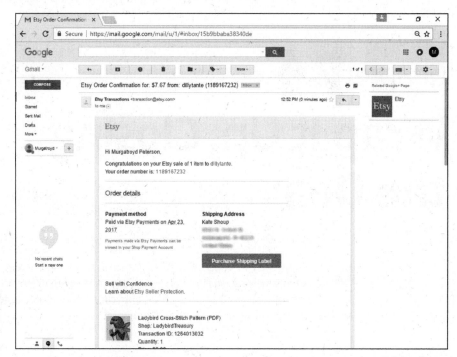

FIGURE 14-1:
Etsy emails you
whenever you sell
an item in your
Etsy shop.

TIP

To make sure your email program's spam filter doesn't come between you and these notification emails, consider adding the email address transaction@etsy.com to your list of safe senders. For details on how to perform this task, see your email program's help information.

Baby Got Track: Keeping Track of Sales

When you know you've sold an item, you can view it in Shop Manager. You can keep track of what sales you've made, which items the buyers have paid for, and whether you've shipped the items. To view a sale in Shop Manager, log in to your Etsy account and follow these steps:

1. **Click the Shop Manager button along the top of any Etsy Marketplace page.**

   The main Shop Manager page appears.

2. **On the left side of the Shop Manager page, click the Orders link.**

   The Open Orders page opens with the Open tab selected, displaying a list of items that you've sold but not yet shipped (see Figure 14-2). (We talk about shipping in detail in Chapter 15.)

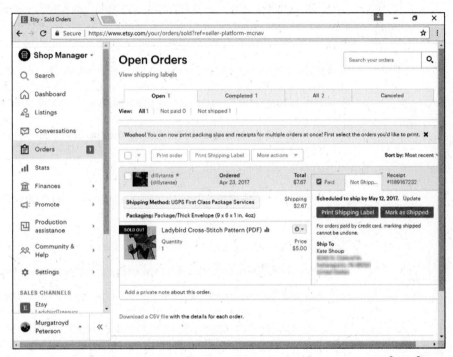

FIGURE 14-2:
View sold items on the Open tab.

TIP

You can view orders you've shipped by clicking the Completed tab. The Canceled tab offers access to canceled orders. Or to see all orders — ones that are open, ones that have shipped, and ones that have been canceled — click the All tab.

Guided by Invoices: Handling Invoices

When someone buys something from your Etsy shop, that person receives an email from Etsy. It's a receipt of sorts and contains all the details of the order. Buyers can click the order number (if purchased via Etsy Payments) or click the View the Invoice link (if they used a different form of payment — say, personal check, money order, frankincense, or myrrh) found in the email to view the order online.

TIP

Even though Etsy sends your buyer a confirmation email, you should still reach out to your buyer to express your thanks. This is an important part of customer service — and it's essential to the success of your shop (see Chapter 17).

Sometimes, you may need to view the invoice from a sale. One way to do this is to click the link featuring the order number found at the top of your notification email message (refer to Figure 14-1). Alternatively, try the following:

1. **Click the Shop Manager button along the top of any Etsy Marketplace page.**

   The main Shop Manager page appears.

2. **On the left side of the Shop Manager page, click the Orders link.**

   The Open Orders page opens.

3. **Locate the listing whose invoice you want to review.**

4. **Click the Receipt link featuring the order number to view the invoice.**

   Etsy displays the invoice for the transaction (see Figure 14-3). It contains key info about the transaction — whether the buyer has paid for the item, whether you've shipped the piece, the buyer's shipping address, how much the item cost, and more. It also features a Print Order button (which you can click to print the invoice for your records or to include in your shipment to the buyer), a Print Shipping Label button, and a Mark as Shipped button.

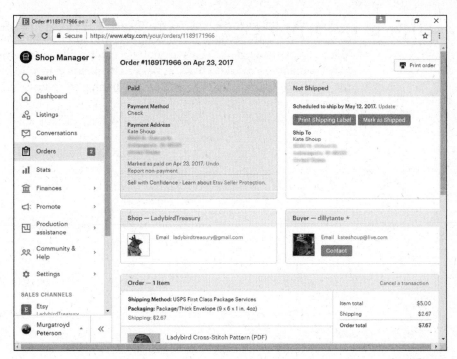

FIGURE 14-3:
View the invoice.

Show Me the Money: Receiving Payment

As you've probably deduced, exactly how you receive a payment depends on the method of payment used. For example, if the buyer opted to pay by check, you'll receive said check in the mail. Ditto for money orders.

REMEMBER

Note that there's a Godzilla-size difference between when a check's funds are released to you and when the check actually clears. Make sure that you ship your item only after the check clears, which can take a week or more. Otherwise, you'll be on the hook for those funds if the check bounces. (Note that the same goes for money orders.)

If you receive a payment via Etsy Payments and your sales history goes back at least 90 days, Etsy will make your money available to you the next business day. If your sales history does not extend back that far, your money will become available three days after the sale, although you may have to wait until the following Monday (or, if that Monday is a holiday, the next business day) for your funds to be disbursed.

If your buyer paid by check or money order and the funds have cleared, you need to do one more thing (apart from shipping the item to your buyer, of course): Mark the item as paid. (This is not necessary if you received payment via Etsy Payments.) To do so, click the Mark as Paid button next to the item listing in the Open Orders page. Etsy updates the listing to indicate that you received payment.

Chapter **15**

The Ship Hits the Fan: Shipping Your Items

The moment you receive payment for your piece (and, if applicable, the check or money order has cleared and you've marked the order as paid), it's time to begin the difficult process of letting it go. As hard as it may be to say goodbye — after all, odds are you slaved over its creation and gave it the best care possible — the time has come to send it on its way. In this chapter, you discover everything you need to know to pack and ship your item to its new happy home.

TIP

If you're worried about protecting your privacy during the shipping process, consider obtaining a post office box and using that to send and receive Etsy-related packages. For information, go to https://poboxes.usps.com.

The Right (Packaging) Stuff: Obtaining Shipping Supplies

Imagine a Venn diagram with one circle representing Etsy users and another representing people who love the environment. Odds are, the part where those circles intersect is pretty huge. No doubt, this explains why so many Etsy sellers prefer to use recycled shipping materials — boxes, bubble wrap, envelopes, packing paper, and the like. Some even go the DIY route, crafting their own mailers and packaging materials from their or others' detritus — for example, running old wrapping paper and magazine sheets through a shredder to create cushioning for fragile items. The great thing about this approach (other than the survival of our planet and its inhabitants) is that it's free!

Speaking of free: If you ship via the U.S. Postal Service (USPS), you can obtain Priority Mail boxes free of charge. Visit the USPS website (www.usps.com) for more info.

Some people would rather just buy shipping supplies for their Etsy shop. That's okay. Even the most devoted recyclers may need to buy certain types of supplies, such as packing tape or the occasional mailer. Whether you seek boxes, bubble wrap, ribbon, or tissue, you can find what you need at these sites:

>> **ULINE:** www.uline.com

>> **Paper Mart:** www.papermart.com

>> **Nashville Wraps:** www.nashvillewraps.com

You can also visit your local office-supply store (think Office Depot, Staples, and the like) to stock up on shipping supplies — although these stores often charge higher prices.

If you have space in your home or studio, set up a shipping station and stock it with all your shipping supplies. Trust us, it'll make packaging your pieces so much easier!

Package Deal: Showing Your Love and Care with Packaging

Yes, everyone knows that it's what's on the inside that counts. But that truism doesn't mean that what's on the outside isn't also important. Translation: When shipping your piece to your buyer, be sure to package it with care. In the following sections, we discuss wrapping different sorts of items, using attractive and brand-friendly packaging, and including goodies.

How you package your items says something about you and your Etsy shop. Make sure it doesn't say, "I'm lazy and careless!"

Protecting the item

When your buyer receives your piece, it needs to be in excellent shape (think Jillian Michaels). To make sure that happens, pack your item carefully — especially if it's fragile. Use cushioning materials such as bubble wrap or shredded paper to prevent breakage, and employ plenty of sturdy packing tape to ensure that your package isn't tattered en route. (See the previous section for more on supplies.) Also, pack bendable booty with a firm, flat backing. Finally, if your item is like the Wicked Witch of the West — in other words, moisture-averse — slip it in a plastic bag and seal it up before sending it on its way.

REMEMBER

Although packaging your items carefully to prevent damage is critical, don't take things too far. Excessive packaging — especially if it doesn't involve recycled materials — is wasteful.

Using attractive, brand-friendly packaging

Don't just stuff your lovingly crafted item in an envelope and plop it in the post. Instead, develop packaging that, in addition to protecting your item, looks good. You don't have to wrap your packages in expensive gift paper with hand-curled ribbon (although some Etsy sellers do); most buyers are perfectly satisfied with a package that has been carefully and securely wrapped with clean, plain, environmentally friendly paper.

In addition, design packaging that reflects your brand. For example, if your brand is froufrou, your packaging needs to be, too. On the flip side, if your brand is all modern minimalism, you want to ensure that your packaging is similarly under-the-top. Also, invest in stickers or a stamp with your shop's logo for use in your packaging. (You find out more about developing your brand in Chapter 16.)

TIP

One way to reflect your brand in your packaging is to use colored tissue paper. For example, if your logo is green and red, you could wrap your items in green and red tissue. If you go this route, be sure to moisture-proof your package by wrapping it in plastic; otherwise, the dye from the paper may bleed onto your piece if the package gets wet in transit.

Including extras in your parcel

It goes without saying that your package needs to include the item your buyer purchased. Beyond that, you may include any (or all) of the following:

>> **A handwritten note:** If you want to make your buyer's day, include a handwritten note in your packaging. It doesn't have to be a 40-page opus; just a few lines thanking the buyer for her purchase and wishing her well will do.

(Be sure to address her by name — it's so much more personal.) You may also use this opportunity to ask your buyer to leave feedback about you on Etsy.

TIP

Invest in special note cards or postcards that reflect your brand — or, better yet, make your own! For example, you could design a note card that includes your shop logo. Or, if you sell art prints, you might design a postcard with one of your bestselling images.

>> **Business cards:** To make sure your buyer remembers you and your store, slip two business cards into your package — one for your buyer and one for her billionaire best friend.

>> **A packing slip:** Unless the package is a gift and it's being sent directly to the recipient, include a packing slip in your package. This is especially important if your buyer lives abroad; it'll keep the package from being held up clearing Customs. We walk you through how to print a packing slip later in this chapter.

>> **Care instructions:** If the item you're sending requires special care — for example, maybe it needs to be washed by hand — include appropriate instructions in your package.

>> **A coupon:** Including a coupon — or, more specifically, a coupon code — in your packaging is a great way to generate sales. For help creating coupon codes, see Chapter 16.

>> **A freebie:** Some Etsy sellers include freebies in their packaging — that is, small, lightweight items tossed in at no additional cost. The best freebies reflect your brand or your inventory in some way — for example, buttons, bookmarks, stickers, or magnets with your shop logo or samples of new or favorite products in your line. Another approach is to include freebies that complement the item purchased. For instance, if you specialize in hand-sewn dog collars, you might toss in some Scooby Snacks. Or if you spin yarn, you may include a printout of a simple pattern you designed.

WARNING

Although some Etsy sellers like to include candy or other treats in their packages, it's not always a great idea. For one thing, some buyers may be diabetic or suffer from nut allergies, and receiving sweets via post could constitute torture (or death!) for them. For another thing, many buyers live in hot climates, meaning that any candy you send could melt, thereby ruining your piece.

Ship Shop: Comparing Shipping Carriers

USPS. FedEx. UPS. DHL. Carrier pigeon. All these are excellent (or at least interesting) ways to ship items to buyers. However, to paraphrase George Orwell, "all shipping carriers are equal, but some are more equal than others" — at least on Etsy. This is because Etsy has established special relationships with certain carriers to help sellers streamline the shipping process and even receive discounts on shipping charges. It's kind of a "friends with benefits" situation — only in this case, the benefits go to you, the Etsy seller!

TIP

We're talking domestic shipping in the United States here. For information about shipping internationally, see the section "Crafters without Borders: Shipping Internationally," later in this chapter.

One of these carriers is USPS. With USPS, Etsy sellers enjoy three key benefits:

>> **Calculated Shipping:** This feature takes the guesswork out of shipping charges by calculating them for you. It would be *literally impossible* for us to overstate how great this feature is. Like, it's the best.

>> **Print Labels:** With this feature, you can print shipping labels right from your computer.

>> **Cheaper postage:** When you use the Print Labels feature, you also save on postage.

For more on Calculated Shipping and Print Labels, read on.

FedEx also enjoys special relations with Etsy. Sellers who choose this carrier can use Etsy's Print Labels feature and receive a discounted rate. However, Etsy's Calculated Shipping tool doesn't work with FedEx.

No matter which carrier you choose, you'll want to be in the know on these key points:

>> How long they take to deliver

>> What shipping options they offer

>> How much the various shipping options cost

>> Whether such services as insurance and delivery confirmation are included (see the sidebar "Insure thing: Insuring your parcel," later in this chapter, for details)

>> Whether they pick up outgoing packages from your place

>> What they do if a package gets lost

Crafters without Borders: Shipping Internationally

Although you can certainly limit your Etsy business to domestic buyers, part of the fun of selling on Etsy is connecting with international customers. First, however, you need to get a feel for the ins and outs of shipping internationally. Keep a few points in mind:

>> **Items shipped to some countries, such as Canada and countries in the European Union, may be subject to duties or taxes.** It's not your responsibility to pay these duties or taxes; it's the buyer's. Still, it doesn't hurt to remind them. Etsy handles this for you by including boilerplate text to that effect in the Shop Policies section of your shop. This text also reminds buyers that it's not your fault if your package gets stuck in Customs.

>> **If your package contains "potentially dutiable contents" (that's post office speak for items subject to duties or taxes), you need to include a Customs form — period, end of story.** Once again, Etsy has your back. When you print an international shipping label through Etsy, it serves as both your shipping label and Customs form.

>> **Shipping certain items — think food products, plant and animal products, precious jewelry, and so on — is prohibited in some countries.** To find out whether your item is verboten, check out the Individual Country Listings page on the USPS website (http://pe.usps.com/text/imm/ab_toc.htm). It contains a list of countries. Click the link for the country in question to view a list of restricted and prohibited items. (Note that these prohibitions and restrictions apply regardless of what carrier you use.)

WARNING

Don't indicate that the item is a gift, even if your buyer asks you to. It's not cricket, and it can get you into trouble. Besides, even gifts may be subject to duties and taxes.

TIP

If you're just getting started, consider shipping to just a few countries — say, Canada, Mexico, Japan, Australia, and European Union (EU) countries. Then, when you're more comfortable with the procedures involved, you can expand to ship everywhere. Just don't indicate that you're willing to ship anywhere on Earth unless you've done the research to find out just what that may involve!

Ship Happens: Choosing Etsy Shipping Options

Your package is ready. You've chosen your shipping provider. It's time to get this show on the road and choose your Etsy shipping options.

Actually, we're lying. The truth is, you choose these options long before you're ready to ship your package. In fact, you choose them when you first create the listing, in the Shipping section of the Add a New Listing page (see Figure 15-1). (We cover them in this chapter instead of in Chapter 13, which walks you through creating a listing, to try to keep things focused.) First, however, you need to make one important decision: whether to use Etsy's Calculated Shipping feature to calculate shipping costs. (In case you forgot, we *really* like the Calculated Shipping feature and urge you to use it.) If so, follow these steps to get started.

REMEMBER

You can use Calculated Shipping only if you plan to ship via USPS. If you want to use a different carrier, you'll have to handle all of this manually.

Note: The Shipping Costs drop-down list is set to Calculate Them for Me by default. Leave that setting as is to use Etsy's Calculated Shipping feature.

1. **In the Origin Zip Code field, type your zip code (or, more specifically, the zip code from which packages from your shop will ship).**

2. **Open the Processing Time drop-down list and choose a processing time.**

   Options range from one business day to six to eight weeks. You can also set a custom processing time or indicate that the processing time is unknown.

3. **Specify where you'll ship to.**

   The default setting is United States and Worldwide. To change this setting, click the Edit link. Then use the drop-down lists that appear to indicate which continents and countries you'll ship to.

Shipping

Set clear and realistic shipping expectations for shoppers by providing accurate processing time and shipping rates.

Shipping options *

Fill out your shipping options for this listing. You can keep these options specific to this listing, or save them as a shipping profile to apply them to future listings.

Shipping costs *
Let us calculate them or enter fixed costs yourself

[Calculate them for me (Recommended) ▾]

Shoppers will see costs based on their location and the weight and dimensions of the listing.
How it works

Origin zip code *
Where do you ship packages from?

[📍 12345]

Processing time *
Once purchased, how long does it take you to ship an item?

[Select your processing time... ▾]

Buyers are more likely to purchase items that ship quickly

Where I'll ship *
What countries will you ship to?

[United States and worldwide Default   ✎ Edit]

Shipping services *
Buyers can choose these at checkout

[6 USPS mail classes Default   ✎ Edit]

Free shipping Optional
Want to offer buyers a free shipping option?

☐ Free domestic shipping
☐ Free international shipping

Handling fee Optional
We'll add this to the buyer's shipping total, they won't see it separately

[$]   Set separate fees for domestic & international

You can save these options to apply to future listings, if you'd like. How shipping profiles work

[**Save as a shipping profile**]

Item weight *
Weight and size are required for calculated profiles. Learn more about calculated shipping.

[lbs] [oz]

Item size (when packed) ⓘ *
Enter the weight and size of the item plus packing materials. This will be used to determine package size.

Length [in]   Width [in]   Height [in]

Preview shipping cost
See what buyers will pay for shipping

To preview calculated shipping costs, enter your item's **weight** and **size**

FIGURE 15-1:
Setting shipping options.

Source: Etsy.com

4. **Specify which shipping services you'll use.**

   When you use Calculated Shipping, all six United States Postal Services shipping options (USPS Priority Mail, USPS Priority Mail Express, USPS First Class Package Services, USPS Priority Mail International, USPS Priority Mail Express International, and USPS First Class International Package Service) are selected by default. To change this setting, click the Edit link and deselect any options you don't want to offer. For even more choices, click the Advanced Shipping Services link to reveal USPS Media Mail and USPS Parcel Select Ground options.

5. **Specify whether you offer free domestic or international shipping.**

6. **If you charge a handling fee, enter it in the Handling Fee section.**

Maybe you want to use a carrier that doesn't support Calculate Shipping, like FedEx. In that case, you'll need to compute shipping costs yourself and enter them by hand. To do so, you open the Shipping Costs drop-down list and choose I'll Enter Fixed Costs Manually. (If you don't see the Shipping Costs drop-down list, click Enter Custom Shipping Options to display it.) Then enter your shipping origin, processing time, and shipping charges for various locations (see Figure 15-2). You can also enter a shipping upgrade — for example, to offer express shipping. (For more on shipping upgrades, see the sidebar "Setting up shipping upgrades," later in this chapter.)

TIP

For help computing shipping costs, visit your carrier's website. Here are the URLs for a few popular carriers:

>> **FedEx:** www.fedex.com

>> **UPS:** www.ups.com

>> **DHL:** www.dhl.com

Regardless of whether you went the Calculated Shipping route or entered shipping info manually, your next step is to enter the weight and size of the package. You do that in the Item Weight and Item Size fields. And that's it! Your shipping settings are complete.

TIP

If you let Etsy calculate the shipping and you enter the weight and size info, you can preview how much it will cost to ship to buyers in various locations. This information appears at the bottom of the shipping section of the Add a New Listing page.

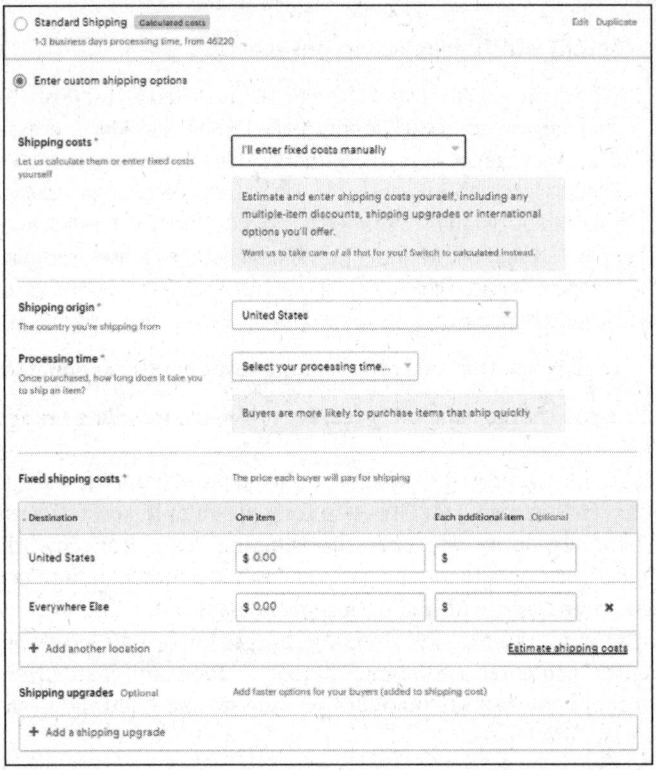

Source: Etsy.com

FIGURE 15-2:
Manual shipping
settings.

Profile Pick: Saving and Selecting a Shipping Profile

Your average Etsy seller uses the same shipping settings most (if not all) of the time. But she doesn't necessarily want to enter all those shipping settings in by hand each time she creates a new listing. Enter shipping profiles. A *shipping profile* is a collection of shipping-related settings that you can apply to a listing in one fell swoop instead of entering them one by one.

After you enter your shipping settings in the Add a New Listing page (as described in the previous section), you can use them to create a shipping profile. To do so, click the Save as Shipping Profile button under the Handling Fee setting (refer to Figure 15-1). When prompted, type a descriptive name for the profile and click Create Profile. The next time you create a listing, you'll be able to choose this shipping profile in the Shipping section of the Add a New Listing page (see Figure 15-3).

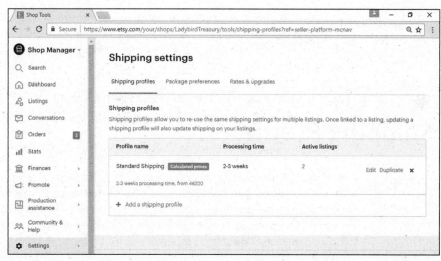

FIGURE 15-3:
Etsy adds the
shipping profile
to the Shipping
section of the
Add a New
Listing page.

Source: Etsy.com

What if you want to create a new shipping profile, but you aren't in the process of generating a new listing? In that case, follow these steps:

1. **Click the Shop Manager link along the top of any Etsy Marketplace page.**

The main Shop Manager page opens.

2. **Click the Settings link on the left side of the page and click Shipping Settings in the pane that appears.**

The Shipping Settings page opens with the Shipping Profiles options displayed (see Figure 15-4).

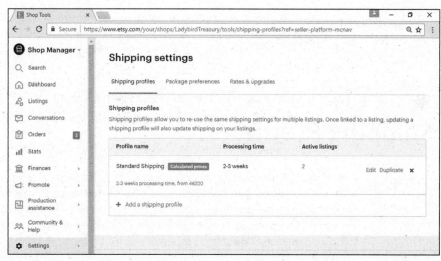

FIGURE 15-4:
The Shipping
Settings page.

Source: Etsy.com

3. **Click the Add a Shipping Profile button.**

The Create Shipping Profile page opens. This page is nearly identical to the Shipping section of the Add a New Listing page (refer to Figure 15-1).

4. **Repeat the steps in the preceding section to set the shipping options.**

   These options will be applied to the shipping profile.

5. **In the Profile Name field, type a descriptive name for this shipping profile.**

6. **Click the Create Profile button.**

   Etsy saves your shipping profile. Again, the next time you create a listing, you'll be able to choose this shipping profile in the Shipping section of the Add a New Listing page (refer to Figure 15-3).

TIP

If you need to, you can edit your shipping profile. To do so, repeat Steps 1 and 2 to access the Shipping Profiles options in the Shipping Settings page. Then click the profile's Edit link. An Edit Shipping Profile window appears. It looks a lot like the Create Shipping Profile page but with all your information filled in. Adjust the settings as needed and click the Save Profile button to save your changes.

SETTING UP SHIPPING UPGRADES

When you use Calculated Shipping and ship via USPS, all six USPS shipping options are selected by default — including Express options. In other words, you're already set up to offer shipping upgrades to buyers. If, however, you've opted out of Calculated Shipping, you'll need to set up upgrades by hand.

First, you need to make sure upgrades are enabled. To do so, click the Shop Manager link along the top of any Etsy Marketplace page, click the Settings link on the left side of the Shop Manager page, and choose Shipping Settings. Then click the Rates & Upgrades link. Finally, click the Enabled option button under Shipping Upgrades to select it.

Now you're ready to set up the upgrade. You can do this when you create a new listing (in which case it will apply to that listing only) or you can add it to a shipping profile (in which case it will apply to any listing that uses that profile). Start by clicking the Shipping Costs drop-down list and choosing I'll Enter Fixed Costs Manually in the Add a New Listing page or the Create Shipping Profile page. After you enter other shipping-related settings, click the Add a Shipping Upgrade link toward the bottom of the page. The Shipping Upgrade section expands to include an Upgrade Name field (go with something descriptive, like "Expedite Shipping"), a Destination drop-down list (your options are Domestic and International), a One Item field (this is where you enter how much it will cost to upgrade shipping for one item), and an Each Additional Item field (here, you indicate how much it will cost to upgrade shipping for additional items). Enter your upgrade details, and you're set.

Print It to Win It: Printing Shipping Labels on Etsy

If you use USPS or FedEx as your shipping carrier, you can print shipping labels right from Etsy. When you print your label from Etsy, tracking and delivery confirmation are included automatically. If you want it, insurance is also available. (See the nearby sidebar "Insure thing: Insuring your parcel.")

Printing a USPS label

Printing a USPS label is a breeze. However, you need to do one thing before you print your first label: Set up Etsy to receive the best USPS shipping rate possible. Otherwise, you won't get that discount we mentioned earlier in the chapter. To do so, click the Shop Manager link along the top of any Etsy Marketplace page, click the Settings link on the left side of the Shop Manager page, and choose Shipping Settings. Then click the Rates & Upgrades link. Finally, click the Etsy Shipping Label Rates option button under Shipping Rates to select it.

After that's done, you're ready to print your first USPS shipping label on Etsy. Here's what you do:

1. **Click the Shop Manager button along the top of any Etsy Marketplace page.**

   The main Shop Manager page appears.

2. **On the left side of the Shop Manager page, click the Orders link.**

   The Open Orders page opens, displaying a list of items that you've sold but not yet shipped.

INSURE THING: INSURING YOUR PARCEL

Remember that movie *Castaway*? In it, Tom Hanks plays a FedEx employee whose cargo plane crashes, marooning him on a desert island with only a volleyball for company. This storyline just goes to show you that sometimes planes carrying packages crash, jettisoning their cargo to the bottom of the sea. To ensure that you're covered if your package goes astray, you may want to opt for insurance from your shipping carrier — especially if your item is on the pricey side. (Insuring packages containing less expensive pieces may be prohibitively expensive; you'll need to decide whether it's worth it to you.) You can also opt for tracking and delivery confirmation — it's free when you ship via USPS and use Etsy's Print Label feature.

3. **Locate the order you want to ship and click its Print Shipping Label button (see Figure 15-5).**

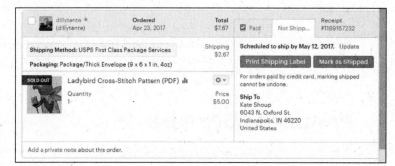

FIGURE 15-5:
Click the Print
Shipping label
button.

4. **The first time you print a shipping label, Etsy prompts you to confirm or update your mailing address and enter your phone number. Do so and click Continue.**

   The Shipping Labels page opens with the Buy Shipping Labels tab displayed (see Figure 15-6).

5. **If you want, enter a note to the buyer in the Add Note field on the left side of the screen (below the buyer's profile picture).**

6. **Review the shipping method, package type, package dimensions, and package weight.**

TIP

   Invest in a postal scale and flexible tape measure. You'll need these to weigh your packages and gauge their dimensions.

7. **If desired, insure your package against loss or damage by typing a monetary value in the Add Insurance field.**

   The value you enter should reflect both the value of the contents and the cost of postage (up to $5,000).

8. **If you want someone to sign for the package, click the Signature Confirmation check box to select it.**

9. **If necessary, click the Ship Date drop-down list and specify the day on which you plan to ship the item.**

10. **Under Download Preference, indicate whether you want to print one or two labels per page or if you want Etsy to format the label for a 4-x-6 label printer.**

FIGURE 15-6:
The Buy Shipping Labels settings on the Shipping Labels page.

Source: Etsy.com

TIP

Notice the View All Open Orders button at the bottom of the Buy Shipping Labels page (refer to Figure 15-6). If you need to print labels for multiple shipments, click this button to do them all at once.

11. **Click the Confirm and Buy button.**

Etsy notifies you that the cost for the label will be added to your Etsy bill. (For info on paying your Etsy bill, see Chapter 18.) Etsy also informs you that they'll email a shipping notification to the buyer right away.

12. **Click the Purchase button.**

Etsy displays the Purchase Complete dialog box (see Figure 15-7).

13. **To print the label, click the Print a Shipping Label button.**

The label is sent to your printer.

TIP

Although you can use regular paper, it's better to use paper with adhesive backing. That way, you don't have to use tape to attach the label to your package.

FIGURE 15-7:
The Purchase
Complete
dialog box.

Source: Etsy.com

14. **Click the Print a USPS SCAN (optional).**

This is handy if you're shipping lots of packages at once. It lets the USPS scan a single barcode for all packages — saving you, and them, time.

15. **Click the Print a Packing Slip button to print a packing slip (optional).**

The packing slip is sent to your printer.

16. **Click the Done button.**

Etsy updates the order's invoice and receipt to show that it has been shipped (see Figure 15-8), essentially closing the order. The item also appears on the Completed Orders tab, which you can access by clicking the Completed tab on the Sold Orders page.

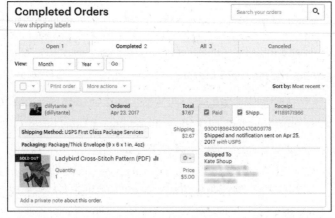

FIGURE 15-8:
Etsy closes out
your order.

Source:Etsy.com

Printing a FedEx label

Printing a FedEx label is a lot like printing a USPS one. You start by locating the order you want to ship and clicking its Print Shipping Label button (refer to Figure 15-5). Then, in the Buy Shipping Labels tab of the Shipping Labels page, next to Shipping Carrier (in the top-left corner of the page), click the FedEx link. The settings in the Buy Shipping Labels tab change to reflect your selection (see Figure 15-9). Some of these settings are the same as the ones for USPS labels — adding a note, insuring the package, setting the ship date, setting your download preferences, and so on. Others are specific to FedEx, like your shipping method and package type, dimensions and weight, and specifying whether you want the buyer to sign for the package. Simply choose your desired settings, click Confirm and Buy, and print.

TIP

If FedEx is your go-to shipper, you can set it up as your default carrier. To do so, click the Options tab on the Shipping Labels page. Then, under Preferred Shipping Carrier, choose FedEx. Finally, choose Save. From now on, when you print labels, you'll see the page shown in Figure 15-9 rather than the one in Figure 15-6 by default.

FIGURE 15-9: Printing FedEx labels.

Source: Etsy.com

Deliverance: Sending Your Package on Its Merry Way

After you securely affix your shipping label to your package (if you opted against an adhesive backing, use clear packaging tape, taking care to avoid obscuring the label bar code), you're ready to send it. One option is to request a free carrier pickup from the USPS website (www.usps.com/pickup); alternatively, you can hand it off to your regular carrier, take it to your local post office, or (if it weighs 13 ounces or less) drop it in a collection box.

TIP

While we're on the subject of your regular mail carrier: Make it a point to buddy up to yours. That way, if you have any shipping-related questions, your carrier will be happy to answer them!

Marky Mark: Marking the Item as Shipped in Etsy

As mentioned, when you print your shipping labels through Etsy, the site automatically marks your item as shipped, essentially closing your order. If you *don't* use Etsy's Print Label function to print shipping labels, you'll need to do this manually. Here's how:

1. **Click the Shop Manager button along the top of any Etsy Marketplace page.**

   The main Shop Manager page appears.

2. **On the left side of the Shop Manager page, click the Orders link.**

   The Open Orders page opens.

3. **Locate the listing for the item you just shipped and click its Mark As Shipped button (refer to Figure 15-5).**

   A Mark As Shipped and Notify Buyer dialog box opens (see Figure 15-10).

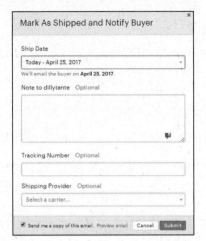

Mark As Shipped and Notify Buyer ✕

Ship Date

Today - April 25, 2017 ▾

We'll email the buyer on **April 25, 2017**.

Note to dillytante   Optional

Tracking Number   Optional

Shipping Provider   Optional

Select a carrier... ▾

☑ Send me a copy of this email.   Preview email   Cancel   Submit

Source: Etsy.com

FIGURE 15-10:
The Mark As
Shipped and
Notify Buyer
dialog box.

4. **Choose a ship date, type a note to the buyer, enter the tracking number, specify the shipping provider, and click Submit.**

   Etsy updates the listing to show that it has been shipped. Etsy also moves the listing to the Completed Orders page.

4

All Up in Your Bidness: Handling Business Matters

IN THIS PART . . .

Get tips on branding and marketing your business like a pro.

Find out how to provide unrivaled customer service.

Discover how to handle financial matters.

Explore ways to grow your Etsy business.

Chapter **16**

High Exposure: Marketing Your Etsy Business

Marketing is as old as dirt. Indeed, the first marketer was most likely the first Cro-Magnon to convince a fellow knuckle dragger to barter for *his* mastodon-fur cape instead of the one offered one cave over. ("But this mastodon-fur cape not stink like one next door!") If you want your Etsy shop to evolve into a thriving enterprise, you need to do the same. This chapter is devoted to the ins and outs of marketing your Etsy business so that it doesn't go the way of the Neanderthal.

TIP

Let's be honest: This chapter constitutes a very basic primer on marketing. If you're serious about your Etsy business, you'll want to study this subject in greater depth. *Small Business Marketing Kit For Dummies*, by Barbara Findlay Schenck (Wiley), is a great jumping-off point!

Brandy, You're a Fine Girl: Building Your Brand

An important part of any business — whether it's a multinational widget-making corporation with more employees than Lichtenstein has citizens, a small mom-and-pop pizzeria that serves the surrounding neighborhood, or your Etsy shop — is its brand.

So what exactly is a brand? Although many people believe that the word *brand* is synonymous with the word *logo*, it's not. Yes, your logo is part of your brand (more on that in a moment), but the brand itself is a much broader concept. Think of your brand as the image your business projects. Your brand is what you're known for.

REMEMBER

Before you begin building your brand, you need to pin down a few key pieces of information:

>> **The brand promise:** Was it Kierkegaard or Dick Van Patten who said, "People don't buy drill bits — they buy holes"? Pinpointing your brand promise means determining what you're *really* selling. You're not selling handmade aromatherapy candles; you're selling unparalleled relaxation. *That's* your brand promise.

>> **The target market:** You want to have some idea of who's likely to be interested in your product so that you can tailor your brand accordingly. That means identifying your target customers — in other words, who you're selling to. Are they male or female? Young or old? Singleton or smug married? Where do they live? How much disposable income do they have? What level of education have they attained?

>> **The competition:** In addition to recognizing your target market, you need to identify your competition. Who are they? What do they offer? How are their brands or products similar to yours? How are they different? Do your target markets overlap? This assessment can help you position your own brand in such a way that you gain an advantage.

>> **The brand personality:** Think of your brand as being like a person (preferably not your mother-in-law). Is it quirky? Refined? Silly? Wise? This personality creates an emotional connection with your target market. You convey your brand's personality through visual elements, such as your logo, and through its voice — that is, your tag line (discussed in the next section), your item descriptions (see Chapter 12), your shop announcement (see Chapter 8), your profile page, your about section, and even your Etsy convos (see Chapter 17).

>> **The unique selling proposition (USP):** Every good brand has at least one characteristic that makes it different from everything else on the market. Using the aromatherapy candle example, maybe your candles burn longer than other candles on the market or smell different or come in super-pretty jars. Whatever special quality your candles have, that's their USP.

With that information in hand, you're ready to start building your brand. In the following sections, we explain how to create tag lines and logos and discuss the importance of infusing your brand into everything related to your Etsy shop.

Composing a tag line

Do you recognize the phrase "You deserve a break today"? What about "Just do it," "Don't leave home without it," "The quicker picker-upper," or "Time to make the doughnuts"? If so, then you know the power of a tag line. A *tag line* is a memorable phrase that expresses who your brand is and what it does. It serves as a marketing slogan and reflects the brand it seeks to promote.

Part of building your brand is composing a tag line of your own. A good tag line

>> **Is short, concise, specific, and, ideally, clever:** The longer the tag line, the more likely people are to lose interest in it.

>> **Speaks to your target market:** If your target market is 20-something hipsters, your tag line shouldn't use language that your 60-year-old dad favors.

>> **Reflects your brand's personality:** If your brand is quirky, you don't want a stuffy tag line!

>> **Hints at your brand promise and its USP:** Take the tag line for M&M's: "Melts in your mouth, not in your hands." It suggests that not only are M&M's super-tasty, but they're also not messy.

TIP

A great place for your tag line is your shop title or your shop's cover photo. For help with changing your shop title and cover photo, see Chapter 8.

Creating a logo

Your logo — along with your tag line — represents your brand. It's critical, then, that your logo (as well as other visual elements, such as the colors and fonts you use in marketing materials like business cards and whatnot) reflects your brand's personality and speaks to your audience.

Keep these points in mind as you develop your logo:

» **Consider your colors.** Different colors evoke different emotions and convey different ideas. For example, if you specialize in custom motorcycle gear, a baby-pink logo may not be the way to go (unless, of course, the custom motorcycle gear is for babies).

» **Make sure you're sending the right message.** Your logo's visual style communicates something about your brand. For example, if your logo has a minimalist style, it suggests that your brand does, too. Be sure that your logo sends the message you want.

» **Be original.** Although it's certainly fine to look to other brands and logos for inspiration, don't copy — especially if the logo in question is a competitor's.

If you're not comfortable developing your logo, don't hesitate to get help. If you're on a strict budget, why not ask a friend with an artistic bent for assistance? Alternatively, try bartering with a professional designer.

Working your brand into all you do

REMEMBER

The key to branding is infusing it in everything you do. Express your brand by using your tag line and logo in your business cards, letterhead, envelopes, postcards, packaging, and other promotional materials. Your brand also needs to permeate your Etsy shop — for example, by appearing in your cover photo and shop icon. You can even communicate your brand by using your tag line and logo on a Facebook page and Twitter feed for your Etsy shop. In this way, you increase the chances of your customers noticing *your* brand among the flotsam and jetsam of Etsy.

Poetry in Promotion: Using Etsy Tools to Promote Your Shop

Etsy recognizes the importance of marketing your shop and offers several built-in promotional tools. Specifically, Etsy enables you to promote listings on Etsy and on Google, create coupon codes for your shop, and post Shop Updates on Etsy to show everyone what's up in your shop.

Advertising your shop

Fun fact: The word *advertise* derives from the Latin *ad vertere*, meaning "to turn the mind toward." And as anyone who's ever suddenly become ravenously hungry after watching a pizza commercial can tell you, it totally works.

Etsy offers two tools to help you advertise your shop. One tool, Etsy Promoted Listings, is, to quote Etsy, "good for improving discoverability within Etsy search results." With Etsy Promoted Listings, you simply note how much you want to spend each day on Promoted Listings, and Etsy does the rest — propelling your listings to the top of the heap (or close to it) when prospective buyers type relevant keywords.

The other tool is Google Shopping. Google Shopping is a type of shopping engine, and it's great if you want to reach prospective buyers outside of Etsy. As with Etsy Promoted Listings, you set an average daily spend. You also specify where you'd like to advertise — for example, in the United States. Then, anytime someone enters certain search criteria into Google, the site displays your listings first-ish.

Setting up Etsy Promoted Listings

To set up Etsy Promoted Listings, follow these steps:

1. **Click the Shop Manager link along the top of any Etsy Marketplace page.**

   The main Shop Manager page opens.

2. **Click the Promote link on the left side of the page and choose Advertising Options in the pane that appears.**

   The Etsy Advertising page appears (see Figure 16-1).

3. **Click the Start Advertising on Etsy button.**

   The Promoted Listings page opens (see Figure 16-2).

4. **Enter your daily budget.**

   This can range from $1 to $10. (The more you spend, the more impressions you'll get.)

5. **If you want new listings to be automatically included in your ad buy, toggle on the Automatically Advertise New Listings setting.**

6. **Click the Start Advertising button.**

   Etsy sets up your Promoted Listings campaign. Then it displays the Advertising dashboard with the Promoted Listings tab displayed (see Figure 16-3). From here, you can view stats on ad performance and sales from ads.

Source: Etsy.com

FIGURE 16-1:
The Etsy
Advertising page.

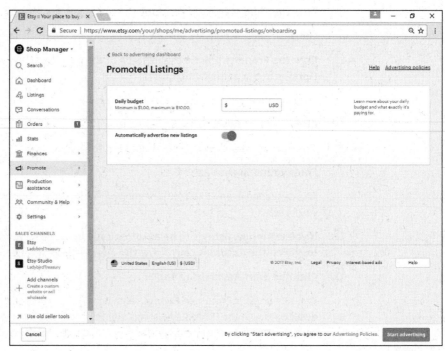

Source: Etsy.com

FIGURE 16-2:
The Promoted
Listings page.

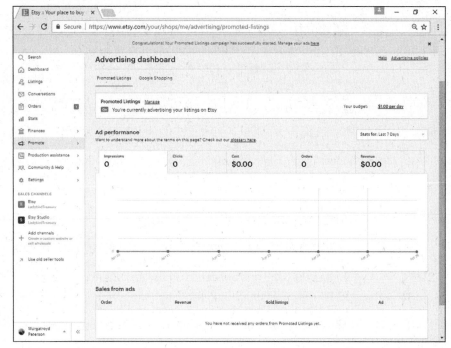

FIGURE 16-3:
The Advertising dashboard with Promoted Listings info displayed.

When you launch Promoted Listings, it will remain in effect until you discontinue it. To do so, click the Manage link near the top of the Promoted Listings page of the Advertising dashboard. The Manage Promoted Listings page opens (see Figure 16-4). Then toggle the Advertise with Promoted Listings setting off to disable it. (To re-enable the feature, you simply toggle the Advertise Promoted Listings setting back on.)

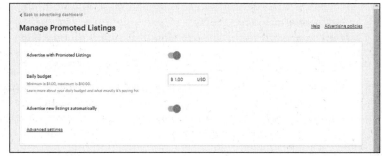

FIGURE 16-4:
The Manage Promoted Listings page.

Setting up Google Shopping

Setting up Google Shopping is just like setting up Etsy Promoted Listings only you choose Start Advertising on Google instead of Start Advertising on Etsy in Step 3, and, in the page that appears, you specify where you want to advertise in addition to indicating your daily budget and whether you want to automatically include new listings. When you're finished, you'll see a Google Shopping page of the Advertising dashboard that is nearly identical to the Etsy Promoted Listings one.

You disable (and re-enable) Google Shopping the same way, too: by clicking the Manage link near the top of the Google Shopping page of the Advertising dashboard and toggling the Advertise with Google Shopping Ads setting in the Manage Google Shopping page off (or on).

Creating coupons

Coupons have come a long way since their invention in 1887, when Asa Candler, an early investor in the Coca-Cola Company, devised a plan to distribute millions of coupons for free servings of the now-famous tonic. In fact, these days, coupons are *everywhere,* including on Etsy. Yes, that's right: You can channel your own inner Asa Candler and offer your Etsy customers discounts on merchandise or free shipping through coupons — or, more specifically, coupon codes. Buyers can then apply these codes to purchases during the checkout process. (When a customer redeems a coupon, Etsy's 3.5 percent transaction fee applies to the discounted price.) You could create coupon codes to celebrate your store's anniversary or an upcoming holiday, to reward repeat customers, or to share with your Facebook fans, Twitter or Instagram followers, Pinterest pinners, or admirers on other social media sites.

TIP

One way to spread the word about your coupon code is to include it in the packaging with any items you sell — say, by writing it on a business card and tucking it in with your piece. Alternatively, if you maintain a newsletter, you may want to include a coupon code there to drive sales in your Etsy shop. (You find out more about newsletters later in this chapter.)

To create a coupon code, follow these steps:

1. **Click the Shop Manager link along the top of any Etsy Marketplace page.**

   The main Shop Manager page opens.

2. **Click the Promote link on the left side of the page and choose Coupon Codes in the pane that appears.**

3. **Click the Create New Coupon button.**

   The Create New Coupon dialog box opens (see Figure 16-5).

Source: Etsy.com

FIGURE 16-5: The Create New Coupon dialog box.

4. **In the Coupon Code field, type the code you want to use for the coupon.**

   This code must contain between 5 and 20 alphanumeric characters (no punctuation), with no spaces. Note that after you use a code, you can *never use it again*. So, you know, no pressure coming up with solid codes.

5. **If you want buyers to receive a coupon automatically upon purchasing an item from your shop, click the Thank You Coupon check box to select it.**

6. **Click the Discount Type drop-down arrow and choose the type of discount you want to offer — Free Shipping, Percent Discount, or Fixed Discount.**

   - If you choose Free Shipping, optionally select the Domestic Addresses Only check box that appears.

   - If you choose Percent Discount, type the discount amount in the % field that appears.

   - If you choose Fixed Discount, type a dollar amount in the field that appears.

7. **If desired, enter a minimum purchase amount.**

Buyers must spend this amount to be able to apply the coupon.

8. **Enter an expiration date (optional).**

9. **Click the Active option button to activate the coupon code.**

10. **Click the Add Coupon button.**

Etsy creates the coupon code and lists it on the Coupon Codes page (see Figure 16-6).

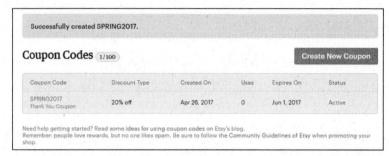

FIGURE 16-6:
Etsy creates the coupon code.

To deactivate a coupon code, simply click the code's Active link in the screen shown in Figure 16-6. Then, in the dialog box that appears, click the Inactive option button and click Save Changes. Etsy deactivates the code for you. You can reactivate the code later by clicking its Inactive link and then clicking Active in the dialog box that appears. You can also simply delete a coupon code by clicking the X button to the right of the code in the Coupon Codes page.

Posting Shop Updates

People love seeing what Etsy sellers are up to. That's why Etsy created Shop Updates. With Shop Updates, you can show every Etsy user who has purchased from you or favorited your shop (or an item you listed in it) what's happening with your Etsy biz. You may use Shop Updates to offer a sneak peek at a new item. Maybe you'll use it to announce an upcoming sale. Or maybe you just want to share a cute picture of your dog in your studio. Whatever's afoot, Shop Updates are a great way to share it — and potentially drive prospective buyers to your shop to boot.

Posting Shop Updates is easy. You can do so by using the Sell on Etsy app on your mobile phone. (Note that only Apple iOS and Android phones offer this app.) Here's how:

1. **Open the Sell on Etsy app, tap the More button in the bottom-right corner, and tap Shop Updates (see Figure 16-7).**

   The Shop Updates page opens.

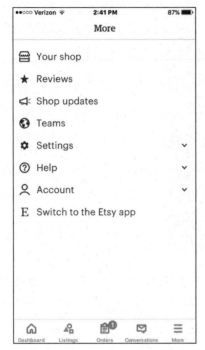

FIGURE 16-7:
Choose Shop
Updates from the
More menu.

Source: Etsy.com

2. **Tap the camera button at the bottom of the page.**

3. **Tap Take Photo or Choose Existing Photo.**

   - If you choose Take Photo, the app will access your phone's camera and allow you to take a photo. Do so, and then choose Use Photo.

   - If you select Choose Existing Photo, the app will display photos already on your camera to choose from. Tap the photo you want to use.

4. **If you want, adjust the photo by zooming in on the subject. Then tap Next.**

5. **Tap the photo. Etsy shows your active listings; tap one to tag it to your Shop Update, and tap Next.**

   Yeah, we know. If you're sharing a photo of a work in progress, you probably don't have any listings that relate to that item yet. The point is just to drive potential buyers to an item — any item — in your shop.

6. **Type a caption for your photo, tap Done, and tap Share on Etsy (see Figure 16-8).**

   Etsy shares your Shop Update.

FIGURE 16-8:
Caption and share your Shop Update.

Source: Etsy.com

7. **Click Continue to complete the Shop Update.**

TIP

You aren't limited to sharing Shop Updates on Etsy. You can also share them on social media, including Facebook, Twitter, and Instagram, as well as send it out via email or text. To do so, tap the appropriate button on the screen that appears when Etsy shares your Shop Update (see Figure 16-9) and follow the prompts. (For more on using social media to market your Etsy shop, see the next section.)

FIGURE 16-9:
Share your Shop
Update on social
media.

Source: Etsy.com

Saving Facebook: Promoting Your Etsy Shop on Social Media

Everybody knows that social media — most notably, sites like Facebook and Twitter — is a super marketing tool. It's particularly great for small businesses, providing significant reach at an excellent price: free. To help you capitalize on the power of social media, Etsy enables you to link your shop to your Facebook page and Twitter feed. When you do, people scrolling through your shop can like you on Facebook or follow you on Twitter.

REMEMBER

To link your shop to Facebook, you must create a Facebook page for your Etsy shop. Note that we said *page*, not *profile*. You can only connect your shop with a Facebook page designed for a business, not to the personal profile you probably maintain to keep up with friends. For help with creating a Facebook page, see Facebook's Help info. (It's not a bad idea to create a separate Twitter feed for your shop as well, although this is not required.)

To link your shop to a Facebook page, follow these steps:

1. **Click the Shop Manager link along the top of any Etsy Marketplace page.**

   The main Shop Manager page opens.

2. **Click the Settings link on the left side of the page and choose Info & Appearance.**

   The Info & Appearance page opens.

3. **Scroll down to the Links section and click the Connect with Facebook link (see Figure 16-10).**

FIGURE 16-10:
Link a Facebook page and Twitter account to your Etsy shop.

Etsy prompts you to allow permission to access your page.

4. **Click Allow.**

   If you have multiple Facebook pages, you'll be prompted to specify which one you want to connect to Etsy.

5. **Click your shop's page.**

   Etsy connects your shop to the Facebook page you selected.

Linking your shop to a Twitter feed is similar. To start, click the Connect with Twitter link shown in Figure 16-10. Etsy prompts you to allow permission to access your feed. Click Authorize App, click your shop's feed, and voilà. Etsy connects your shop to the Twitter feed you selected.

Connecting your Etsy shop to your Facebook page or Twitter feed doesn't just help Etsy shoppers connect with you on social media; it also helps your social media followers connect with you on Etsy. Etsy facilitates this by enabling you to share listings on Facebook or Twitter (as well as Pinterest) either when you first publish them or after they're live. Here's how:

1. **Click the Share button that appears when you publish a listing (see Figure 16-11). Alternatively, click a listing's Manage This Listing button (it looks like a gear) and choose Share.**

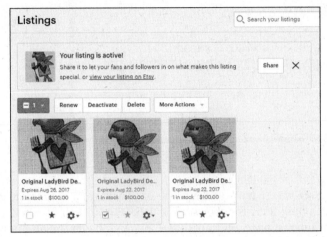

FIGURE 16-11:
Share a new listing on social media.

The Share This Listing dialog box opens (see Figure 16-12).

FIGURE 16-12:
The Share This Listing dialog box.

2. **Click the Twitter, Pinterest, or Facebook button (see Figure 16-12).**

   A platform-specific dialog box appears, where you can enter text to post alongside the listing (or, in the case of Pinterest, choose a board to pin it to). Figure 16-13 shows the Facebook dialog box.

3. **Type your text and click the Post to Facebook (or whatever platform) button to share your listing.**

FIGURE 16-13:
Share the listing
on Facebook.

One more way to harness the power of social media to promote your Etsy shop is by including links to other social media pages, such as your Instagram feed or your Pinterest page, on your shop's main page. You can also provide links to any blogs or personal web pages you maintain. Here's how:

1. **Click the Shop Manager link along the top of any Etsy Marketplace page.**

   The main Shop Manager page opens.

2. **On the left side of the page, under Sales Channels, click the Edit button (it has a pencil on it) for your Etsy shop.**

   A page opens where you can edit your shop.

3. **Scroll down to the Around the Web section.**

4. **Click Add a New Link.**

   A drop-down list and blank field appear.

5. **Click the drop-down list and choose the desired option — Facebook, Twitter, Instagram, Pinterest, Website, or Blog (see Figure 16-14).**

6. **Enter the URL for your Facebook page, Twitter feed, Instagram feed, Pinterest page, website, or blog and click Save.**

   Etsy adds the link you entered to your shop's About section.

You can repeat these steps as often as you need to for any additional sites you want to link to in your Etsy shop.

FIGURE 16-14:
Choose an option from the Around the Web drop-down list.

Source: Etsy.com

SALE SISTER: PUBLICIZING SALES

Running the occasional sale in your Etsy shop is a great way to pull in customers and move merchandise — but only if other people know about it. Fortunately, social media is an easy and free way to spread the word. All you need to do is share a post about your sale on whatever social media platforms you use — Facebook, Twitter, Instagram, whatever — and provide a direct link to your shop. For best results, include some Etsy-related hashtags, such as #Etsy, #EtsySeller, #EtsySale, #EtsyFinds, #ShopEtsy, and #EtsyHunter. That way, people who don't currently follow you on social media will get wind of your sale (and maybe give you a follow)!

In addition to using social media to publicize your sales, consider doing the following:

- Talk up your sale in the Etsy community. (For more on the Etsy community, see Chapter 20.)

- Share the news on any blogs you maintain.

- Upload a special "sale" graphic for your cover photo and/or shop icon. (See Chapter 8 for details on creating cover photos and shop icons.)

- Post a notice about your sale in your shop announcement. (See Chapter 8 for information on how to create a shop announcement.)

- Include the word "SALE!" in your item title and description, and add a Sale tag. (You find out about item titles and descriptions, as well as tags, in Chapter 12.)

Go Postal: Sending an Email Newsletter

A great way to keep in touch with your customers is to send periodic email newsletters. For example, you may send an email newsletter to announce an upcoming sale, to spread the word about a new product, or to share a coupon.

WARNING

Who should receive your email newsletter? If your answer is "anyone and everyone who has ever ordered from my Etsy shop," stand down. Etsy considers that behavior spamful, and it's against their House Rules. The right answer is, "anyone who has added their name to my email list and has consented to receive newsletters." (This doesn't mean you should convo all your past customers to see whether they want a seat on your bandwagon, however. *That's* a violation of Etsy's House Rules, too.)

Here are three ways to build your mailing list without honking off Etsy:

>> Include a link to sign up for your newsletter in the About section of your shop page (for more on populating the About section of your Etsy shop, see Chapter 8).

>> Include a link to sign up for your newsletter in your shop announcement (for more on adding a shop announcement, see Chapter 8).

>> Include a link to sign up for your newsletter in the "thank you" message you send to a buyer when she buys something in your shop (for more on this communique, see Chapter 17).

When it comes to composing and distributing your newsletter, we recommend that you use an email newsletter service such as MailChimp (www.mailchimp.com). Not only does MailChimp enable you to manage subscribers and employ different templates to add some visual spice to your newsletter, but it also allows you to send up to 12,000 emails per month to as many as 2,000 subscribers for free. Other email newsletter services include Constant Contact (www.constantcontact.com) and Vertical Response (www.verticalresponse.com).

TIP

Make it a point to send your newsletters on a regular — but not overwhelming — basis, like biweekly, monthly, or quarterly. If you're planning a sale or launching a new product line, you can pepper in a few extra missives.

» **Communicating clearly with customers**

» **Handling a bungled transaction**

Chapter **17**

You've Been Served: Providing Excellent Customer Service

Running your own Etsy shop is a little like being the Wizard of Oz: You preside over your own Emerald City from behind a curtain of sorts, working the wheels and levers of your online craft business while hidden from view.

If you truly want to be a great and powerful Etsy seller, however, you must pull back the curtain and interact with your Ozmites — er, customers. It's not enough to craft or curate gorgeous items and list them in your shop; you must also provide excellent customer service — before, during, and after each sale. In this chapter, we stress the importance of clear communication and prompt shipping. We also provide guidance on how to gracefully deal with bungled transactions.

Pros and Convos: Accessing Etsy Convos

A *convo* — short for "conversation" — is a communication with another member using Etsy's internal messaging system. You can use convos to communicate with any other Etsy member. To access your convos, click the Shop Manager link that appears along the top of any Etsy Marketplace page, and choose Conversations in the main Shop Manager page. The Conversations page appears (see Figure 17-1), listing your convos.

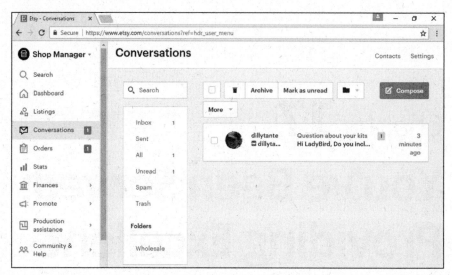

FIGURE 17-1:
Access your Etsy convos here.

TIP

If you use the Sell on Etsy app, you'll receive a notification on your mobile phone when you receive a message via convo. To make sure you don't miss a missive, you can also set up Etsy to email you anytime someone sends you a message on the site. Here's how:

1. **Click the Settings link in the top-right corner of the Shop Manager Conversations page.**

   The Emails tab opens (see Figure 17-2).

2. **In the General Notifications section of the Emails tab, click the Someone Sends Me a Convo check box to select it.**

3. **Click the Save Settings button at the bottom of the page.**

   Etsy saves your settings.

TIP

Set up a separate email address for correspondence on Etsy. That way, you can keep all your business-related messages in one place.

Account | Preferences | Privacy | Security | Addresses | Credit Cards | Emails | Taxpayer ID

Email settings for ladybirdtreasury@gmail.com

General Notifications

EMAIL ME WHEN...
- ☑ Someone sends me a convo
- ☐ I send a convo
- ☑ Someone follows me
- ☑ My listings are about to expire

Source: Etsy.com

Let's Talk: Communicating with Buyers

Communication is *the* single most critical factor for ensuring the success of your Etsy business. After your fabulous inventory catches your buyers' attention, your prompt and friendly communication — via Etsy convo, email, carrier pigeon, or whatever — will keep them coming back for more (not to mention recommending your shop to their friends).

When communicating with buyers, you must strike a balance. Communicate too little, and your buyers could conclude that you don't care about them. Communicate too much, and your buyers may think you're annoying. So when exactly should you reach out to buyers? And what exactly should you say? For guidance, read on.

Answering customer questions

Even if you upload five spectacular photos of your item and compose a listing description with Tolstoyan detail, prospective buyers will still have questions about your piece. Queries may range from "How big is it?" to "What does it smell like?" to "How fuzzy is it?" to "Um, what is that thing?" to "Can you make this in puce?"

Whatever the question, it's critical that you answer it — the sooner, the better. Unless you're stranded on a desert island or in labor, try to respond to all questions within 24 hours. Quickly replying to emails and convos containing queries from potential buyers does more than just help them determine whether your item is right for them; it reassures them that you're a seller they can count on.

REMEMBER

When communicating with customers, keep things simple. Providing too much information may confuse them. Focus on communicating the information that will be most helpful to the customer. For example, if a customer asks how quickly you can put an item in the post, simply respond by telling her, "Tomorrow." Don't say, "Well, I'd do it today, but my dog just ate my cactus, and I have to take her to the vet, so it will have to be tomorrow." TMI.

Giving thanks

As you may know, Etsy sends you a notification email when someone purchases an item from your Etsy shop. When you receive this email, you should contact the buyer to thank her for her purchase and to confirm that you've received payment for it (assuming you have). While you're at it, give the buyer some idea of when she can expect to receive the item and invite her to drop you a line if she has any questions. (We provide a sample note covering this and additional info later in this chapter.)

REMEMBER

On Etsy, as in life, simple courtesy goes a long way! Saying thank you is key to keeping your customers happy.

You can contact the buyer in one of two ways (the method you choose depends simply on which one you prefer). One is to email her. As shown in Figure 17-3, Etsy includes the buyer's email address in its notification email. Or you can access the buyer's email this way:

1. **Click the Shop Manager link along the top of any Etsy Marketplace page.**

2. **On the left side of the main Shop Manager page, click the Orders link.**

   The Open Orders page opens.

3. **Find the listing for the item in question, click the buyer's username, and click her email address in the list that appears (see Figure 17-4).**

FIGURE 17-3: Locate the buyer's email address on your notification email.

Another way to contact the buyer is to hold a convo with her (or any other Etsy user) right on the Etsy site. To initiate a convo with your buyer, click the Send Buyer a Convo link in the notification email (refer to Figure 17-3) or click her name in the Open Orders page but choose Contact from the menu that appears (see Figure 17-4). The New Conversation dialog box opens (see Figure 17-5); type your message and click Send.

TIP

To launch an Etsy convo with any other Etsy member (not just someone who has purchased something from your Etsy shop), open that person's Etsy profile page and click the Contact link under his name. The same box from Figure 17-5 appears.

FIGURE 17-4:
Access the buyer's email address from the Open Orders page.

New conversation
with dillytante

Re: Order #1189167232 on Apr 23, 2017

Invoice:
https://www.etsy.com/your/orders/1189167232

Attach image

Send   Cancel

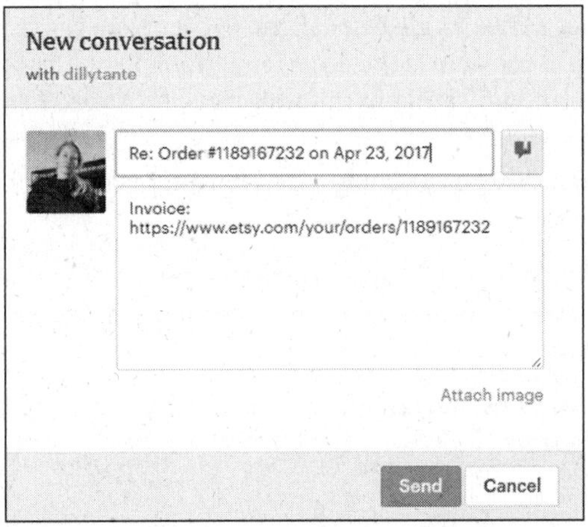

FIGURE 17-5:
The New Conversation dialog box.

Finding out how they found you

In the course of communicating with your buyers, whether it's in your initial convo or later in the process — for example, when you ship the item — ask how they found you. Did they happen upon your store while browsing Etsy? Did they see your work on a blog? Or did an ad pique their interest? This info can help you determine how well your marketing strategy is working — which is critical to the long-term success of your Etsy shop. (Flip to Chapter 16 for the scoop on marketing your Etsy shop.) While you're at it, consider asking whether they want to opt in to your mailing list (also discussed in Chapter 16).

Communicating with foreign buyers

Especially if you sell internationally, you must be prepared to correspond with buyers who are not native English speakers. (Of course, even if you sell only in the United States, you'll run across the occasional transplant.) To ward off misunderstandings when communicating with foreign buyers, keep these points in mind:

>> **Keep messages brief and simple.** Using long, complex words and sentences will almost certainly create confusion.

>> **Steer clear of slang.** Including nonstandard English is just asking for trouble. At best, your customers may misunderstand you. At worst, you may inadvertently offend them.

>> **Avoid abbreviations and jargon.** Spell out what you want to say, using clear, standard language.

Covering all your bases in one short, pleasant message

Still a bit stymied over what your initial message needs to contain? Here's a sample note that combines all the elements you should cover:

Hi [Buyer]!

Just a quick note to thank you so much for your purchase. You made me smile!

Payment has been received, and your treats will ship to the following address:

[Insert Address Here]

I'll send you an email when your package is ready to ship.

Also, may I ask where you found my shop — from an ad maybe, or just browsing around Etsy? And while I have you, are you interested in signing up for my monthly newsletter?

Thanks again, and I hope you have a fabulous day!

Kate

Shipping it quickly

If you've ever ordered anything on Etsy — and, let's face it, who hasn't? — you're no doubt familiar with the sweet torture of waiting for that prettily packaged parcel to pop into your postbox. To keep your buyers from expiring from anticipation, and to improve your chances of getting excellent feedback, be a dear and ship their goodies as soon as is feasibly possible (after they've paid for them and, if applicable, the check or money order has cleared). See Chapter 15 for more info on shipping options and packaging your parcel like a pro.

TIP

Touch base with your buyers after you ship their package to let them know it's on its way. Etsy makes this easy by enabling you to send a message right from the Open Orders page. Simply click the Mark as Shipped button next to the item in question to open the Mark As Shipped and Notify Buyer dialog box (see Figure 17-6). Then type a note to the buyer, indicate the tracking number and shipping carrier, and select the Send Me a Copy of This Email checkbox. (That way, you'll receive a copy of the email for your records.) Finally, click the Submit button. Message sent!

FIGURE 17-6:
Notify buyers that their item is on the way.

Source: Etsy.com

BABY GOT FEEDBACK: ETSY'S REVIEW SYSTEM

After purchasing an item from you, buyers have 60 days (starting from the estimated delivery date) to rate and review the transaction. Other Etsy users can then peruse this review to determine whether you are aboveboard. (Users can see reviews of your shop by clicking the stars at the top of the shop's main page.)

Leaving reviews isn't mandatory. If buyers opt out, Etsy doesn't send a gaggle of intimidating fellows to their door to harass them. But hopefully your buyers will leave a review anyway. This helps ensure that future buyers will feel safe shopping on Etsy — and that's good for everyone. If after a reasonable period of time has passed a buyer has not left a review, it doesn't hurt to politely remind her. Don't do this more than once, however. Otherwise, you'll officially become a pest.

Bungle Fever: Handling a Bungled Transaction and Other Tough Issues

Despite our best efforts, transactions occasionally do go to heck in a handbasket. Payments get lost, parcels go AWOL, and people get angry. To inoculate against this, read on.

Prompting a buyer to pay up

Most of the time, buyers pay right away when they purchase from an Etsy shop. In fact, if they opt to use Etsy Payments, they *must* pay right away. But occasionally, you may encounter buyers who take their sweet time when it comes to tendering the Benjamins. If that happens, you must take matters into your own hands by issuing a polite reminder for them to pay up.

Not sure what to write? Try something like the following:

> Dear [Buyer],
>
> Just a quick note to thank you for your purchase. I'm so glad you found some goodies to love!
>
> Whenever you get a chance, please send me your check (the total is $44.50) so that I can put your piece in the mail.

Thanks so much, Loretta! I can't wait until you see your treats. Have a lovely day!

Kate

If your buyer fails to respond to your gentle nudge within a reasonable time frame, you may relist the item and cancel the sale. For more information, see the upcoming section "Canceling an order."

Dealing with lost shipments

"Neither snow nor rain nor heat nor gloom of night," my eye! It's an unfortunate fact that sometimes the postal service and other delivery companies simply fail to deliver. If one of your packages has gone the way of Amelia Earhart, you have a few options:

>> **Ask your buyer to give it a few days.** More often than not, "lost" packages are merely delayed. Shipping times vary depending on destination and time of year.

>> **Ask your buyer to check with his neighbors.** It may be that the package was delivered there instead.

>> **Track the package.** If you sprang for package tracking (which, if you used Etsy's Calculated Shipping feature and shipped via USPS, you did by default), you can track the package. To do so, open Shop Manager, click Orders, click the Completed tab, and locate the order in the Completed Orders page. The order's Shipped tab features a link with a zillion digits. Click the link to open the Track Package dialog box. This dialog box indicates whether the package is shipped, in transit, out for delivery, or delivered. There's even a little map to pinpoint the package's exact location!

TIP

The buyer can also track the package. One way is to click the You menu and choose Purchases and Reviews, locate the order on the Purchases page, and click the order's Track Package button. Or he can click the Track Package link in the email notification he received when you shipped the package.

>> **Report the missing package.** If you sent the package via USPS, you can report it missing after seven business days. If you're lucky, the USPS will find your package. If not, well, at least you'll have done your part to improve the system. To report a missing package, go to www.usps.com/help/missing-mail.htm, click the Start Your Missing Mail Search button, and follow the prompts.

What if all these efforts fail? In that case, you'll unfortunately have to send a replacement item or refund the buyer's money (or if you're feeling especially customer-friendly, both). Yes, it hurts — but it's part of running a legitimate Etsy shop. Even if you suspect you're being scammed, refunding a buyer's dough may be worthwhile for the sake of your own review score (and sanity). It's your call. Our advice? Trust your gut.

TIP

If you do refund a buyer's money for an item lost in the mail, you need to cancel the order. That way, you'll at least receive a refund from Etsy for your transaction fee. For help canceling an order, see the section "Canceling an order."

Responding to a negative review

Earlier, we mentioned that buyers can leave reviews about transactions with Etsy sellers. Assuming that you deliver what you promise and treat your buyers kindly, these reviews will likely be overwhelmingly positive. Every so often, however, you may wind up with less-than-stellar feedback.

If you receive a negative review, launch a convo with the buyer to see whether you can resolve the matter (and thereby convince her to edit her review). To initiate this convo, open Shop Manager, click Orders, and click the Completed Orders tab. Then locate the order, click the buyer's username, and choose Contact from the menu that appears (refer to Figure 17-4).

If that doesn't work, Etsy gives you one chance to publicly respond to any review with a rating of three or fewer stars. (Note that if you go this route, the buyer will no longer be allowed to edit her rating or review, and you won't be able to edit your response, either.)

Dealing with a reported case

Although Etsy urges buyers and sellers to work through problems related to non-delivery themselves via civilized means such as with convos or emails, buyers sometimes feel compelled to report nondelivery cases to Etsy. (Buyers may also launch a case if the item received didn't match its description.) If a buyer launches a case against you, you'll receive an email from Etsy outlining the details of the case and instructions for resolving it. To view details about the case, do the following:

1. **Click the Shop Manager link that appears along the top of every Etsy Marketplace page.**

2. **Click the Community & Help link on the left side of the main Shop Manager page and choose Cases from the list of options that appears.**

    The Your Cases page opens.

3. **Click the Cases Reported About Your Shop tab.**

    A page appears with a link to the case.

4. **Click the link to the case.**

    A page containing information about the case appears, as shown in Figure 17-7.

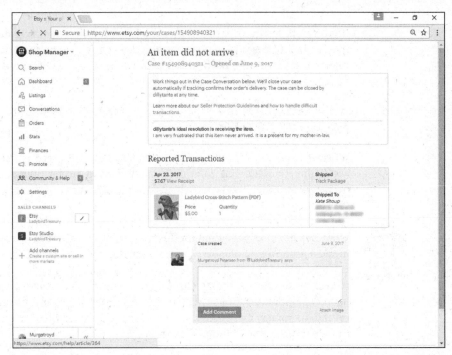

FIGURE 17-7:
View information about your case.

To resolve your case, you'll need to work directly with your buyer — and you should do it sooner rather than later. All correspondence pertaining to the open case should occur on the case's page. Simply type your message in the Comments box. Note that you can also upload images or photos — say, a scanned image of your delivery confirmation receipt or something similar — directly to the case's page by clicking the Attach Image link under the text box. In the end, you may need to refund the buyer's money. For help, see the next section. When the buyer is satisfied with your actions, she can close the case.

PROTECTIVE CUSTODY: ETSY'S SELLER PROTECTION PROGRAM

As noted in Chapter 6, Etsy offers a Seller Protection program, which guarantees that your account status will remain unaffected if a buyer reports a problem with a transaction with your shop. As a bonus, Etsy's Seller Protection program fully covers items purchased via Etsy Payments. So if a good transaction goes bad, you'll be in the clear. To find out whether you're eligible, flip to Chapter 6.

If you fail to resolve the case within a week, the buyer can escalate it for review by Etsy's Dispute Resolution team, in which case you may be contacted for additional information. If the team deems it necessary, they may issue a refund on your behalf.

Issuing refunds

When it comes to refunds, different sellers have different policies. Some sellers are happy to issue full refunds for any reason, other sellers allow buyers to exchange for other goods in their shop, and still others hold a firm "all sales final" stance.

REMEMBER

Whatever position you adopt on this matter, be certain that your shop policies are marked accordingly. Flip to Chapter 9 for more about setting up shop policies.

If you do decide to allow refunds, how you process them depends on which payment option your buyer chose. For example, if he sent a check, you'll likely refund his money by sending him one back. If he used Etsy Payments, you'll need to follow these steps to refund his money:

1. **Click the Shop Manager link that appears along the top of every Etsy Marketplace page.**

2. **Click the Orders link on the left side of the Shop Manager page.**

   The Open Orders page opens. If you're refunding the money after the item has been shipped, click the Completed Orders tab.

3. **Click the Receipt number link on the right side of the listing entry.**

   A page containing information about the order opens.

4. **Click the Manage Order menu and choose Issue a Refund (see Figure 17-8).**

   The Issue a Refund page, shown in Figure 17-9, opens.

5. **Click the Reason for Issuing a Refund drop-down list and choose the appropriate option from the list.**

6. **If you want, type a message to your buyer.**

7. **To issue a full refund, select the Issue a Full Refund check box; otherwise, enter the desired amounts in the appropriate fields in the Amount to Refund column.**

8. **Click the Review Refund button.**

   Etsy asks you to confirm the refund.

FIGURE 17-8:
The item's
order page.

Source: Etsy.com

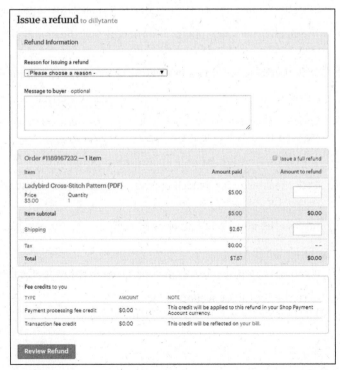

FIGURE 17-9:
Issue a refund.

Source: Etsy.com

9. **Click the Submit button.**

   Etsy refunds the buyer's money. The amount will be deducted from the available balance in your Shop Payment account or charged to your credit card. (Any processing fees associated with your card will be refunded proportionally. You'll see an adjusted transaction fee on your bill.)

Canceling an order

In certain circumstances, you, as a shop owner, can cancel an order. For example, you may cancel an order if the buyer fails to pay, if both you and the buyer agree to cancel the transaction prior to shipment, if you can't complete the transaction (for example, due to inventory problems), if the item was lost in the mail, or if the buyer returned the item to you. When you cancel an order, Etsy refunds your transaction fee. Note that you can cancel an order only after refunding the buyer's money (see the preceding section).

To cancel an order, follow these steps:

1. **Click the Shop Manager link that appears along the top of every Etsy Marketplace page.**

2. **Click the Orders link on the left side of the Shop Manager page.**

   The Open Orders page opens. If you're refunding the money after the item has been shipped, click the Completed Orders tab.

3. **Click the Receipt number link on the right side of the listing entry.**

   A page containing information about the order opens (refer to Figure 17-8).

4. **Click the Cancel a Transaction link. (This link appears in place of the Manage Transaction link after you issue a refund.)**

   The Cancel Transactions page appears (see Figure 17-10).

5. **Click the Reason for Canceling Transaction drop-down list and choose the reason for the cancellation.**

6. **Answer the questions that appear.**

   The precise questions that appear depend on the reason you select in Step 5.

7. **If you want, type a message for the buyer in the Message to Buyer field.**

8. **Click the Submit Cancellation button.**

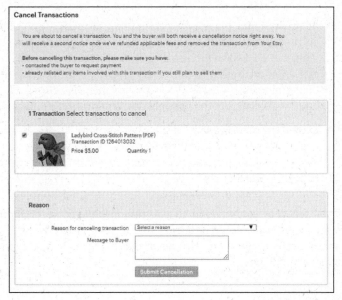

Cancel Transactions

You are about to cancel a transaction. You and the buyer will both receive a cancellation notice right away. You will receive a second notice once we've refunded applicable fees and removed the transaction from Your Etsy.

Before canceling this transaction, please make sure you have:
• contacted the buyer to request payment
• already relisted any items involved with this transaction if you still plan to sell them

1 Transaction Select transactions to cancel

Ladybird Cross-Stitch Pattern (PDF)
Transaction ID 1264013032
Price $5.00   Quantity 1

Reason

Reason for canceling transaction   Select a reason
Message to Buyer

Submit Cancellation

Source: Etsy.com

FIGURE 17-10:
Cancel a
transaction.

After you submit the form, Etsy finalizes the cancellation (it may take up to 48 hours), notifies you and the buyer that the cancellation has occurred, credits your account with the listing fees associated with the order, and moves the listing to the Canceled Orders page.

REMEMBER

Occasionally, you may come across buyers who request a cancellation. It's up to you whether you grant their request. If you do, you can follow the same steps outlined here.

Dealing with a difficult customer

Honestly, nearly everyone on Etsy is great. For real. But every so often, you're bound to run into someone who, well, *isn't*. Whether someone on Etsy is rude, demanding, or simply a pain in the patootie, keep these points in mind:

» **Polish your policies.** Clear, concise shop policies can go a long way toward heading off problems down the road. Be sure that your shop's policies are as clear as possible. (For guidance on creating your shop's policies, see Chapter 9.)

» **Don't take it personally.** If, after receiving your beautiful baubles, your buyer doesn't appreciate their magnificence, that's on him, not on you.

>> **Be professional.** However tempting it may be to uncork on a difficult buyer, don't — at least, not where that person can hear you. Keep all communications firm, polite, and to the point. Oh, and resist the temptation to air your grievances on the Etsy forums. Everything you write there is visible to anyone on the Internet — including your grandmother. Plus, calling out a buyer by name is a violation of the site's policies, which can lead to your expulsion.

>> **Extend the olive branch.** Most buyers aren't evil. They just want to feel like you're willing to work with them to achieve a happy, speedy transaction. Kindly communicate to them that you'll do everything possible to make that happen — and then do it.

If you feel that you've done all you reasonably can to rectify a problem with a buyer to no avail, don't be afraid to cut your losses by refunding the buyer's money. Better to get a problem buyer out of your hair than to kill yourself trying to make him happy.

Refusing service to a buyer

Although Etsy asks that sellers do everything they can to honor a sale, on extremely rare occasions, you may feel that you must refuse service. For example, if you feel you're being harassed by a buyer, or if a buyer becomes belligerent — or if, say, you're a Hatfield and the buyer is a McCoy — you do have the right to refuse service, no questions asked. You may also refuse service if your gut instinct tells you that the buyer isn't on the up and up — for example, if you sense that she has paid with a stolen credit card or is attempting to commit some other type of fraud.

Refusing service is a rare event, indeed. It's something you want to do only as a last resort.

REMEMBER

To refuse service to a buyer, simply use an Etsy convo to politely inform the buyer that you won't be able to send the item she purchased. You don't need to explain yourself. In fact, the less you say, the better. Then take the necessary steps to refund the buyer's money and cancel the sale (as we describe earlier in this chapter).

After you refuse service to a buyer, if that person continues to contact you, you can report the problem to Etsy Support.

TIP

IN THIS CHAPTER

» **Settling your Etsy bill and paying taxes**

» **Keeping good records and tracking and analyzing shop data**

» **Choosing a business structure**

» **Using Etsy apps**

» **Going on hiatus and closing your Etsy shop**

Chapter **18**

Business as Usual: Managing Your Etsy Store

f you're a fan of Chinese food, you're probably familiar with the pu-pu platter — you know, the appetizer that features a little bit of everything. This chapter is the literary equivalent. It covers an assortment of topics that relate to managing your Etsy business. They include exploring the Shop Manager dashboard, paying your Etsy bill, handling taxes, keeping good records, analyzing shop data, turning your thriving shop into a legit business, and more.

REMEMBER

On top of all the Etsy-specific info, we've tried to cram several books' worth of business information into this one wee chapter. We strongly urge you to educate yourself further on all these matters and more. A good place to start is *Starting a Business All-in-One For Dummies* (Wiley), which packs content from eight whole business-related books into one.

Paradise by the Dashboard Light: Using the Shop Manager Dashboard

You manage your shop from . . . well, Shop Manager. You've already seen how Shop Manager enables you to manage your listings, convos, and orders as well as your promotional activities. In this chapter, you find out how to use it to manage your shop finances, track stats, and more.

As you've no doubt noticed, when you open Shop Manager (by clicking the Shop Manager link that appears along the top of any Etsy Marketplace page), the Shop Manager dashboard appears. This dashboard provides several key pieces of information, all accessible at a glance (see Figure 18-1):

>> An overview of orders received and active listings

>> A list of unread convos

>> A stats overview (including views, favorites, orders, and revenue)

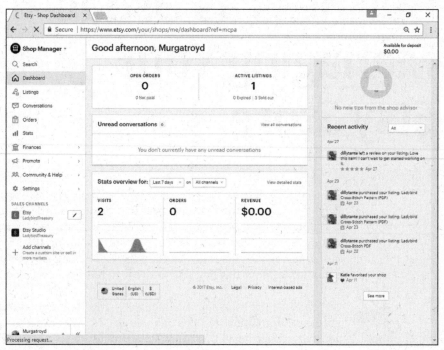

FIGURE 18-1:
View the Shop Manager dashboard.

Source: Etsy.com

>> Updates from the Shop Advisor (these may flag a listing that's about to expire, alert you to a new case, or just share useful info to help you run your shop more efficiently)

>> Recent shop activity, including people favoriting a listing in your shop (or the shop itself) as well as purchases made in your shop

"I'm Just a Bill": Paying Your Etsy Bill

You're not the only baby who needs a new pair of shoes. The folks at Etsy have their own financial obligations. As we mention in Chapter 1, Etsy stays afloat by charging sellers a listing fee (currently 20¢) for each item listed on the site. In addition, Etsy collects a commission from the seller for each item sold — currently, 3.5 percent of the total price of the item (not counting shipping) — as well as fees for shipping labels and search ads.

Etsy keeps a running tab of these fees on the Your Bill page (see Figure 18-2). To access this page, click the Shop Manager link that appears along the top of any Etsy Marketplace page, click the Finances link on the left side of the main Shop Manager page, and choose Your Bill.

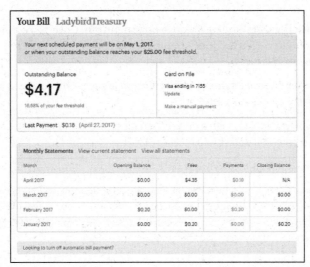

FIGURE 18-2: View your Etsy bill.

Source: Etsy.com

Etsy sends you a bill via email for these fees each month or when you exceed your fee threshold. (New sellers have a fee threshold of $25. As you sell more on Etsy, this fee threshold will rise.) By default, this happens automatically. That is, Etsy charges whatever credit card you have on file to cover your fees. We like this system because it prevents us from falling behind, but we get that it may not be for everybody. If you'd prefer to pay your bill manually, you can disable automatic payment. To do so, click the Looking to Turn Off Automatic Payment? link at the bottom of the Your Bill page and click the Turn Off Automatic Bill Payment button in the confirmation dialog box that appears. Then pay your bill, like so:

1. **On the Your Bill page, click the Make a Manual Payment link.**

   The Make a Payment page opens (see Figure 18-3).

FIGURE 18-3:
Pay your bill.

2. **Click the Outstanding Balance option button. Or to pay a different amount, click the Other Amount option button and type the amount in the box below it.**

3. **Under Choose Payment Method, choose the credit card you have on file with Etsy or select PayPal.**

   If you want to pay with a different credit card, click the Change Card on File link and enter the details for a new card.

4. **Click the Submit Payment button.**

   If you opted to pay with PayPal, Etsy directs you to the PayPal site (www.paypal.com), where you're prompted to log in. After you do so, review the payment information. Assuming that it's correct, click the Continue button. PayPal processes your payment and directs you back to Etsy.

REMEMBER

To remain in good standing with Etsy, you must pay the amount due on your Etsy bill by 7 p.m. EST on day 15 of the month. If you don't, Etsy may restrict your site privileges and could even suspend your account.

If you change your mind and decide you'd rather pay your Etsy bill automatically after all, just click the Enroll Now button on the Your Bill page; specify whether you want to pay using the credit card you have on file, a new card, or PayPal; and click the Enroll in Automatic Bill Pay button.

Taxing Matters: Appeasing Uncle Sam

A world with no taxes would be lovely indeed — except for the fact that it would also be a world with no roads, public school teachers, firefighters, air traffic controllers, or snowplows. Indeed, without taxes, there would be no Internet — and, by extension, no Etsy! After all, taxpayers bankrolled the U.S. government's Advanced Research Projects Agency (ARPA), which, in 1969, created the network that would eventually become the Internet. (Thanks, Al Gore!) To make sure you're square with Uncle Sam, read on.

REMEMBER

We're not licensed accountants or lawyers, nor do we play them on TV. To be absolutely certain you're in compliance with local and federal tax laws, seek the advice of these experts.

Collecting sales tax

You need to collect sales tax at least some of the time on your Etsy sales (unless you live in Alaska, Delaware, Montana, New Hampshire, or Oregon — five states that don't impose a statewide sales tax). Specifically, you must collect sales tax (sometimes called a *franchise tax, transaction privilege tax,* or *use tax,* among other aliases) on most goods and some services delivered to a customer who lives in a U.S. state where your business maintains a physical presence, or *nexus.* So, for example, if you run your Etsy shop from your fifth-floor walkup in Brooklyn, and someone from the state of New York buys something from your shop, you need to hit that person with sales tax. But if your buyer lives in California, you're both off the hook.

Sales tax rates vary widely from state to state. Plus, some cities, counties, and jurisdictions impose sales tax above and beyond the state rate. To get a handle on your state's requirements — including whether you're obligated to charge a sales tax; what sales tax rate(s) you must charge; how to register with your state for a sales tax license or permit; and where, when, and how to remit sales tax you've collected to your state — nothing beats consulting a fancy-pants accountant for guidance.

In general terms, the sales tax process works like this:

1. **You get a sales tax ID number from your state (check your state government's website for details).**

   But good news! This sales tax ID number entitles you to buy supplies and other items for your Etsy business wholesale — which is typically at least half off the retail price. Holy bonus, Batman!

2. **Each time you conduct a taxable transaction, you calculate the tax owed and collect it from the buyer.**

3. **You keep excellent records about the tax that you've collected through your Etsy business (we advise you on this later in this chapter).**

4. **Each month, quarter, or year (depending on your level of sales), you file a tax return and submit the sales tax that you've collected to your state.**

5. **You stay out of jail.**

If, after checking the local laws in your area and consulting a fancy-pants accountant, you've determined that you must collect sales tax, you can easily set up your shop to do so. In fact, with Etsy's tax calculator (available for Etsy sellers in the United States and Canada), you can collect sales tax during the checkout process. That way, Etsy will automatically assess a sales tax for buyers in your region. It's like magic! Here's how it works:

1. **Click the Shop Manager link along the top of any Etsy Marketplace page.**

2. **Click the Finances link on the left side of the main Shop Manager page and choose Payment Settings.**

   The Payment Settings page opens.

3. **Click the Sales Tax tab.**

   The Sales Tax Settings page opens (see Figure 18-4).

4. **If you live in the United States, click the State drop-down list and choose your state.**

   If you live in Canada, choose a province from the drop-down list in the Canada section. If you live in another country, select it from the drop-down list under Other Countries.

5. **Click the Add Tax Rate button.**

6. **Enter the appropriate tax rate in the Tax Rate box.**

7. **If the laws in your area require you to charge sales tax on shipping fees, select the Apply Rate to Shipping check box.**

FIGURE 18-4:
Set up the Etsy
tax calculator to
automatically
collect taxes.

8. **If local laws require you to assess a sales tax on buyers from specific zip codes, click the Zip Code Range or Zip Codes tab, enter the applicable zip code range or zip code, and repeat Steps 5 through 7.**

9. **Click the Update Tax Settings.**

   Etsy saves your settings.

Paying quarterly income tax and filing your annual tax return

If you run your Etsy business as a sole proprietorship (covered later in this chapter), you expect to owe more than $1,000 in taxes for the year, and you live in the United States, you have the distinct pleasure of paying estimated income taxes not once, not twice, not three times, but *four times* per year — on April 15, June 15, September 15, and January 15 (unless any of those days falls on a weekend or holiday, in which case you must pay up on the next business day).

Paying these quarterly estimated taxes is a breeze. You can download the necessary form (called a 1040-ES) from the IRS's website, here: www.irs.gov/pub/irs-pdf/f1040es.pdf. You need to download a similar form from your state government's site. Then fill out the forms, cut your checks, and send them to the appropriate office. (Check the form for details.) Alternatively, you can pay your quarterly estimated taxes online using the Electronic Federal Tax Payment System (EFTPS): www.eftps.gov/eftps. (EFTPS is for federal taxes only; check with your state to see what resources are available for paying your state taxes online.)

PERFECT 1099: FILING YOUR 1099-K

If your Etsy shop's sales are high enough — that is, you process more than 200 payments through Etsy Payments and gross more than $20,000 by the end of the year — Etsy is required by federal law to file a 1099-K form on your behalf with the IRS and to send you a copy so you'll have it when you file your taxes. (If you don't make those numbers, Etsy won't file a 1099-K.) For all this to work, Etsy needs your taxpayer ID. To provide it, click the Shop Manager link that appears along the top of any Etsy Marketplace page. Then click the Finances link and choose Taxpayer ID. Click the Social Security Number or Employer Identification Number (EIN) option button, enter your taxpayer ID, and click the Submit button. Finally, click Confirm when prompted to confirm that the number you entered is correct.

REMEMBER

Estimating how much you should pay each quarter can be tricky. One approach is to simply look at your prior-year tax return to see how much you paid in taxes, divide that number by four, and send that amount for each quarterly installment. (Of course, that strategy won't do if you expect your income to be vastly different from one year to the next.) Our advice? Don't take our advice. Seek the guidance of a qualified accountant.

Of course, you'll also have to file an annual tax return (and make up the difference on your annual taxes if your quarterly payments fell short). That happens on April 15 like always (or, again, the next business day if April 15 falls on a weekend or holiday). This involves filing a Schedule C "Profit or Loss from Business" form as well as a Schedule SE "Self-Employment Tax" form (because income from your Etsy shop is considered "self-employment income").

Identifying tax deductions

Your taxable income is the *net profit* from your Etsy business — in other words, the amount of money you hauled in from sales minus the amount of money you paid out for business expenses. These expenses are called *deductions*. Here are a few examples (again, for a complete list, hit up a qualified accountant):

>> **Cost of goods sold (COGS):** This category is the cost of the materials you purchased to craft your inventory. For example, if you make jewelry, your COGS may include the price you paid for beads, thread, findings, and so on. The COGS may also include what you shelled out for pretty packaging and shipping costs.

>> **Equipment:** Did you buy a kiln to fire the ceramic bowls that you list in your Etsy shop? Or a laptop to help run your Etsy business? Or a printer to print

invoices for your Etsy customers? If so, you can deduct the cost of these items from your taxable income.

- **Office expenses:** These purchases include pens and pencils, paper, letterhead, printer supplies, and so on.

- **Home office:** If you use a portion of your home to run your Etsy shop — maybe you devote a special room to crafting the pieces that you sell or for handling administrative tasks — you can claim a home-office deduction. Or if you rent studio space, you can deduct that instead.

- **Selling expenses:** These expenses include Etsy fees, banking fees, and the like.

- **Advertising fees:** Say that you printed some snazzy business cards for your Etsy shop. These and other marketing expenses are fair game. (Chapter 16 provides a general introduction to marketing materials.)

- **Mileage:** Do you regularly drive to your local craft store to stock up on supplies for your Etsy shop? Or to the post office to ship items to Etsy buyers? If so, you can deduct your mileage for those outings. The current rate, as of this writing, is 53.5¢ per mile. Any tolls or parking fees that you incur en route are also deductible.

- **Legal or professional services:** If you follow our advice and hire an accountant, you can deduct her fee. Ditto for any fees associated with other professionals who serve your business — attorneys, graphic designers, and the like.

REMEMBER

If you forked over more than $600 to a particular person for services rendered — for example, your attorney or graphic designer — you must send that person a 1099 form if you intend to deduct the expense. Ask your tax consultant for more information.

Recording Artist: Keeping Accurate Records

Yes, we know. Record keeping is for squares. But if you want to avoid getting sideways with the IRS — not to mention stay on top of your business — you'll want to be scrupulous about your record keeping, however tedious it may be. That means keeping careful track of all your sales and expenses and keeping *all* receipts — even the little ones. All those road tolls and parking fees add up! You'll also want to hang on to invoices, bank statements, and any other financial-type documents that cross your desk.

SEPARATION ANXIETY: SEPARATING YOUR PERSONAL AND BUSINESS FINANCES

Especially if you plan to grow your Etsy business into a full-time operation, do yourself a favor: Open a business bank account for your Etsy shop, preferably with a credit or debit card. Then use that account to handle all expenses related to your Etsy shop. At tax time, you won't have to cull your business transactions from your personal ones to report your business expenses. Plus, if you ever need to verify your income — say, if you're taking out a loan to make a major purchase — you'll be able to provide the lending authority with everything it needs. Depending on your location, you may need to show your business license to open a business account with your bank. (You find out more about business licenses later in this chapter.)

TIP

It's smart to put all this information in one place. An accordion file is a good way to go; it enables you to separate your receipts and other documents by month or by category. Also keep an eye on your inventory as part of your record keeping so you don't run low. One approach may be "one out, one in" — that is, as soon as you sell an item, you make and list a new one.

Using QuickBooks for Etsy

Maybe you've heard of QuickBooks. It's an accounting software package that's great for small businesses (like your Etsy shop). Well, good news: QuickBooks has partnered with Etsy to offer QuickBooks for Etsy. With QuickBooks for Etsy, you can export your Etsy sales and seller fees right into QuickBooks (specifically, to a cloud-based version of QuickBooks called QuickBooks Self-Employed). That's not all, though. You can also export other sales and expenses into QuickBooks Self-Employed — for example, from Square, from PayPal, and even from your business bank account and credit card. And with the QuickBooks Self-Employed app, you can snap and store business-related receipts and track mileage. But wait, there's more! QuickBooks Self-Employed automatically categorizes your expenses to help you maximize your business deductions and calculates your quarterly estimated taxes.

TIP

If you *really* want to go crazy, you can upgrade to the QuickBooks Self-Employed + TurboTax bundle. Then you can use TurboTax to pay your quarterly estimated taxes and to prepare and file your state and federal taxes online.

To try QuickBooks for Etsy, click the Shop Manager link along the top of any Etsy Marketplace page. Then click the Finances link on the left side of the Shop

Manager page and choose QuickBooks for Etsy. Finally, click the Get Started button to sign up for a free trial. (At the time of this writing, Etsy sellers get half off on QuickBooks Self-Employed as well as on the QuickBooks Self-Employed–TurboTax bundle for the first year.)

Using spreadsheet software to manage your shop

Maybe you'd rather do your own bookkeeping using Excel or something similar. In that case, you'll be glad to know that Etsy enables you to download sales data in comma-separated value (CSV) form and save it on your hard drive. You can then view this data by opening the CSV file in a spreadsheet program. To download this data, follow these steps:

1. **Click the Shop Manager link that appears along the top of every Etsy Marketplace page.**

2. **Click the Orders link on the left side of the Shop Manager page.**

   The Open Orders page appears.

3. **Click the Download a CSV File link at the bottom of the page to initiate the download.**

   The Download Shop Data page appears.

   - To download a CSV containing all listings currently for sale, click the Download CSV button under Currently for Sale Listings. Then follow the onscreen prompts to save the file to your hard drive. (The steps differ by operating system.)

   - To download a CSV with order information, click the CSV Type drop-down list and choose Order Items, Orders, Etsy Payments Sales, or Etsy Payments Deposits. Then select the desired month and year, click Download CSV, and follow the prompts.

You can also download your monthly Etsy bill in CSV format. To do so, click the Finances link on the left side of the Shop Manager page, choose Finances, and select Your Bill. Then, on the Your Etsy Bill page, click the desired month, click the Download This Entire Monthly Statement as a CSV File link at the bottom of the page that appears, and follow the prompts.

One Track Mind: Tracking and Analyzing Shop Stats

Statistics. They're not just for baseball fanatics and Nate Silver. They're also for Etsy shop owners like you, thanks to Etsy Shop Stats. With Etsy Shop Stats (see Figure 18-5), you can track a plethora of information.

Etsy divides Shop Stats into three main categories, each with its own page in Shop Manager:

>> **Traffic:** These statistics reveal how many visits and orders your shop has received as well as the amount of revenue earned. They also reveal traffic sources — where visitors are coming from and what search terms they're using to find you. This can help you assess how effective your marketing efforts both on the site and off are. Figure 18-5 shows the Etsy Stats Traffic page.

>> **Listings:** This page shows which listings potential buyers are looking at most. It also reveals how many people have favorited each listing and how many orders each listing has received.

TIP

>> Tracking order data over time — by day, week, month, and beyond — can help you identify fluctuations, which can help with planning. With this information, you know when your high and low cycles are, so you can plan for them (for example, ordering supplies before they get critically low).

>> **Customers:** This page reveals additional search terms used by customers (helpful information if you're considering expanding your product line), where your customers are located geographically, and what devices your customers are using.

To access Etsy Shop Stats, follow these steps:

1. **Click the Shop Manager button that appears along the top of every Etsy Marketplace page.**

2. **Click the Stats link on the left side of the Shop Manager page.**

   The Shop Stats page opens with the Traffic page displayed.

3. **Click the Last 30 Days button in the upper-right corner of the page and choose the desired time period — for example, Last 7 Days or Last 12 Months.**

4. **To view stats on listings or customers, click the Listings or Customers link in the upper-left corner of the page.**

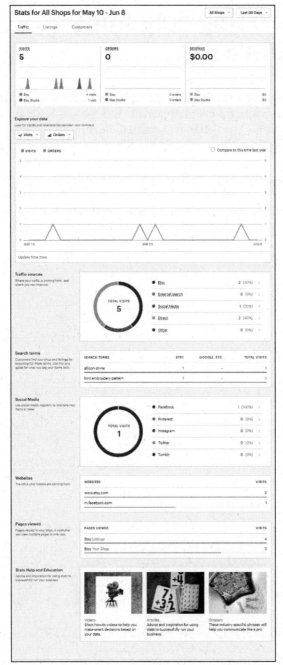

Source: Etsy.com

FIGURE 18-5:
Checking your
shop sales stats
is a cinch.

An App a Day: Using Etsy Apps to Run Your Store

You don't have to be "at work" to manage your Etsy shop. With the Sell on Etsy app, available for Android and Apple iOS devices, you could be *literally anywhere*. Antarctica? Check. The Sahara? Check. The hammock in your backyard? Check, check, and check (as long as you have a cell or Wi-Fi signal, of course).

The main page of the Sell on Etsy app looks a little like the main Shop Manager page. It features a dashboard as well as links to a Listings-type page, Open Orders and Completed Orders pages, and convos (see Figure 18-6).

FIGURE 18-6: The Sell on Etsy app works a lot like Shop Manager.

Source: Etsy.com

Clicking the More button reveals even more options (see Figure 18-7):

- **Your Shop:** Tap this option to view your shop.
- **Reviews:** To peruse your reviews, tap this option. (For more on reviews, see Chapter 17.)

>> **Shop Updates:** Tap this to post Shop Updates. (Flip to Chapter 16 for more on posting Shop Updates.)

>> **Teams:** Your Etsy Teams are just a tap away. (We talk about Etsy Teams in Chapter 20.)

>> **Settings:** Access shop and notification settings here.

>> **Help:** Tap Help for help using the Sell on Etsy app, to view the Seller Handbook, or to check out Etsy policies.

>> **Account:** When you tap Account, you see options to open profile settings, access additional Etsy accounts, and sign out.

>> **Switch to the Etsy App:** Tap this if you want to take off your "seller" hat and put on your "buyer" one and do a little shopping yourself.

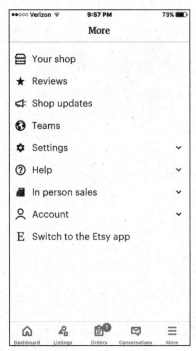

FIGURE 18-7:
Tap More for more options.

You're not limited to using the Sell on Etsy app to manage your store, however. Tons of third-party vendors have built apps to help Etsy sellers manage their shops. Some of these apps are for Android and Apple iOS devices. Others are meant for a desktop or laptop computer. These apps handle all sorts of tasks, like selling Etsy products directly through Instagram and Facebook (Spreesy), managing your inventory (RunInventory), pricing your items (PriceWoot), and more. You can browse Etsy's App Gallery to find out which apps are available. To access it, follow these steps on the Etsy website:

1. **Click the Shop Manager link that appears along the top of any Etsy Marketplace page.**

2. **On the left side of the Shop Manager page, click the Community & Help link and choose App Marketplace.**

   The Apps You Use page opens.

3. **Click the App Gallery link.**

   The Apps for Etsy page opens (see Figure 18-8).

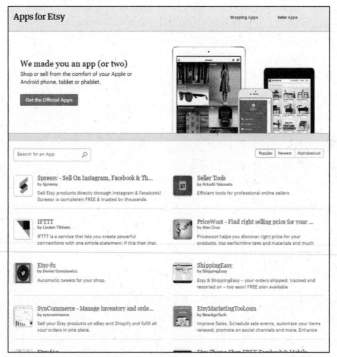

FIGURE 18-8: The Etsy App Gallery.

4. **To find out more about an app, click the app's link.**

   A page containing information about the app opens.

5. **To download the app, click the Visit Website button that appears on the app's page and follow the instructions. (We'd walk you through the process, but the precise steps vary by app.)**

REMEMBER

Like we said, these apps are developed by third-party vendors. That's a techy way of saying that although you can access the apps from Etsy's website, for the most part, Etsy didn't build them. And *that's* a polite way of saying that if you have a problem with an app, don't bug Etsy about it; bug the company that actually *made* the app.

Too Legit to Quit: Making Your Business Legit

If you're starting your Etsy shop as a hobby, you probably haven't given much thought to the structure of your Etsy business. It's just you, creating or curating stuff and putting it up for sale. But if your Etsy shop grows into a full-time operation — or if you want it to — you'll need to consider what business structure is best for you. The structure that you choose affects both your personal liability if your business is sued and the taxes you'll have to pay.

REMEMBER

Depending on your location, you may be required to obtain a business license to operate your Etsy shop in an aboveboard manner. You may also need a business license to open a business checking account. For information about business license requirements in your area, visit www.sba.gov/localresources.

When it comes to business structures, you have a few main options:

>> **Sole proprietorship:** If you're just starting out with your Etsy business, odds are you're running a *sole proprietorship*, sort of by default. That is, you own your business outright and you're solely responsible for all decisions and debts that pertain to it. This type of business is by far the easiest to start, but it's also the riskiest type to run. This is because you'll be held personally accountable if something goes wrong. For example, if someone using your product becomes sick or injured, that person could sue you, personally, placing your assets (and any assets that you hold jointly with a spouse) at risk. You're also personally accountable for any debt that the business assumes.

>> **General partnership:** A *general partnership* consists of two or more co-owners. Typically, the parties in a general partnership split the profits from the business equally, although that's not always the case. For example, if you and your friend go into business together but you invest more in startup costs, you may agree to a different split of the profits — say, 60/40. General partnerships are similar to sole proprietorships in that you and your partner(s) are personally responsible for any debt that the business incurs.

>> **Limited partnership:** In addition to general partnerships, limited partnerships exist. In that case, one partner contributes funds and shares in profits but assumes no role in the workings of the company.

>> **Corporation:** A *corporation* is a legal entity all its own, separate from its founders (you), managers, and employees, and owned by its shareholders (again, you, along with anyone else you decide to bring into the fold). Operating as a corporation means, among other things, that your personal assets are protected in case the company is sued. Two types of corporations exist: C-corporations and S-corporations. Although C-corporations provide the most financial protection to shareholders and offer other advantages, many small businesses go the S-corporation route because they're cheaper to start and easier to maintain. To avoid running afoul of the IRS, speak to your accountant in detail about how to deal with profits if you opt to form a corporation.

SWEET CHARITY: HANDLING CHARITABLE GIVING

Some kindly Etsy sellers use their shops as fundraising vehicles — for example, donating proceeds from certain listings to a particular charity or even devoting an entire shop to a cause. However, because fundraising is subject to many laws, and because the occasional bad apple may confuse "charity" with "larceny," Etsy has established strict policies on charitable listings and shops. Members who fail to comply are subject to suspension of account privileges and/or termination (of their account, not their corporeal existence).

Here are the high points of Etsy's policies on charitable giving:

- All charitable fundraising that occurs on Etsy must comply with applicable laws.

- Any seller who publicizes that his Etsy shop engages in charitable fundraising on behalf of a recognized tax-deductible charitable organization must receive appropriate consent from the charitable organization.

- The seller must include clear information about the charitable organization in question, as well as donation details, in the listing and/or other public areas of the shop.

- It's no fair generating listings solely to solicit donations. All listings must be for a tangible item available for sale.

- Sending unsolicited donation requests to other Etsy users via convos or in the forums is verboten.

>> **Limited liability company (LLC):** A popular choice for many business owners, a *limited liability company (LLC)* is a sort of hybrid between a partnership and a corporation. An LLC not only limits your liability for business debt but also allows you to choose whether you want to be treated as a partnership or as a corporation, depending on which has the lower tax burden.

So what type of business structure is right for you? That's an excellent question — and one that you want to direct to a lawyer or accountant. (Also, be sure to seek the help of a lawyer or accountant when it comes to actually setting up your company because the precise steps for doing so differ depending on where you live.)

The Artist Is Out: Switching to Vacation Mode

It's a well-known fact that vacations are as good for you as Brussels sprouts. Vacations do more than help you rest and relieve stress. They promote creativity — which is pretty important when the success of your Etsy shop depends a great deal on your ability to create!

Of course, the key to getting the most out of any vacation is being able to put aside your work while you're away. To facilitate this, you can switch your shop to vacation mode. When your shop is in vacation mode, your listings aren't visible to anyone who visits your shop. In addition, you can add a special vacation-mode notice to replace your shop announcement or upload a special "on vacation" cover photo (see Chapter 8 to find out how). And anyone who attempts to convo you in your absence will receive an auto reply containing the text that you specify.

TIP

You don't have to actually be "on vacation" to put your shop in vacation mode. You can use this feature any time you need a break from your Etsy shop.

It's not a bad idea to put your shop in vacation mode a day or two before you leave. That way, you have time to handle all your orders before you depart. You may also leave your shop in vacation mode for a day or two after you get back so that you can ease into things. To put your shop in vacation mode, follow these steps:

1. **Click the Shop Manager button that appears along the top of every Etsy Marketplace page.**

2. **Click Settings on the left side of the Shop Manager page and select Options.**

   The Shop Settings page opens.

3. **Click the Vacation Mode tab.**

The Vacation Mode page opens (see Figure 18-9).

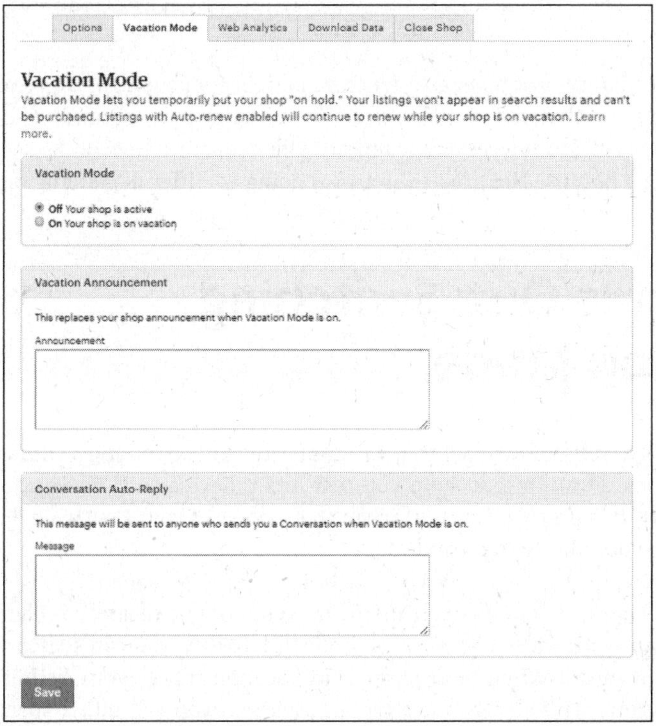

| Options | **Vacation Mode** | Web Analytics | Download Data | Close Shop |

Vacation Mode

Vacation Mode lets you temporarily put your shop "on hold." Your listings won't appear in search results and can't be purchased. Listings with Auto-renew enabled will continue to renew while your shop is on vacation. Learn more.

Vacation Mode

○ Off Your shop is active
○ On Your shop is on vacation

Vacation Announcement

This replaces your shop announcement when Vacation Mode is on.

Announcement

Conversation Auto-Reply

This message will be sent to anyone who sends you a Conversation when Vacation Mode is on.

Message

Save

FIGURE 18-9:
Put your shop in vacation mode any time you need a break.

4. **Click the On Your Shop Is On Vacation option button under Vacation Mode.**

5. **Type the desired text — how long you'll be away, when you'll be back, and so on — in the Vacation Announcement field.**

This text replaces your shop announcement.

6. **In the Conversation Auto-Reply field, type the message that you want prospective customers to receive if they convo you while you're away.**

7. **Click the Save button.**

Etsy puts your shop in vacation mode.

If you fly to Rome on a moment's notice, fret not. You can use your Sell on Etsy app to switch to vacation mode. To do so, tap the More button on the app's main screen, choose settings, select Shop Settings, and toggle the Vacation Mode setting on.

TIP

Hanging It Up: Closing Your Etsy Shop

If — God forbid — you decide that running an Etsy shop just isn't for you, you can close your Etsy shop (assuming you've closed all unresolved cases and paid any overdue fees). When you close your shop, your shop and listings will no longer appear on Etsy. If someone tries to view your shop, she will be redirected to your profile. Anyone who attempts to view a listing from your shop will see a "Page Not Found" error.

To close your shop, follow these steps:

1. **Click the Shop Manager button that appears along the top of every Etsy Marketplace page.**

2. **Click Settings on the left side of the Shop Manager page and select Options.**

   The Shop Settings page opens.

3. **Click the Close Shop tab.**

   The Close Your Shop page opens (see Figure 18-10).

Source: Etsy.com

FIGURE 18-10: Things not working out? You can close your Etsy shop.

4. **Click the Select a Reason drop-down list and choose the reason that best explains why you are closing your shop.**

   Options include business reasons, Etsy just isn't right for you, personal reasons, and other. (After you make a selection, you'll see additional options to further explain your reason for leaving.)

5. **Click the Close Shop button.**

   Etsy prompts you to confirm the closure.

6. **Click the Close Shop button again.**

   Etsy closes your shop. (Note that it may take 30 minutes or so for your request to be processed.) Your Etsy account will now be for buying only.

If — hallelujah! — you later change your mind and want to reopen your shop, you can easily do so. Follow these steps:

1. **Open the You menu that appears along the top of any Etsy Marketplace page and choose Account Settings.**

   The Account page opens.

2. **Click the Your Closed Shop link on the left side of the page.**

   The Reopen Your Shop page opens.

3. **Click the Reopen Shop button.**

   Etsy reopens your shop. (Again, it may be a half-hour or so before your request is processed.)

Chapter **19**

Growing Your Etsy Business

Maybe you're content to run your Etsy shop as a hobby or a side hustle. Lots of Etsy sellers are. But maybe — just *maybe* — you'd like to grow your Etsy business to be your sole source of income. That's what this chapter is about: taking your Etsy shop to the next level.

You Got the Whole(sale) World in Your Hands: Selling Wholesale on Etsy

One sure-fire way to grow your Etsy business is to become a wholesaler — that is, to sell the products you make to other retailers. To facilitate this, Etsy has created Etsy Wholesale. Etsy Wholesale gives Etsy sellers (read: you) access to more than 20,000 registered retailers. Plus, with Etsy Wholesale, you can integrate your wholesale business with your Etsy shop for easy management.

REMEMBER

When you sell goods through Etsy Wholesale, Etsy charges a 3.5 percent transaction fee. This fee will be added to your Etsy bill.

Before you launch your wholesale business, Etsy suggests that you do a little soul-searching. That means making sure of the following:

>> You've developed a product line with an assortment of items that will appeal to a range of retailers.

>> You've developed a solid brand that is expressed both in your product line and in your packaging.

>> You can slash retail prices in half (or more) for wholesale clients *and* turn a healthy profit. (For more on pricing, see Chapter 10.)

>> You have the cash flow to cover the upfront costs associated with producing your product line.

>> You have a streamlined and scalable production process.

>> You have enough space in your studio to stow stock and supplies as well as crank out your creations.

TIP

If you decide to sell wholesale, you may need to hire help or partner with an outside manufacturer. We dig into both of these options later in this chapter.

Although literally anyone can become president of the United States, not everyone can become an Etsy wholesaler. Etsy vets all prospective wholesalers to ensure that they (you) meet a few key criteria:

>> **Your pricing structure passes muster.** Your wholesale prices must be at least 50 percent less than each item's suggested retail value, and each item's suggested retail value must match up with its price in your Etsy shop. (Again, for more on pricing, see Chapter 10.)

>> **Your Etsy record is clean as can be.** If you don't have a solid review score, you have a history of delinquency paying your Etsy fees, or you fail to demonstrate compliance with Etsy's policies, you won't make the cut.

>> **Your Etsy shop is the real deal.** Don't just throw together an Etsy shop and expect to be cleared to sell wholesale. Your shop should offer a solid assortment of products and reflect a unified brand. (For more on branding, see Chapter 16.)

Visit www.etsy.com/wholesale/designers and click the Apply button to begin the approval process.

Assuming that you make the cut, setting up your Etsy Wholesale storefront involves three key steps:

>> **Outlining your Etsy Wholesale policies:** As shown in Figure 19-1, these are similar (though not identical) to the policies you set for your Etsy retail shop.

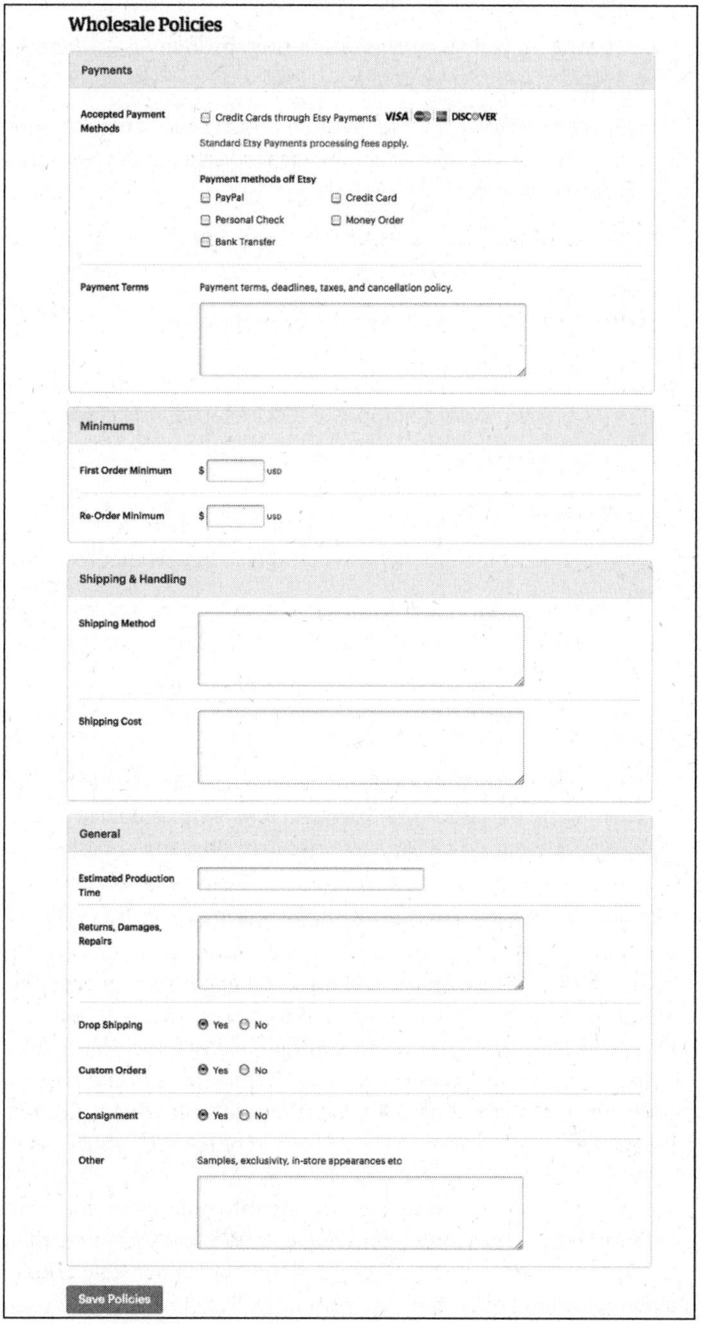

Wholesale Policies

Payments

Accepted Payment Methods	☐ Credit Cards through Etsy Payments **VISA** ⬤ ▦ DISC**O**VER
	Standard Etsy Payments processing fees apply.

Payment methods off Etsy

☐ PayPal   ☐ Credit Card

☐ Personal Check   ☐ Money Order

☐ Bank Transfer

Payment Terms   Payment terms, deadlines, taxes, and cancellation policy.

Minimums

First Order Minimum $ [   ] USD

Re-Order Minimum $ [   ] USD

Shipping & Handling

Shipping Method

Shipping Cost

General

Estimated Production Time

Returns, Damages, Repairs

Drop Shipping   ⦿ Yes   ○ No

Custom Orders   ⦿ Yes   ○ No

Consignment   ⦿ Yes   ○ No

Other   Samples, exclusivity, in-store appearances etc

Save Policies

FIGURE 19-1:
Outline your Etsy Wholesale policies.

Source: Etsy.com

>> **Setting up your Etsy Wholesale shop profile:** Again, this is a lot like the profile you set up for your Etsy retail shop (see Figure 19-2).

Speaking of the profile for your Etsy retail shop, it doesn't hurt to include a sentence or two on that shop's page indicating that you're an approved Etsy Wholesale seller.

>> **Generating a linesheet:** A *linesheet* is a little like a catalog. It contains information about each product you carry, including the following:

- A clear image of each product you sell

- The product's name

- A unique product number or stock keeping unit (SKU)

- Available sizes

- Available colors

- Materials used to make the product and how they're sourced

- Pricing information (both the wholesale price and the recommended retail price)

- Info about you, such as a bio, and how to contact you

- Info about your ordering process, including minimum quantities

Etsy automates the process of generating your linesheet with the Linesheet Organizer (see Figure 19-3). All you have to do is upload your photos, type in a description for each product, specify pricing, and publish.

You aren't limited to sharing your linesheet with registered Etsy Wholesale buyers. You can also share it with buyers who aren't on Etsy's wholesale platform by providing them with a guest pass. To generate a guest pass, click on the Shop Manager link. Then click the pencil icon next to the Wholesale entry under Sales Channels. The Linesheet Organizer opens. Click the Share with Buyers link in the upper-right corner. Then copy the link that appears and paste as needed. This link takes buyers to your linesheet as well as to your wholesale shop policies and profile. (Buyers will need to register with Etsy to start a purchase order.)

You probably feel like we haven't gone into enough detail to really get you up and running with Etsy Wholesale. We get it. We feel that way, too. The problem is, if we tried to cover everything there is to know about Etsy Wholesale, we'd wind up writing a whole other book. Fortunately, Etsy has lots of resources to help you set up your wholesale operation, including a four-week email course on the subject. To sign up for the course, visit www.etsy.com/emails/wholesale_courses.

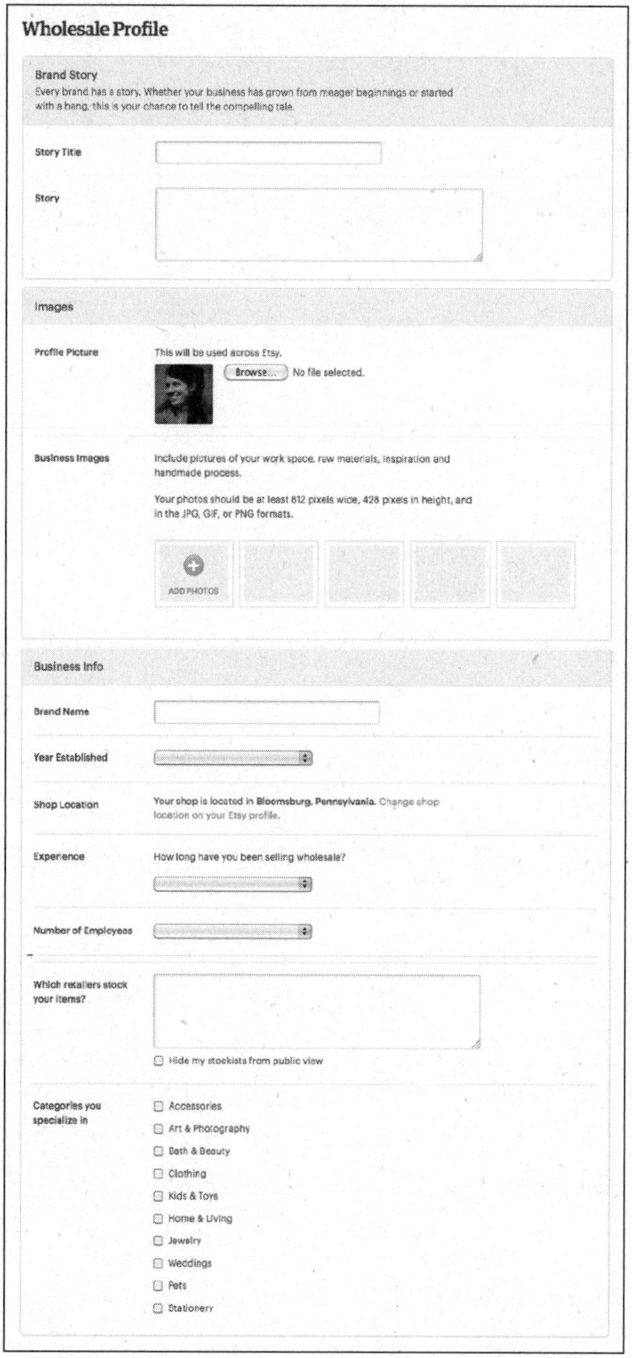

Wholesale Profile

Brand Story

Every brand has a story. Whether your business has grown from meager beginnings or started with a bang, this is your chance to tell the compelling tale.

Story Title

Story

Images

Profile Picture
This will be used across Etsy.

[Browse...] No file selected.

Business Images
Include pictures of your work space, raw materials, inspiration and handmade process.

Your photos should be at least 812 pixels wide, 428 pixels in height, and in the JPG, GIF, or PNG formats.

⊕
ADD PHOTOS

Business Info

Brand Name

Year Established

Shop Location
Your shop is located in **Bloomsburg, Pennsylvania**. Change shop location on your Etsy profile.

Experience
How long have you been selling wholesale?

Number of Employees

Which retailers stock your items?

☐ Hide my stockists from public view

Categories you specialize in
☐ Accessories
☐ Art & Photography
☐ Bath & Beauty
☐ Clothing
☐ Kids & Toys
☐ Home & Living
☐ Jewelry
☐ Weddings
☐ Pets
☐ Stationery

FIGURE 19-2:
Creating an Etsy Wholesale shop profile.

Source: Etsy.com

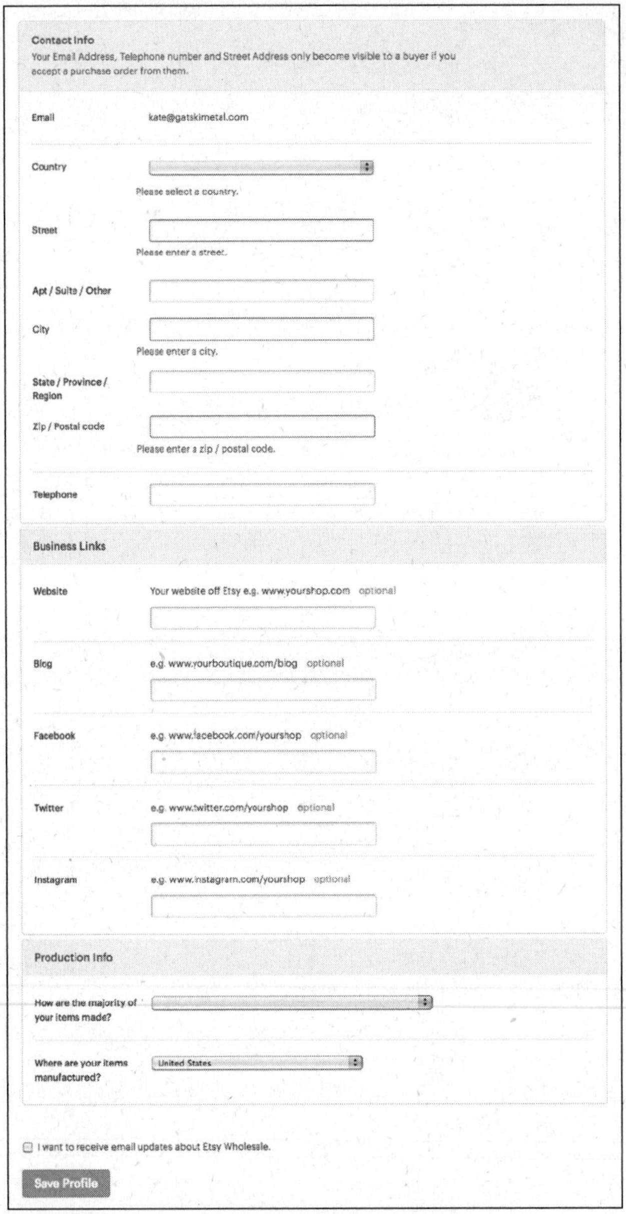

Contact Info
Your Email Address, Telephone number and Street Address only become visible to a buyer if you accept a purchase order from them.

Email	kate@gatskimetal.com
Country	Please select a country.
Street	Please enter a street.
Apt / Suite / Other	
City	Please enter a city.
State / Province / Region	
Zip / Postal code	Please enter a zip / postal code.
Telephone	

Business Links

Website	Your website off Etsy e.g. www.yourshop.com optional
Blog	e.g. www.yourboutique.com/blog optional
Facebook	e.g. www.facebook.com/yourshop optional
Twitter	e.g. www.twitter.com/yourshop optional
Instagram	e.g. www.instagram.com/yourshop optional

Production Info

How are the majority of your items made?	
Where are your items manufactured?	United States

☐ I want to receive email updates about Etsy Wholesale.

Save Profile

FIGURE 19-2:
(Continued)

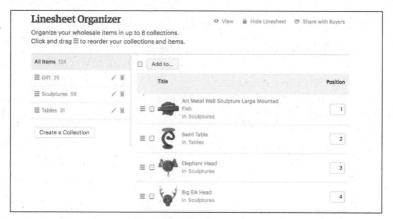

FIGURE 19-3:
The Linesheet
Organizer.

Howdy Partner: Finding Shop Helpers and Production Partners

If you're like most Etsy sellers, you're probably a one-man band. You design and make (or curate) every product in your shop, post every listing, process every order, and ship every package. This may work great — until Kendall Jenner posts an insta of herself wearing one of your baubles and drives 50 million of her closest followers to your shop.

When (not *if*) your Etsy shop takes off, you may find yourself experiencing mixed feelings. On the one hand, your newfound success may enable you to truly earn a living as an Etsy seller (thanks for everything, Kendall!). On the other hand, you're likely drowning in incoming orders — unable to maintain your inventory of current products (let alone develop new ones) or provide the level of customer service you'd like (thanks for nothing, Kendall!). One thing's for sure, though: You're going to need some help.

Hiring shop helpers

One way to get help is to hire a part-time, full-time, or seasonal employee. This person can act as your assistant, customer-service rep, marketer, photographer, shipper, or all of the above. Or you can bring someone on board to help you design and produce or curate goodies for your shop.

REMEMBER

Etsy's all for you getting help running your shop. They just ask that you disclose any helpers — Etsy calls them *shop members* — in your shop's About section. (For help updating the About section of your shop to include shop members, see Chapter 8.)

Using Etsy Manufacturing to find production partners

Maybe hiring a few employees isn't gonna cut it. Maybe that shout-out from Kendall Jenner means you need even more help. In that case, you'll want to look into Etsy Manufacturing.

Etsy Manufacturing is a little bit like Tinder — but instead of helping you meet people who bear no resemblance whatsoever to their profile pictures, it hooks you up with a production partner who can help you grow your business.

Before you use Etsy Manufacturing to connect with prospective production partners, Etsy recommends that you complete a couple of important steps:

>> **Take stock.** Make sure your business, concept, and initial designs are really and truly ready for production. That means answering a few tough questions:

- Do you already make (or are you thinking of making) a product that may lend itself to manufacture by an outside party?

- Do you know what processes and machinery are needed to meet your manufacturing needs?

- Do you have the technical skills to communicate your designs to a manufacturer?

- Have you decided what types of materials to use for your designs?

- What types of quantities are you after?

- Do you have the cash flow to pay a manufacturer upfront?

>> **Build a budget.** Figure out whether your profit margin can absorb manufacturing-related costs.

Next up: research. Here you use Etsy Manufacturing to pinpoint prospective producers and pair up with your perfect partner. Follow these steps:

1. **Click the Shop Manager link that appears along the top of every Etsy Marketplace page.**

2. **On the left side of the Shop Manager page, click Production Assistance. Then choose Find a Partner in the list of options that appears.**

   The Etsy Manufacturing page opens (see Figure 19-4).

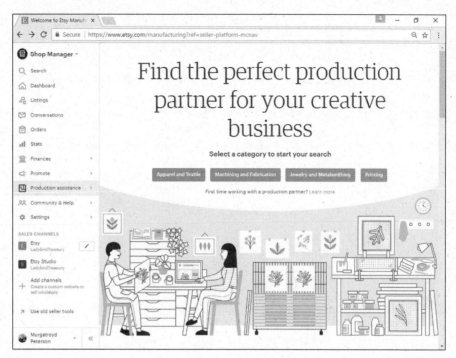

FIGURE 19-4:
Get started
with Etsy
Manufacturing.

Source: Etsy.com

3. **Click a category.**

   Options include Apparel and Textile, Machining and Fabrication, Jewelry and Metalsmithing, and Printing.

   A category-specific page opens to help you narrow your focus (see Figure 19-5). Each of these pages contains two main sections: Capabilities (which is further subdivided into Process, Materials, and Products sections) and Production Partner Location.

4. **In the Capabilities section, select at least one process, material, and product.**

5. **In the Production Partner Location section, specify where you want your production partner to be located (or choose Anywhere).**

6. **Click See Results.**

   As shown in Figure 19-6, Etsy displays a list of manufacturers that meet your criteria. (For the moment, these are limited to manufacturers in the United States and Canada.)

   Some manufacturers offer development services. That is, they work with Etsy sellers like you to standardize the specifications for your product.

TIP

Apparel and Textile

Capabilities *
Select at least one process, material or product from the options below.

Process

☐ Cut and Sew   ☐ Direct to Garment
                            (DTG)
☐ Dye Sublimation   ☐ Dyeing
☐ Embellishment   ☐ Embroidery
☐ Finishing   ☐ Knitting
☐ Millinery   ☐ Screenprinting
☐ Textile Printing   ☐ Weaving

Want to know more
about a process listed
here? Download our
new Manufacturing
Glossary.

Materials

☐ Knits   ☐ Leather
☐ Natural Fibers   ☐ Performance &
                            Specialty Fabrics
☐ Synthetic Fibers   ☐ Wovens
☐ Sustainable Materials
   ⓘ

Products

☐ Accessories   ☐ Apparel
☐ Bags   ☐ Hats
☐ Leather Goods   ☐ Packaging/Labels
☐ Scarves   ☐ Shoes
☐ Socks   ☐ Housewares
☐ Yardage

Production partner location
You can search for production partners in the United States and Canada.

Show me production   ◉ ⦿ Indianapolis, IN, United States
partners near
                        ○ Anywhere

[See results]

Source: Etsy.com

FIGURE 19-5:
Use the options
on this page to
narrow your
focus.

7. **Click a manufacturer in the list of results to find out more about it.**

8. **If you like what you see, click the Contact Manufacturer button on the business's page.**

   A contact form opens (see Figure 19-7).

9. **Fill in the requested info (including a description, photos or sketches, what you need help with, what you already have, how many you need, how much you want to spend, when you need the finished product, and any notes you want to add) and click Submit.**

   Etsy creates a "project" from the information you submitted and forwards it to the manufacturer. You can access this project anytime by opening Shop Manager, clicking the Production Assistance link, and choosing Manage Projects.

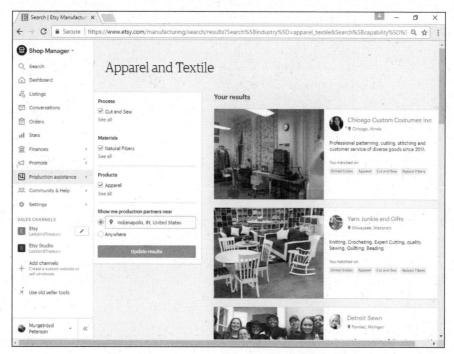

Apparel and Textile

Source: Etsy.com

FIGURE 19-6:
Etsy displays a list
of businesses
that match your
criteria.

TIP

Don't just "swipe right" on the first manufacturer you find. Contact several to see which ones can meet your needs, offer the best terms on your project, and have received positive feedback from other Etsy sellers. Also, before you and a prospective partner say "I do," have them do a sample run of your product. And, to be 100 percent sure they're the right fit, it doesn't hurt to conduct an on-site visit.

As with shop members, Etsy asks that you disclose any production partners you use. This information will appear on your shop's About page as well as in listings for any items the production partner helped to create. First, however, you must build a production partner profile for each of your production partners. Here's how:

1. **Click the Shop Manager link that appears along the top of every Etsy Marketplace page.**

2. **On the left side of the Shop Manager page, click Settings. Then choose Production Partners.**

    The Production Partners page appears.

FIGURE 19-7:
Fill out the
contact form.

3. **Click the Add a New Production Partner button.**

   An Add a New Production Partner form appears (see Figure 19-8).

4. **Enter your production partner's name and location and say a little bit about it.**

5. **Indicate why you are working with this production partner, what your role in the design process is, and what your partner's role in the production process is. Then click Save Partner.**

   Etsy saves the production profile.

FIGURE 19-8:
Create a
production
partner profile.

Source: Etsy.com

To add this production profile to an existing item listing, follow these steps:

1. **Click the Shop Manager link that appears along the top of every Etsy Marketplace page.**

2. **On the left side of the Shop Manager page, click Listings.**

   The Listings page appears.

3. **Click the check box for each listing to which you want to apply the production partner profile.**

4. **Click the More Options button and choose Production Partners (see Figure 19-9).**

   The Update Production Partners dialog box opens (see Figure 19-10).

5. **Click the check box next to the production partner you want to add and click Update.**

   Etsy adds the production partner profile to the selected listing(s) (see Figure 19-11).

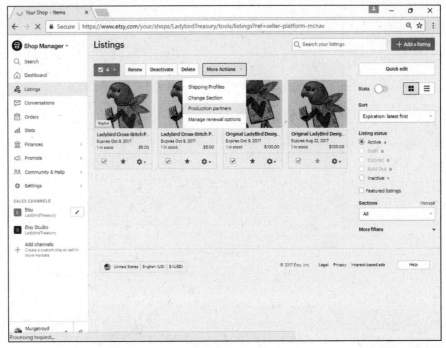

FIGURE 19-9:
Click the More
Actions button
and choose
Production
Partners.

Source: Etsy.com

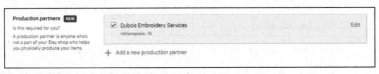

FIGURE 19-10:
The Update
Production
Partners
dialog box.

Source: Etsy.com

FIGURE 19-11:
Etsy adds the
production
partner profile
to the selected
listing(s).

Source: Etsy.com

Adding a production partner to a new listing is even easier. As you create the listing, open the Who Made It drop-down list and choose Another Company. You will then be prompted to select the production partner profile (or create a new profile) to add it to your listing.

REMEMBER

If you work with multiple production partners, you should create a profile for each one.

You aren't limited to working with manufacturers that Etsy suggests. You can work with any manufacturer you like — *if* they meet certain ethical criteria. First, the manufacturer must be in compliance with all applicable laws, including safety, labor, and employment laws. In addition, manufacturers should

>> Not employ child labor or youth labor

>> Not employ involuntary labor

>> Not engage in discriminatory practices

>> Provide humane working conditions

>> Use sustainable materials to reduce environmental impact

Pattern-Cake, Pattern-Cake: Building a Custom Shop with Pattern

As your Etsy shop thrives, you may find yourself wanting to expand beyond the Etsy Marketplace. Enter Pattern. Pattern is a new service by Etsy that enables you to set up your own custom e-commerce website to reflect your shop's brand — right down to its URL. This isn't just *any* custom e-commerce website, though — it's one that integrates with your Etsy shop. In fact, you stock the website with listings from your Etsy shop (although you can create Pattern-only or Etsy-only listings), and you manage the site using Etsy's Shop Manager. Etsy puts it this way: "Pattern uses all of your existing Etsy inventory, payments and order management tools" — we're talking Etsy Payments, Etsy Shipping Labels, and so on — "so all of the work you've put into your Etsy shop will be applied directly to your new standalone website."

At the time of this writing, Etsy allows shop owners to test out Pattern for 30 days free o' charge. After that, it's $15 a month. To get started using Pattern, follow these steps:

1. **Click the Shop Manager link that appears along the top of every Etsy Marketplace page.**

2. **On the left side of the Shop Manager page, under Sales Channels, click Add Channels.**

   The Add Channels page appears.

3. **Under Pattern, click the Get Started link.**

   The Pattern website opens and prompts you to select from several shop-layout themes.

4. **Select a theme and click the Start with This Theme button.**

   The Pattern dashboard opens (see Figure 19-12). Here you'll find links to tools to customize your theme (for example, change colors, fonts, and so on), buy a domain name (or connect to one you already own), write your first blog post for the site (did we mention you can include a blog on your site?), and explore marketing tools.

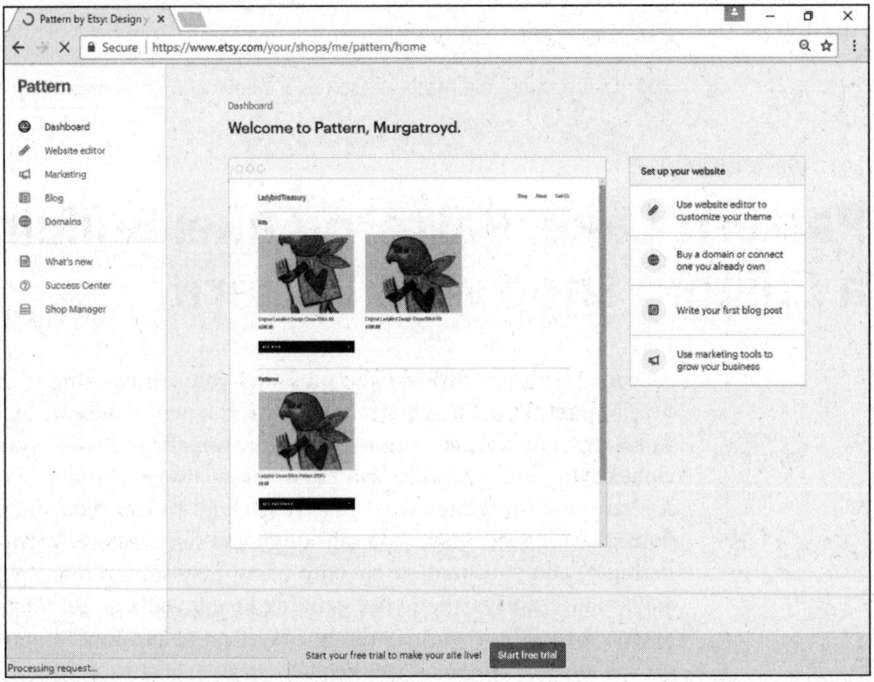

FIGURE 19-12: The Pattern dashboard.

Source: Etsy.com

5. **Click the Start Free Trial button**

   Pattern launches your site.

REMEMBER

To use Pattern, you must enable Etsy Payments.

Going Mobile: Taking Your Etsy Show on the Road

These days, you're no longer limited to conducting Etsy business online. Now, with the Sell on Etsy mobile app, you can do it in person, too — assuming that you use an Apple iOS or Android device and you live in the United States. (Etsy hopes to expand the service to more locations soon.) For example, you may use the app to handle transactions at a local art fair or farmers' market.

You can use the Sell on Etsy app to peddle items already listed in your Etsy shop in person. Etsy updates your shop inventory in real time to reflect the sale. Or you can use the app's Quick Sale feature to sell items you haven't listed. Just enter an item name and price. (After you've entered details for a Quick Sale, you can access them by selecting Sell from History. That way, you don't have to enter the same title and price over and over again until your fingers fall off.) Either way, your shop's total sales will reflect these transactions.

What's super great about the Sell on Etsy app is that you can use it in combination with an Etsy credit card reader — which you can order free from Etsy at www.etsy.com/reader — to process Visa, MasterCard, American Express, and Discover transactions. (Etsy charges just 2.75 percent per swipe and waives all other transaction fees.) Funds from in-person transactions will appear in your Etsy account alongside monies from online sales.

REMEMBER

You don't have to use the Etsy card reader. You can also accept in-person payments in cash.

Before you can use the Sell on Etsy app (with or without the card reader), you need to do a few things. First, make sure your Etsy shop is set up to accept Etsy Payments. (For help, see Chapter 8.) Second, make sure that you have the latest version of the Sell on Etsy app installed on your mobile device. Third, if this is your first time using the Sell on Etsy app, you need to accept the Terms of Use and enable location services. Fourth, set the app to apply the appropriate sales tax to your in-person sales. Here's how:

1. **Launch the Sell on Etsy app.**

2. **Tap the More button in the lower-right corner of the app's main screen.**

3. **Tap the In Person Sales option.**

4. **Tap the Sales Tax option.**

5. **Tap the Add Sales Tax Rate button.**

6. **Tap the Name option and type a descriptive name for the tax rate (such as the state for which it applies).**

7. **Type the Tax Rate option and enter the desired rate.**

8. **Click Done.**

   Etsy will apply this rate to all in-person transactions with the Sell on Etsy app.

With that done, you're ready to make in-person sales. Here's how it's done:

1. **Launch the Sell on Etsy app.**

2. **Tap the Sell Now link in the upper-right corner of the app's main screen.**

   The Sell in Person screen opens (see Figure 19-13).

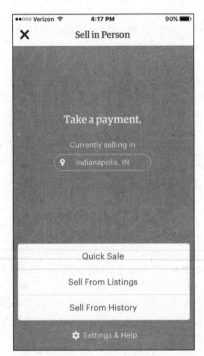

Source: Etsy.com

FIGURE 19-13:
Make an
in-person sale.

3. **Do one of the following:**

   • **Tap Quick Sale.** Then type a name for the item, type a price, and tap Continue (see Figure 19-14).

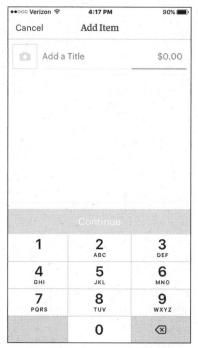

FIGURE 19-14:
Process a
Quick Sale.

Source: Etsy.com

- **Tap Sell from Listings.** The app displays your shop's active listings (see Figure 19-15). Tap the one for the item you want to sell.

- **Tap Sell from History.** If you're selling an item for which you've already entered the details in the Quick Sale screen, you can access it here.

4. **To add more items to the sale, tap Add Another Item. Then repeat Step 3.**

5. **To apply a discount, tap Add Discount. Specify whether the discount should be a cash amount or a percentage, enter the discount value, and tap Apply Discount.**

6. **Tap the Charge button at the bottom of the screen (see Figure 19-16).**

7. **Tap Cash or Credit.**

8. **Indicate the amount of cash received or swipe the credit card using the card reader.**

   If the buyer is paying by credit card, the app will prompt her for a signature.

9. **If the buyer wants a receipt, ask her to type in her email address in the screen that appears.**

   That's it! You're done.

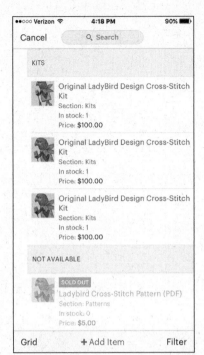

FIGURE 19-15:
Sell an existing
listing via
Quick Sale.

FIGURE 19-16:
Process the
transaction.

LA VIDA LOCAL: CONNECTING WITH BUYERS VIA ETSY LOCAL

If you know you'll be setting up shop at an art fair, farmers' market, or other local event, you can use Etsy Local to spread the word. To do so, open the Etsy Local page (www.etsy.com/local), enter the name of the town where the event will take place, and choose a time frame from the drop-down list. (Choices include This Week, This Month, and This Year.) It may be that someone has already added the event to Etsy Local. In that case, click the event and, in the event page that opens, click the I'm Participating button and follow the prompts.

If the event doesn't appear on the Etsy Local page, you can add it. To do so, click the Create an Event button. Next, in the Create an Event page, shown here, enter a name, date, and time for the event and specify its location. Then enter a description. (If the event has its own web page, add that, too.) Finally, click Submit. Etsy will add the event to the list of events on the Etsy Local page and to the Local section on your shop's main page.

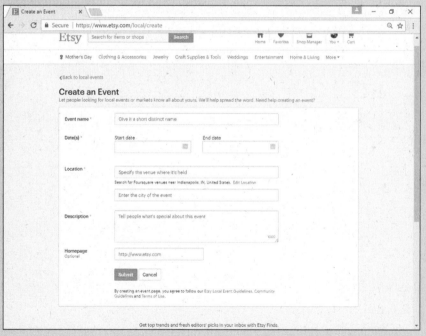

Source: Etsy.com

5

Commune System: Exploring the Etsy Community

Chapter **20**

Community Building: Joining the Etsy Community

Anyone who has spent more than 30 seconds on Etsy knows that it's a bang-up place to buy and sell gorgeous handmade, vintage, and otherwise interesting items. But Etsy is more than just an amazing online marketplace; it's also a vibrant community of fascinating, creative people. On Etsy, connections are created, friendships are formed, love matches are made, and lives are enriched. In this chapter, you discover how you can participate in this lively Etsy community.

Talk among Yourselves: Using Etsy Forums

The *Merriam-Webster Dictionary* defines *forum* as "a public meeting place for open discussion," derived from the marketplaces and public places found in ancient Roman cities across that great empire. Similarly, Etsy's forums serve as meeting places for Etsy members. In essence, Etsy forums are public message boards where members can discuss all manner of topics.

Etsy supports five main forums:

>> **Questions:** You got questions? The Etsy community has answers. This forum offers an easy way to ask general questions about how to use Etsy, questions about site features, or questions related to site policy. Odds are, someone in the Etsy community can — and will — answer your question!

>> **Discussions:** Maybe you're in the hunt for some tips and tricks for buying or selling on Etsy. Or maybe, in your infinite wisdom, you have some tips or tricks to share. Either way, this forum is for you. This forum also offers you the ability to bring up any other Etsy-related topic for discussion among the Etsy community.

>> **Bugs:** If you come across some part of the site that's not working as intended, check the Bugs forum to see whether anyone else has experienced the same glitch. If not, use the forum to report it.

>> **Chitchat:** Maybe you're not in the mood to talk about anything Etsy related. Maybe you're in the mood for a bit of a diversion instead. In that case, check out the Chitchat forum. Here, anything goes (provided it meets Etsy's etiquette and ethical standards).

>> **Promos:** This forum provides Etsy users with an easy way to promote their items.

In addition to these forums, there's often an additional forum to support a current Etsy initiative. There's also an Announcements forum, which Etsy staff uses to post site-related announcements, such as upcoming site changes.

REMEMBER

None of Etsy's forums is meant to serve as a complaint desk. If you need to air a grievance, you can bring it straight to Etsy via its contact page, located at www.etsy.com/help/contact.

Accessing Etsy forums

To participate on an Etsy forum, follow these steps:

1. Scroll down to the footer on any Etsy Marketplace page and click Forums in the Join the Community category of links.

The Forums page opens (see Figure 20-1).

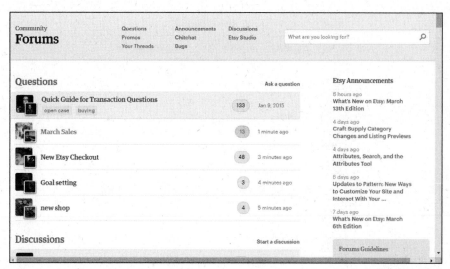

Source: Etsy.com

FIGURE 20-1:
The Etsy forums.

2. **Click the title of the forum that you want to visit.**

   The forum page opens.

REMEMBER

Links to Etsy's five main forums — Questions, Discussions, Bugs, Chitchat, and Promos — are prominently listed on the forums page. You can also access these five forums, as well as the Announcements forum and a page showing all your threads (more on this in a minute), from the links along the top of the page. (Recent Etsy announcements also appear along the right side of the main Forums page.)

Viewing and responding to posts in a thread

The posts in any Etsy forum are divided into threads (Figure 20-2 shows threads in the Discussion forum). You can view and respond to any thread you want. Here's how:

1. **Click a thread that interests you.**

   A page opens, showing the post that started the thread, along with any responses to that post (see Figure 20-3).

2. **To respond to the original post, click the Add Your Response link at the bottom of the post.**

   An Add Your Response box appears at the bottom of the page (see Figure 20-4).

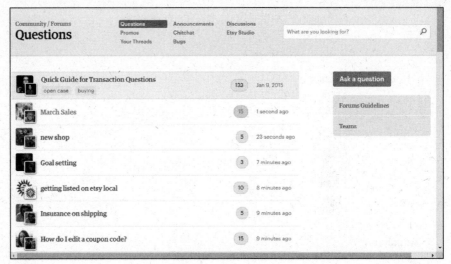

FIGURE 20-2:
An Etsy forum.

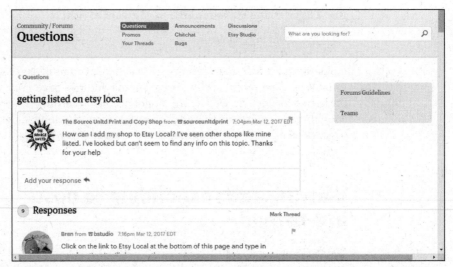

FIGURE 20-3:
An Etsy thread.

REMEMBER

Alternatively, to reply to one of the responses rather than to the main post, click the Reply to *User Name* link (where *User Name* is the user name of the person who wrote the reply to the original post). Reply to *User Name* box appears under the post you're responding to.

3. **Type your reply and then click Add Your Reply.**

   Your post appears at the end of the list of replies.

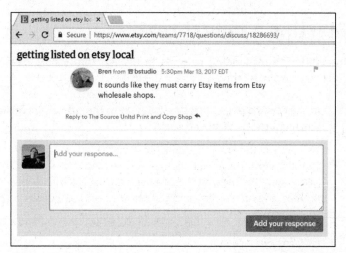

FIGURE 20-4:
Reply to a post.

Source: Etsy.com

To view threads in which you've posted a reply, click the Your Threads link at the top of any forum screen. Then, in the Your Threads page, click the Threads You've Posted In tab. Etsy displays a list of threads you've posted in (see Figure 20-5). To revisit the thread, simply click it in the list.

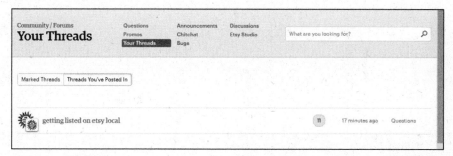

FIGURE 20-5:
View your forum threads.

Source: Etsy.com

If you find a thread that's particularly interesting but that you haven't engaged in personally, you can mark it. That way, you can easily keep track of new posts in that thread. To mark a thread, open the thread and click the Mark Thread link (refer to Figure 20-3). To view threads you've marked, again click the Your Threads link at the top of any forum screen, click the Marked Threads tab, and click the thread you want to view.

REMEMBER

Before you reply to a thread in an Etsy forum or start a new thread of your own (see the next section), be sure your post doesn't violate Etsy etiquette (discussed later in this chapter).

Starting a new thread

In addition to responding to posts in threads that others have started, you can start your own new thread. Here's the drill:

REMEMBER

1. **In the Forums page, click the link next to the title of the forum in which you want to start a new thread.**

   The name of this link varies depending on the forum. The link for the Questions forum is Ask a Question. For the Discussions forum, it's Start a Discussion. The Bugs forum has a Report a Bug link. Finally, the Chitchat, Promos, and rotating Etsy initiative forums each has a Create a Thread link.

   The page opens that contains a Title field, a Post text box, and a Tags field (see Figure 20-6).

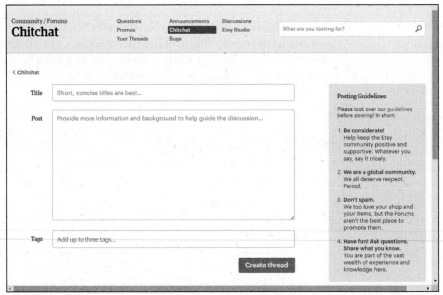

FIGURE 20-6: Create a new thread in a forum.

Source: Etsy.com

2. **Type a descriptive, relevant title for your thread in the Title field.**

   Short, concise titles are best.

3. **Type your post in the Post field.**

4. **Enter as many as three tags to describe your thread.**

   For example, if you have a question about Shop Manager, you might add a "Shop Manager" tag.

5. Click the button at the bottom of the page.

As with the link in Step 1, the name of this button depends on the forum you're posting in.

Etsy creates a new thread, with your post at the top (see Figure 20-7). If you click the forum's link at the top of the page, you'll see your thread listed in the forum.

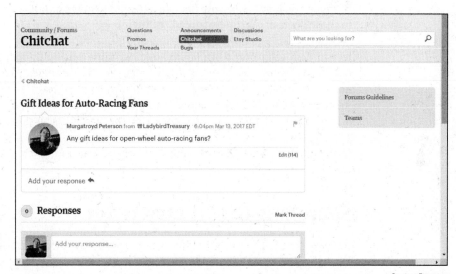

FIGURE 20-7:
Create a new thread.

REMEMBER

When you start a new thread, be sure to start it in the correct forum. For example, don't start a thread asking for advice about your Etsy shop in, say, the Bugs forum. That discussion belongs in the Discussions forum. Be aware that if you do start a thread in the wrong forum, Etsy may move it to the appropriate forum without notice.

TIP

Before you start a new thread, try searching for existing threads that cover your topic of interest. To do so, open the main Forums page, type a relevant keyword or phrase in the What Are You Looking For? field at the top of the page, and click the Search button. Etsy searches existing forum threads for the keyword or phrase that you entered and displays a list of matches.

Go Team! Exploring Etsy Teams

Etsy's forums are splendid — if your area of interest is questions, discussions, bugs, chitchat, promo, or announcements. But what if you're itching to explore some other topic — say, product photography, quilting, Bauhaus style, or even a charitable cause? Or maybe you just want to connect with other Etsy members in your geographic area. In that case, Etsy's teams are for you.

Etsy teams act a lot like Etsy forums. People start discussion threads, and others add their two cents. The difference? With teams, you must join to participate. Although non-team members may be able to view posts in a team — when team members start new threads, they specify whether those threads are public (visible to anyone on Etsy) or private (visible to team members only) — they can't respond to those posts or start new threads of their own.

In addition, each Etsy team has its own captain (usually the person who started the team), who may appoint other members as "leaders." The team captain and team leaders are responsible for administering the team — that is, approving membership applications (some teams are open to any and all Etsy members; others require that you apply), moderating the team's discussion forum, and so on.

In the following sections, we show you how to search for a team, join a team, and start your own team.

Searching for an Etsy team

Literally thousands of Etsy teams exist, so you can surely find one for you. For example, you can join a team based on the type of items you sell, your particular interests, or your geographic location. To find a team, log in to your Etsy account and follow these steps:

1. **Scroll down to the footer on any Etsy Marketplace page and click Teams in the Join the Community category of links.**

    The Teams page opens (see Figure 20-8).

2. **Type a keyword in the Search in Teams box and click the Search button.**

    Etsy searches teams for the keyword that you entered and displays a list of matches (see Figure 20-9). You can sort your matches by Relevancy, Most Recent, and Least Recent by selecting the desired option from the Sort By drop-down list next to the Search in Teams box.

3. **Click a team in the list of matches to learn more about it.**

    The team's page opens (see Figure 20-10). This page includes information about the team and who's eligible to join; a Discussions area, which lists recent threads (click the Discussions link to view more); and a sampling of team members.

FIGURE 20-8:
The Etsy
Teams page.

Source: Etsy.com

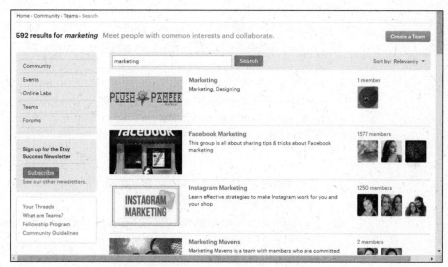

FIGURE 20-9:
View your
search results.

Source: Etsy.com

Joining an Etsy team

As mentioned, some teams are open to any and all Etsy members. Others are moderated, meaning that they limit their membership based on certain criteria.

To join a team that's open to all, simply click the Join This Team button that appears in the top-left corner of the team's page (refer to Figure 20-8). Then, when prompted, click Join This Team again. A welcome message appears at the top of the team page, and your profile picture appears in the list of team members. The team that you joined also appears near the top of your main Teams page.

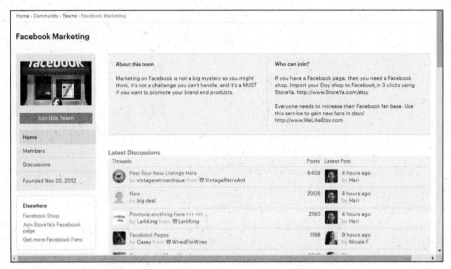

Source: Etsy.com

FIGURE 20-10:
An Etsy team
page.

Joining a team that restricts membership, called a *moderated team,* is a bit more involved. Instead of simply clicking a button, you must apply for membership, which sometimes means jumping through a few hoops. To join a moderated team, follow these steps:

1. **Click the Apply to Team button. (It appears in the same spot as the Join Team button shown in Figure 20-8.)**

2. **Read the information in the dialog box and answer any questions in the field at the bottom.**

3. **Click the Apply to Team button to apply.**

Assuming that you meet the membership criteria, as determined by the team captain and laid out in the team charter, you'll likely be accepted — although the team leadership may deny membership at its discretion. Either way, after the team makes a decision, it'll notify you via email.

When you become a member of a team, you can view and respond to posts in existing threads and create new threads, as described earlier in this chapter in the section "Talk among Yourselves: Using Etsy Forums." You can also view discussion activity on the Sell on Etsy app with a simple tap of the Teams link.

You can also opt to subscribe to team digest emails, which contain a summary of the team's most recent discussion activity. That way, you can keep track of the team's goings-on without having to log in to Etsy first. To subscribe to a team's digest email, simply click the Subscribe to Email Digest link on the left side of the team's main page after you become a member. Then, when prompted, click the Subscribe button. (You'll have to do this for each team individually.) To unsubscribe, simply click the Unsubscribe from Digest link, which replaces the Subscribe link you clicked earlier.

Starting your own Etsy team

If you don't find a team that meets your needs, you can start one of your own. For example, you may want to start a team for other Etsy members who share your passion for your medium, who live in your geographic area, who are devoted to a particular style of design, who share similar goals with their Etsy shops, or what have you. Note that when you create a team, you automatically become its captain, so administrative duties fall to you (unless you delegate them to other members).

To create a team, click the Create a Team button in the top-right corner of the main Teams page (refer to Figure 20-8). Etsy prompts you to enter the team details (see Figure 20-11):

>> The name and team type

>> A short description and (optionally) a long description

>> Team access options and (optionally) who can join

>> Application questions (if needed)

>> The team's logo

>> Tags to describe your team (Check out the sidebar "Tag, you're it! Tagging your Etsy team" for details on tags.)

>> Related links (For example, you might include a link to your own personal website or to some other relevant page online.)

After you fill in the requested information, click Create Team.

TAG, YOU'RE IT! TAGGING YOUR ETSY TEAM

When you create your team, you're prompted to enter tags that describe it — for example, where your team is based, the focus of your team, and so on. These tags act a lot like the tags that you add to your item listings. That is, when someone searching for a team enters keywords that match your tags, your team appears among the matches.

Note that the tags you enter to describe your Etsy team are different from what Etsy calls *team tags*. A team tag is a tag that team members use to tag their item listings to identify themselves and their listing as being affiliated with a particular Etsy team. These tags must be unique terms — say, your team's name — and must contain the word *team* in them. When you create a team, you can establish a team tag for it, noting it in the team's description.

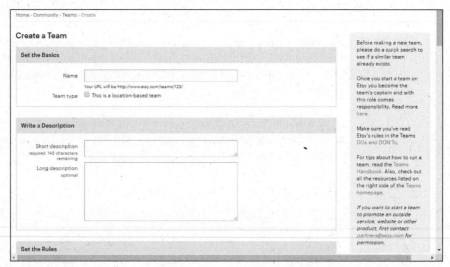

FIGURE 20-11:
Create a
new team.

Source: Etsy.com

Event Horizon: Staying Apprised of Etsy Events

You aren't limited to connecting with Etsy users online. You can also attend real-world events organized by Etsy, such as craft- and business-related gatherings both at its Brooklyn-based offices and at various locations worldwide. To stay apprised of Etsy events, visit www.eventbrite.com/o/etsycom-312100517. This opens a special page that lists upcoming events all over the world (see Figure 20-12). To see information about an event, simply click it in the list.

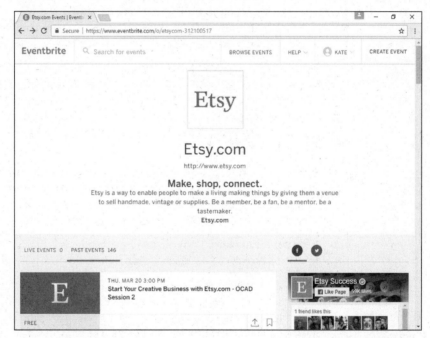

FIGURE 20-12:
View a list of Etsy events.

Source: Etsy.com

Miss Manners: Respecting Community Etiquette

When it comes to interacting with the Etsy community — for example, in the forums or within a team — some important ground rules apply. Etsy's Community

Policy, found in its House Rules, spells out these rules in detail (see www.etsy.com/legal/community). If you violate any of these rules, Etsy may take action, ranging from removing your post or closing your thread to revoking certain privileges.

REMEMBER

Chief among these rules is this: For Pete's sake, *be nice.* It should go without saying that you need to treat all Etsy members with respect, but we're saying it anyway, just so there's no confusion. Also, never knowingly harass, insult, abuse, or otherwise dis another site user. Finally, don't "call out" an Etsy member, shop, or item — that is, discuss him, her, or it in a negative manner. (Duh.)

Beyond that, keep a few other points in mind as you mingle in the Etsy community (for a complete list, check out the aforementioned Community Policy):

» **Don't post angry.** Yes, discussions in Etsy's community spaces sometimes get testy. After all, the Etsy community consists of millions of passionate, creative types. But if you find yourself getting your dander up, step away from the keyboard. In the history of the world, no good ever came from firing off a message in anger! Besides, if you do, you'll likely violate the aforementioned "Be nice" rule.

» **Stay on topic.** Sure, tangents happen. But if the tangent intensifies to such a degree that it threatens to smother the main discussion, others interested in the "real" topic can't find the info they need. If you find yourself part of a discussion that's gone off the rails, consider starting a new thread to handle that tangential issue.

» **Protect your privacy.** Don't share private information of any type, such as your (or someone else's) email address, phone number, address, or what have you, on Etsy's public spaces. Also, put the kibosh on public discussions about specific transactions or feedback that you've received.

» **Posts are permanent.** They say nothing lasts forever . . . but your Etsy posts do. There's no way to take down an Etsy community post.

» **Don't solicit.** Even if you're raising money for the best, most important charity on the planet, Etsy members are prohibited from trolling for donations or engaging in other types of fundraising on the Etsy teams and forums. Similarly, spamming Etsy teams and forums — that is, posting unsolicited advertisements — is prohibited.

REMEMBER

To maintain order, Etsy employs moderators. They're a little bit like hall monitors. They keep an eye on the Etsy community to make sure no one breaks the rules — and take action if someone does. Be aware that if a moderator takes action against you, it's final. What they say goes.

Chapter **21**

OMG, Did You Hear? Keeping Up with Etsy News

As big and active as Etsy is, staying abreast of all its goings-on can be as challenging as solving a Rubik's Cube during a blackout. Fortunately, Etsy maintains several resources to help members stay on top of Etsy-related info, including a blog, multiple email newsletters, and various social media pages. You can also stay on Etsy's cutting edge by joining Prototypes, which are special projects run by Etsy admin that explore using Etsy in different ways. In this chapter, you discover all the ways you can keep up with Etsy news.

All the News That's Fit to Print: Exploring the Etsy Blog

Maybe you're looking for tips to improve your Etsy shop. Or perhaps you want to explore a new craft medium. Or perchance you want a glimpse into the lives of other Etsy sellers. Or suppose you just need some inspiration already. Whatever the case may be, the Etsy Blog is for you. To access the Etsy Blog, click the Read the Blog link in the Fresh from the Blog section of Etsy's home page. Or scroll down to the footer area on any Etsy Marketplace page and click Blog in the Discover and Shop category of links. Figure 21-1 shows the main page of the Etsy Blog.

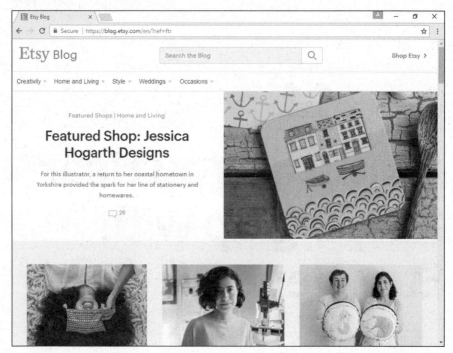

FIGURE 21-1:
The Etsy Blog.

Of course, you could just scroll through this main page of the Etsy Blog to see what's new. Or you can try a more targeted approach by using the drop-down menus in the top-left corner of the main Etsy Blog page. These drop-down menus offer easy access to blog posts in the following categories:

» **Creativity:** If you're ready to try your hand at a new skill, click the Creativity drop-down menu and choose DIY Inspiration. You'll find blog posts with step-by-step instructions for all kinds of killer projects. You can also view featured shops to get your creative juices flowing.

» **Home and Living:** Click this drop-down menu to find blog posts with decorating ideas, shopping guides, and featured shops.

» **Style:** Like the Home and Living drop-down menu, the Style drop-down menu offers easy access to shopping guides and featured shops. The only difference is that these posts focus on clothing and accessories rather than home goods.

>> **Weddings:** People say getting married is more stressful than being fired and only slightly less stressful than suffering a personal injury or illness. We say those people haven't discovered the Weddings section of the Etsy Blog. Here, you can find posts on planning and etiquette, inspiring stories of real weddings that did not end in disaster, and DIY projects to help make your wedding uniquely (and cheaply) your own. Shopping guides and featured shops only add to the offerings.

>> **Occasions:** Party people rejoice! Whether you're the host of an upcoming shindig or merely an attendee, the Occasions area of the Etsy Blog has you covered. You'll find posts that relate to gift-giving as well as decorating and entertaining, and of course, inspirational featured shops.

Etsy also hosts blogs for members in other countries — namely, Australia Edition, Blog Français, Deutscher Blog, and UK Edition. To access these, click the appropriate link at the very bottom of any Etsy Blog page.

To read any post on the Etsy Blog, regardless of category, simply click the post's title. Etsy opens the post in its own page, as shown in Figure 21-2.

FIGURE 21-2: Read a post on the Etsy Blog.

Source: Etsy.com

BABY, YOU'RE A STAR: CHECKING OUT FEATURED SHOPS

Every few days, Etsy staffers introduce a new featured shop on the Etsy blog — one that displays ingenuity, sells well-made items, and populates each listing with interesting descriptions and top-notch photos. To access these featured shops, click any entries on the Etsy blog page whose headlines contain the words "Featured Shop." If you're just starting out on Etsy, reading up on featured shops is a great way to ferret out tips and tricks for becoming a successful seller — not to mention be totally inspired!

To search for an article in any of Etsy's blogs, follow these easy steps:

1. **Type your keyword in the Search the Blog box at the top of any Etsy Blog page and press Return or Enter on your keyboard.**

   Etsy displays a list of blog posts containing the keyword you typed.

2. **Click a post title to view the post.**

TIP

In addition to reading the posts on the Etsy Blog, make it a point to peruse the comments left by other Etsy members. These comments are often as enlightening as the post itself. If you have something to add, don't hesitate to weigh in; just type your two cents in the text box at the top of the comments list and click the Add Your Comment button.

Mail Bonding: Signing Up for Etsy Email Newsletters

If you've ever felt overwhelmed by the sheer number of fantastic items on Etsy, or wished you could employ a personal shopper to sift through them for you, or if you just feel adrift on the Etsy sea, you'll want to sign up for Etsy email newsletters. When you do, you'll receive handy messages featuring all manner of kicky items, right in your email inbox. Click any entry in an Etsy email to launch Etsy in your web browser and view the associated item listing.

In the following sections, we describe the kinds of email newsletters that are available and explain how to sign up to receive them.

Sifting through different types of email newsletters

You can choose to subscribe to any or all of the following Etsy email newsletters:

- » **Etsy Finds:** This daily email is chock-full of clever goodies from a variety of Etsy sellers.

- » **Etsy Gifts:** This email is stuffed with gift ideas for everyone on your list.

- » **Etsy Fashion:** If fashion's your bag, you'll enjoy tracking fashion trends on Etsy with this biweekly email newsletter.

- » **Etsy Weddings:** Sure, all weddings are special. But let's face it: Weddings featuring handmade or vintage items are even more so. If you're in the midst of planning your own nuptials or you craft items that are made just for brides, grooms, or other members of the bridal party, this weekly email newsletter is for you.

- » **Etsy Dudes:** Yes, it's true, Etsy members are overwhelmingly female. But when you're talking about a community as large as Etsy, you'll still find thousands of guys around. If you have a Y chromosome (or buy presents for someone who does), you'll love this weekly email newsletter geared toward dudes.

- » **Etsy Studio Interest:** This newsletter highlights new and unexpected materials, from a global community of sellers.

- » **Etsy Success:** For tips from top sellers, subscribe to the Etsy Success email. There's also an Etsy Success Email Courses newsletter, which offers focused courses to help get your shop in shape, and an Etsy Wholesale Email Course, which delivers eight targeted lessons on the subject of wholesale straight to your inbox.

TIP

In addition to the email newsletters listed here, Etsy sends newsletters in French and German as well as ones for crafting communities in the United Kingdom, Australia, and New Zealand.

Subscribing to email newsletters

To sign up for Etsy email newsletters, follow these steps:

1. **Open the You menu on any Etsy Marketplace page and choose Account Settings. Then click the Email tab in the page that appears.**

   Etsy presents you with a list of newsletters to which you can subscribe (see Figure 21-3). (Notice that in addition to enabling you to choose what newsletters you want to subscribe to, you can perform other email-related actions, such as indicating which types of email notifications you want to receive from Etsy.)

FIGURE 21-3:
Sign up for Etsy email newsletters here.

2. **Click the check box next to each newsletter to which you want to subscribe.**

3. **Click the Save Settings button.**

   Etsy signs you up to receive the newsletters you selected.

TIP

If you decide that you no longer want to receive a newsletter, simply click the blue Unsubscribe link that appears along the bottom of every Etsy newsletter. Alternatively, manage your subscriptions by returning to the page shown in Figure 21-3, deselecting the check boxes next to the newsletters to which you want to unsubscribe, and clicking the Save Settings button.

Social Skills: Staying in Touch Using Social Media

If you're like 1 billion or so other people, you maintain a Facebook account. Not surprisingly, Etsy does, too! If you're on Facebook — or you use Pinterest, Twitter, or Instagram — you can stay on top of Etsy's goings-on even when you're not on Etsy.

To connect with these other sites, simply scroll down to the bottom of any Etsy Marketplace page and click the logo for the desired site in the Follow Etsy section of the footer links. When you do, you'll be taken to Etsy's presence on the site in question, which you can "like," "follow," or otherwise sign up for. Figure 21-4 shows Etsy's Instagram page.

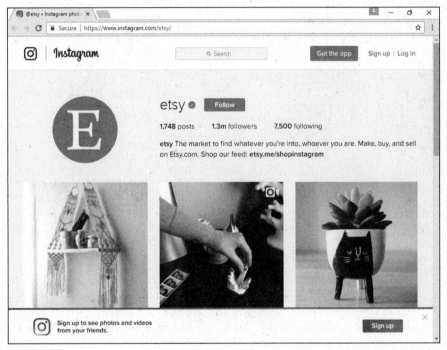

FIGURE 21-4: "Follow" Etsy on Instagram.

Source: Etsy.com

Proto Baggins: Joining Etsy Prototypes

Want to be on the cutting edge on Etsy? Then look into Prototypes. *Prototypes* are projects run by Etsy Admin that explore different ways of using Etsy. The idea behind Prototypes is to gather data and observe how people use the tools offered in the Prototype. Figure 21-5 shows the Prototypes page, which you access by visiting www.etsy.com/prototypes.

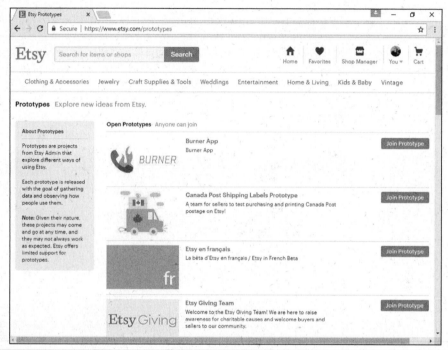

FIGURE 21-5:
Etsy Prototypes.

Source: Etsy.com

To participate in an Etsy Prototype, you must join it. To do so, click the Join Prototype button next to the Prototype on the main Etsy Prototypes page. You'll be prompted to confirm your choice; click Join Prototype again. Note that when you join a Prototype, you're automatically added to a team dedicated to that Prototype. This enables you to discuss the Prototype and interact with Etsy Admin.

Be warned: Because of their experimental nature, some Prototypes don't work as planned. Don't panic — it's not like anything's going to explode. It's just that some Prototypes end up being somewhat of a bust, in which case they may be discontinued by Etsy. On the plus side, if a Prototype works exceptionally well, it may be incorporated into the larger Etsy site — in which case, you'll have the advantage of already knowing how to use it!

Chapter **22**

A Love-Love Relationship: Showing Your Love for Other Etsy Sellers

Have you ever noticed how the plot of literally every romance novel is that person A loves person B, and person B loves person A, but neither person A nor person B is aware of the other person's feelings? On Etsy, that never happens. Love flows freely — and visibly. That's because Etsy gives members the tools to show their love.

One way you can show love on Etsy is to "favorite" the items and stores you adore. Another is to "follow" (not to be confused with "stalk") Etsy sellers so you stay apprised of their goings-on. This chapter is devoted to the ways you can love — and be loved — on Etsy.

Por Favorite: Favoriting on Etsy

If you've spent any time at all on Etsy, you've no doubt run across a bazillion items and shops that you positively adore. Fortunately, Etsy enables you to keep track of all these gorgeous goodies by *favoriting* them. When you favorite an item or shop, Etsy adds it to the Your Favorites page.

Why favorite an item or shop? Lots of reasons. For example:

>> You may favorite an item that you're dying to buy but that'll have to wait until your next payday.

>> You could favorite your favorite supplier's shop so that the next time you need to stock up, you'll be able to find it more easily.

>> You may favorite an item or shop simply to let another Etsy seller know that you appreciate her work.

In the following sections, we explain how to favorite items and shops and view them in the Your Favorites page.

Favoriting items and shops

Favoriting an item is simple. First, make sure you're signed in to your Etsy account. Then click the Favorite button on the right side of the item's listing page (see Figure 22-1). Etsy adds the item to the Your Favorites page.

As an aside, you can also click the Tweet, Pin It, Tumblr, or Like button in the item listing to share the item on Twitter, Pinterest, Tumblr, or Facebook.

Favoriting an Etsy shop is just as easy: Simply click the Favorite Shop button at the top of the shop's main page (see Figure 22-2) or beside the shop icon in the upper-left area of any shop listing (see Figure 22-1).

Viewing favorited items and shops

To revisit your favorite items and shops, click the Favorites button in the header bar that appears along the top of every Etsy Marketplace page. The Your Favorites page opens, with lists of favorite items displayed. (At first, there's just one list here, called "Items I Love," as shown in Figure 22-3; we show you how to add more lists in the next section.) You can click one of these lists to see the items it contains (see Figure 22-4). Or to view your favorite shops, click the Shops button (see Figure 22-5).

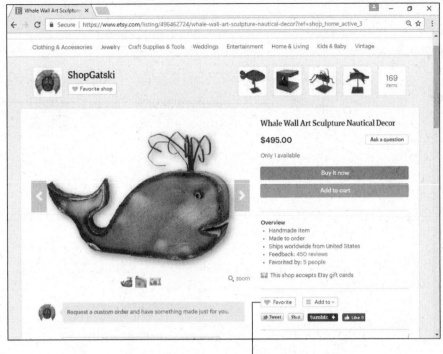

FIGURE 22-1:
Click the Favorite button to add an item to the Your Favorites page.

Favorite button

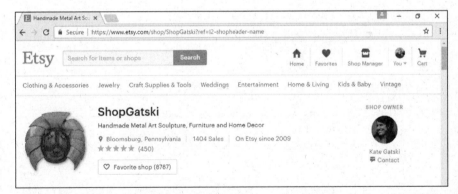

FIGURE 22-2:
The Favorite Shop button on a shop's main page.

TIP

REMEMBER

The Your Favorites page also includes links to items Etsy has picked for you based on your Favorites and your purchases and to new listings from your favorite shops.

The Etsy app also offers easy access to your Favorites. Simply tap the Favorites button (the one with a heart on it) at the bottom of the screen to view your favorite items and shops.

Organizing favorite items

As mentioned, the Your Favorites/Items page includes just one list, called "Items I Love." That's where your favorite items are stored by default. But if you find yourself favoriting lots of different types of items — say, goodies for your home, nifty gift ideas, tempting trinkets, or what have you — you can organize them into different lists, or collections. To create a new list, follow these steps:

1. **In the Your Favorites/Items page (refer to Figure 22-3), click the Create New List button.**

   Etsy prompts you to type a name for the list (see Figure 22-6).

FIGURE 22-6:
Create a new list.

Source: Etsy.com

2. **Type a name for the list and click Create.**

   Etsy creates the list, which, for now, is empty.

3. **To add an item to the list, open the item's listing, click the Add To button (to the right of the Favorite button), and choose the list from the menu that appears, as shown in Figure 22-7. (Notice that you also have the option of creating a new list on the fly.)**

   Etsy adds the item to the list (see Figure 22-8).

What if you've already favorited something and you want to move it to a different list? To do so, open the list that currently contains the item. Then hover your mouse cursor over the item. A drop-down arrow appears; click it and choose the desired list from the menu or opt to move it to a new list entirely (see Figure 22-9).

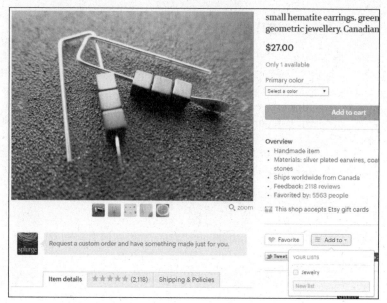

FIGURE 22-7:
Add the item to
the list.

Source: Etsy.com

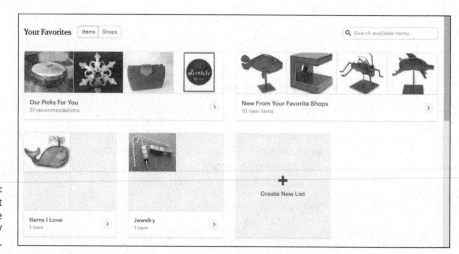

FIGURE 22-8:
The new list
appears on the
Your Favorites/
Items page.

Source: Etsy.com

TIP

Even if you organize your favorite items into collections, you may still collect so many that it becomes difficult to find the one you want. In that case, you can search for items in your Favorites by using the Search Available Items field in the Your Favorites/Items page (refer to Figure 22-3). Simply type a relevant keyword and press Enter or Return, and voilà! Etsy displays items you've favorited that match your criteria. (Note that only those items that are still available are displayed. If the item you're looking for has been sold or its listing has expired, you won't see it in the list of results.)

FIGURE 22-9:
Move a Favorite
to a different list.

Source: Etsy.com

Removing a Favorite

Look, it happens. People fall out of love. It's nothing to feel bad about. If you find yourself disenchanted with one of the items or shops you've favorited, you can always break up with it — er, remove it from your list. To do so, open the list that contains the item you want to remove, hover your mouse cursor over the item, and click the heart button that appears (refer to Figure 22-9).

Removing a favorite shop is just as easy. Simply switch to the Your Favorites/Shops page (refer to Figure 22-5), hover your mouse cursor over the shop you want to remove, and click the X button that appears (see Figure 22-10).

SECRET ADMIRER

By default, your Favorites are public. Other Etsy users can see which shops and items you've favorited by opening your profile and clicking the Favorites option below your profile picture on the left side of the screen. In addition, anyone who follows you on Etsy (more on that later in this chapter) will be able to see what items and shops you've favorited in her home page feed. And if someone visits an Etsy shop or views an item listing you've favorited, you'll be listed among that shop's or item's "admirers."

If you'd prefer to keep your Favorites private — maybe you're a secret agent or a ninja, or perhaps you're just shy — you can do so. To hide a particular list of Favorites from prying eyes, follow these steps:

1. **Click the list in the Your Favorites/Items page to open it.**

2. **Click the Edit button in the upper-right corner of the list's main page.**

3. **The Edit List dialog box appears. Click Only I Can See This List and click Save.**

The steps for hiding your list of favorite shops are nearly identical. You click the Edit button in the Your Favorites/Shops page (refer to Figure 22-5), click the Only I Can See My Favorite Shops option in the Edit Privacy dialog box that appears, and click Save.

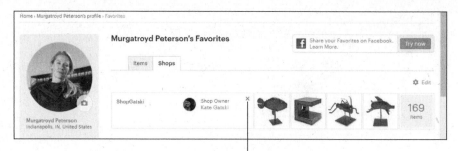

FIGURE 22-10:
In this case,
breaking up is
easy to do.

Click the X to remove the shop

Source: Etsy.com

Follow Me! Following Others on Etsy

Etsy's raison d'être is to serve as a marketplace for artisans and other creative types. But as you find out in Chapter 20, Etsy also supports a vast and vibrant community of fascinating individuals.

To help you build your own place in this larger Etsy community and generally share the love, Etsy enables you to follow other Etsy members — say, family members on the site, friends who run their own Etsy shops, or other Etsy members you admire. When you follow someone, you can stay on top of that person's activity on Etsy — for example, if that person favorites an Etsy store or item or starts following someone else.

Following another Etsy member

Following someone on Etsy is a cinch. To do so, first make sure that you're signed in to your Etsy account. Then click the name of the person you want to follow in the Shop Owner section of her shop's main page to open her profile page. Finally, click the Follow button on the left side of the profile page, under the profile picture. (See Figure 22-11.) When you follow someone, Etsy notifies that person via email.

FIGURE 22-11:
Follow another
Etsy member.

Source: Etsy.com

FIND YOUR FRIENDS

TIP

A great way to find people to follow is to use Etsy's Find Your Friends feature. With Find Your Friends, you can search your Google or Yahoo! accounts to locate people in your address book who are also on Etsy. To use Find Your Friends, click the Following button in the upper-right corner of the Your Favorites/Items page (refer to Figure 22-3). Then, in the Following page (see Figure 22-12), click the Find Your Friends tab. Finally, select either Google or Yahoo! and follow the onscreen prompts. Alternatively, you can use Etsy's People Search tool to search for other Etsy members by name. The People Search tool is available here: www.etsy.com/search/people.

Viewing your Etsy "circle"

It's easy to survey your Etsy "circle" — that is, the members you're following as well as any who are following you. To see the members you're following, click the Following button in the Your Favorites/Items page. The Following page opens, displaying any Etsy members you've followed. (See Figure 22-12.)

FIGURE 22-12:
View your
Etsy circle.

Source: Etsy.com

To stop following someone on Etsy, locate her entry in the Following page and click the Following button. The Following button turns into a Follow button, indicating that you are no longer following this person.

Interested in finding out who's following you? You're in luck. By default, Etsy notifies you via email any time someone follows you. (If you don't want to be notified, click the You drop-down menu that appears along the top of every Etsy Marketplace page, choose Account Settings, click the Emails tab, deselect the Someone Follows Me check box, and click the Save Settings button at the bottom of the page.)

You can also track who's following you by clicking the Followers tab in the page shown in Figure 22-13. (You can access this tab directly by clicking the Followers button in the Your Favorites page.)

REMEMBER

If you go the secret-admirer route with your Favorites (as we describe earlier in this chapter), anyone who follows you won't be able to see items and shops you've favorited. Otherwise, this info is visible for all to see.

Checking your activity feed

To keep abreast of goings-on among the people you follow on Etsy — for example, who in your circle has increased her own circle by following new members — you can check your activity feed. To view your activity feed, locate the From People You Follow section of Etsy's home page. Then click the See More Activity link. The Your Activity Feed page opens (see Figure 22-13). Note that if the members you follow haven't been particularly active on the site, Etsy may supplement your feed by recommending other members to follow.

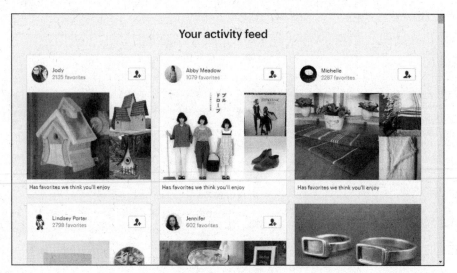

FIGURE 22-13:
View your
activity feed.

Source: Etsy.com

Chapter **23**

Help! Getting It When You Need It

Yes, Etsy is super easy to use. But that doesn't mean you won't ever need a little help. Fortunately, Etsy maintains copious resources to help members find answers to all their burning questions (the ones about using Etsy, anyway). This chapter covers getting help on Etsy.

Handy Dandy: Reading the Seller Handbook

If you're looking for guidance running your Etsy shop, look no further than Etsy's Seller Handbook. (You access the Seller Handbook by scrolling down to the footer area on any Etsy Marketplace page and, under Sell on Etsy, clicking the Seller Handbook link.) This deep-dive resource, shown in Figure 23-1, contains links to hundreds of articles, with new ones added every week. For ease of navigation, Etsy has organized these articles into categories, from photography to shipping to marketing and beyond. Or you can search for articles by topic by entering a keyword in the Search field at the top of the Seller Handbook page.

FIGURE 23-1:
The Seller Handbook.

Source: Etsy.com

TIP

The Seller Handbook is also available on the Sell on Etsy app. To access it, tap Settings & Help, and then tap Seller Handbook.

Search and Rescue: Searching for Help on Etsy

Given the proclivity of Etsy users for DIY, it's no surprise that the site offers tools for finding help on your own. Perhaps the easiest of these is the Search Help tool, which enables you to search the site's Help information for the answers you need by entering a keyword or phrase.

To use the Search Help tool, follow these steps:

1. **Click the Help button in the bottom-right area of any Etsy Marketplace page.**

   The Help page opens (see Figure 23-2).

Source: Etsy.com

FIGURE 23-2:
The Help page.

2. **Type a topic, keyword, or phrase in the Search for Help field at the top of the page, and then click the Search Help button.**

   Etsy displays a list of articles, or answers, that match your criteria (see Figure 23-3).

3. **Click the link for the article that appears most likely to contain the information you need.**

   Etsy displays the article (see Figure 23-4).

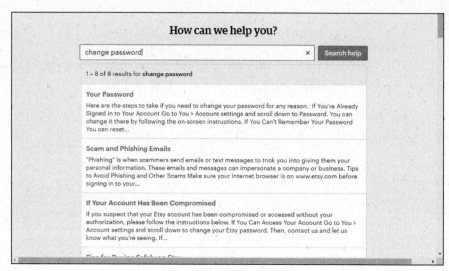

FIGURE 23-3:
View your
matches.

Source: Etsy.com

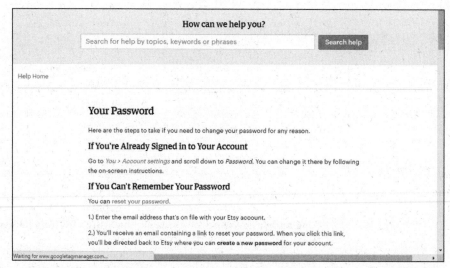

FIGURE 23-4:
View the article.

Source: Etsy.com

At the bottom of the page, Etsy displays links to other articles related to the one you just read. Simply click an article's link to view it.

TIP

If your search efforts fail to yield useful results — for example, Etsy returns too many matches — try the search techniques discussed in Chapter 5.

People Person: Getting Personalized Help

Sometimes you just want to ask a question and have it answered by an actual person. Fortunately, Etsy can accommodate you! You can use Etsy's Questions forum to get help from other Etsy users. If that doesn't work, you can contact Etsy Support to get the answers you need.

Using the Questions forum

As we explain in Chapter 20, Etsy's forums serve as public message boards where members can discuss all manner of topics. Specifically, Etsy's Questions forum, shown in Figure 23-5, is a great resource if you have general questions about how to use Etsy, questions about site features, or questions related to site policy. Odds are, someone in the Etsy community or on the Etsy staff can — and will — answer your question.

You can access the Questions forum directly from Etsy's Help page. Simply click the Ask in the Forums link toward the bottom of the main Help page. Alternatively, scroll down to the footer area of any Etsy Marketplace page, click the Forums link under Join the Community, and click the Questions forum to view it. For info on using the forum, see Chapter 20.

TIP

If you're looking for help because you're experiencing a bug on the site, then drop in on the Bugs forum instead of the Questions one.

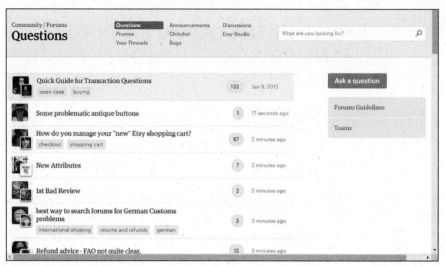

Source: Etsy.com

FIGURE 23-5:
The Questions
forum.

Contacting Etsy Support

Suppose that you have a problem with your account. Or maybe you need help with a transaction. In either case, you can send a message to Etsy Support. You can also send a message to Etsy Support to notify Etsy of a problem on the site. To start, click the Contact Us . . . link at the bottom of the main Help page. Alternatively, click Shop Manager, click the Community & Help link, and choose Contact Us. Then use the drop-down lists that appear to select from a series of categories and subcategories to define your query. When you finish, Etsy displays links to articles that may answer your question (see Figure 23-6).

Odds are, the answer to your question lies in one of these articles. But on the off chance it doesn't, you can email Etsy for additional help. Simply click the Contact Us by Email button at the bottom of the Contact Etsy Support page (see Figure 23-6). The page expands to include a Subject and a Message field as well as an Attach a File button, which you can use to attach supporting information if needed. (For example, if you're experiencing a problem with your shop page, you might capture a screenshot of the page and attach that image file to your message.) When you've entered the requested info, click the Get in Touch button at the bottom of the page. Etsy notifies you that your question has been submitted and sends you a confirmation email to that effect. After Etsy tracks down the answer to your question, a member of the site's support staff will email you with the information.

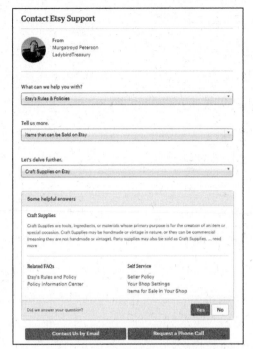

Contact Etsy Support

From
Murgatroyd Peterson
LadybirdTreasury

What can we help you with?
Etsy's Rules & Policies ▾

Tell us more.
Items that can be Sold on Etsy ▾

Let's delve further.
Craft Supplies on Etsy ▾

Some helpful answers

Craft Supplies

Craft Supplies are tools, ingredients, or materials whose primary purpose is for the creation of an item or special occasion. Craft Supplies may be handmade or vintage in nature, or they can be commercial (meaning they are not handmade or vintage). Party supplies may also be sold as Craft Supplies. ... read more

Related FAQs   Self Service
Etsy's Rules and Policy   Seller Policy
Policy Information Center   Your Shop Settings
                                    Items for Sale in Your Shop

Did we answer your question?   Yes   No

Contact Us by Email   Request a Phone Call

FIGURE 23-6:
See whether you can find an answer to your question in one of the articles listed.

Source: Etsy.com

Maybe you'd rather talk to a living human on the phone. In that case, you can request a phone call with a member of Etsy's staff. Just click the Request a Phone Call button at the bottom of the Contact Etsy Support page (refer to Figure 23-6). Etsy prompts you to enter your full name, your phone number, and a brief description of your issue. Do so, and then click Request a Phone Call. Someone from Etsy will then contact you at the phone number you provided within 30 minutes (unless Etsy is experiencing an unusually large number of call requests).

TIP

You can also contact Etsy support from the Sell on Etsy app. To do so, tap Settings & Help, tap the Sell on Etsy Help Center, and scroll all the way down to Contact Us. You'll be prompted to select the category that best describes your question or issue; you can then contact Etsy by email or request a phone call.

6

The Part of Tens

Chapter **24**

Ten Terrific Tips for Etsy Sellers

Running an Etsy shop — even if it's just a hobby — is no small undertaking. Organization is critical, as is offering top-notch customer service. Here's the place where we offer a neat, concise roll call of ten terrific tips for Etsy sellers. Drum roll, please!

Have a Place for Everything

Nothing is as frustrating as trying to find just the right bead, button, ribbon, or supply when you have 82 orders breathing down your neck. Do yourself a favor: Get organized! Figure out the best way to store all your supplies, both for your craft and for your business. First, sort all your supplies by type or color. Then stash everything in a place where you can easily find it.

TIP

In our experience, clear boxes with labels are the only way to go.

Save Time with Twosies

We've wasted too much time looking for scissors, and then tracking down tape, and then wondering where the heck that marker went. Save yourself a ton of time and aggravation by buying many, *many* multiples of oft-used supplies.

Our advice? Head to a discount store and knock yourself out. Get a dozen pairs of scissors, a zillion rolls of tape, and lots of whatever else you need.

TIP

Organize Your Paperwork

Even if it's just a shoe box, have a place to stick all your business-related receipts, whether they're for crafting tools, packaging supplies, or what have you. Then have *another* place for your other paperwork — invoices, bank statements, and such. Tax time is tough enough without having to sort through all that stuff at the 11th hour! (Flip to Chapter 18 for more details on handling paperwork and other business-related issues.)

Use What You Discover from Other Shops

Before you start selling on Etsy, buy a handful of items from a handful of sellers. Pay attention to the way each seller communicates with you, the packaging he uses, how long it takes for him to ship to you, and so on. What are the sellers doing right? Where can they improve? Then put what you learn to work in your own Etsy shop.

Offer Service with a Smile

No, your online customers can't see you. But that doesn't mean you can cop an attitude with them. In fact, even though you're "out of sight," your lousy outlook will ooze into everything you do. Remember, on Etsy, it's all about the customer service! Offering service with a smile is a good way to ensure that you get a smile in return. (Check out Chapter 17 for more customer service tips.)

Network, Network, Network

Networking is a wonderful way to grow your Etsy business. Whether you're interacting with others in the Etsy community (see Part 5) or just going about your day in the real world, make it a point to connect with people. Ask questions. Coax those you meet to share their stories. Offer to help others. Engage in the kinds of behaviors that let people know who you are, what you're about, and, eventually, what you do.

Send an Email Newsletter

If you're serious about your Etsy shop, consider publishing a newsletter. A newsletter can serve as an excellent marketing tool to help you grow your customer base. Newsletters are a great way to share tips and ideas. You can even run contests and giveaways.

Learn to Say No

As an Etsy seller, you'll almost certainly be inundated with requests for freebies, donations, and discounts. You know what? It's perfectly okay to say no to some or even all of these requests. Pick and choose. Say yes to the requests that make you feel good and that are good for your business; to everything else, say no.

Never Give In

Take a lesson from the great British Prime Minister Winston Churchill: "Never give in. Never give in. Never, never, never, never." Although Churchill uttered those words in an attempt to galvanize the British against their Axis foes, they apply equally to Etsy sellers — with a spin: If you have an original idea for a product that you love, never stop developing and finessing and improving and learning and changing and working hard. Never, never, never, *never.*

Have Fun!

You're not out to change the world here, one beaded necklace at a time. Selling your work on Etsy should be fun! Do your best to maintain perspective. Chortle on the inside when a customer requests a gum-wrapper purse made entirely of Clark's Teaberry wrappers, and enjoy yourself!

Chapter **25**

Ten Strategies for Marketing Your Etsy Shop

Marketing is the key to any successful business, your Etsy shop included. Here, we offer ten tips you need to know to successfully market your Etsy shop (flip to Chapter 16 for even more guidance).

Offer Tiered Pricing

If all you had to offer were $25 gumball machines, you'd really be limiting your customer base. By offering a $5 item as well as a $100 item, you open your shop to buyers with different-sized pocketbooks. With so-called "tiered pricing," you can include big-ticket items to make your shop seem more exciting, while at the same time offering goodies for entry-level shoppers.

Understand That Giving Begets Giving

Helping someone by giving her more than she asked for makes that person want to return the favor. Build trust and develop relationships with your customers by offering something for nothing — say, a gift with a purchase or a coupon code for their next purchase.

WARNING

But don't go the cheap route — it may actually work against you by turning off customers. Make sure you offer only good-quality stuff.

Provide a Guarantee

No doubt about it, you can engender a lot of trust by offering to replace or refund an item if the customer isn't happy for any reason. Buying online can be a scary proposition; you can break down a barrier by letting shoppers know that you're willing to work with them. We guarantee it!

Consider a Loyalty Program

Loyalty programs, or frequent-customer cards, can be a great way to bring back return customers. Your loyalty program may offer prizes, future discounts, and other incentives designed to keep customers doing business with you.

TIP

As you develop your loyalty program, don't forget your branding. Design customer cards that reflect your shop's color, logo, design, and feel.

Impose a Deadline

Overcome the customer's natural tendency to put things off by offering a sale with a deadline. Add a sense of urgency to your marketing message, and customers will respond.

Create a Great Email Signature

Most email programs enable you to create an email signature — a bit of text or an image that appears at the bottom of every email message you send. Take advantage of this feature! Creating an email signature gives you a chance to share your contact info and reinforce your branding.

TIP

Your email signature is the last thing the person reading your message will see — you want it to reflect your brand and personality!

Connect with Social Media

It's really easy to get so caught up in sharing our own stories online that we forget to listen to others. Instead of using Facebook, Twitter, and other forms of social media as one big free-for-all to advertise your wares, use them to reach out to others. Read and comment on others' posts. Congratulate a fellow seller on her successful sale or cheer up a Twitter buddy who's down in the dumps. It's karma, baby!

Make Google Your Best Friend

With this newfangled interweb thingy, you can find the answer to literally any question you have (including marketing questions). Don't be afraid to turn to Google as you grow your Etsy shop! You'll find everything from tips on developing a logo to the best marketing strategy for your Etsy business.

Use Your Items in the Real World

One of the simplest ways to promote your work is to use or wear your pieces in everyday life, and to always have a business card handy. That way, when your barista compliments you on your beautiful bedazzled bracelet, you can hand her your business card and tell her where to get one of her very own.

Help Your Community

Get your craft business some publicity by doing something to benefit your community. For example, create a special breast cancer awareness necklace to honor a neighbor, or hold a special sale to help someone in the area. Make sure you let the local paper know what you're up to!

Index

About the Authors

Kate Shoup: Kate Shoup has authored more than 45 books, including *Not Your Mama's Beading, Not Your Mama's Stitching,* and *Rubbish: Reuse Your Refuse* (all published by Wiley), and has edited scores more. Kate also co-wrote (and starred in) a feature-length movie and worked as the sports editor for *NUVO Newsweekly*. When not writing, Kate, an IndyCar fanatic, loves to ski (she was once nationally ranked), read, craft, and ride her motorcycle. She also plays a mean game of 9-ball. Kate lives in Indianapolis with her husband, her daughter, and their dog.

Kate Gatski: Kate is a handmade entrepreneur. She and her husband, Ben, make sculpture and furniture full-time in their rural shop. Their business, Gatski Metal, is celebrating its 13th year. They enjoy working with a growing group of fantastic customers via their Etsy shop www.shopgatski.etsy.com. Kate enjoys supporting others in their entrepreneurial pursuits. She loves to provide guidance and support to others in the business. Kate was born into craft, raised by a full-time rag-rug weaver. Kate is mother to three children who keep her from going all crafts, all the time. Kate savors a strong cup of tea and a good mystery book.

Dedications

Kate Shoup: For my darling Heidi-bird.

Kate Gatski: To all of you — crafters, artists, makers, designers — who quietly labor away, creating something beautiful to share with the world. May this make some part of your efforts a little easier.

Authors' Acknowledgments

Kate Shoup: The publication of any book is an enormous undertaking, and this one was no exception! Thanks go first to my excellent coauthor, Kate Gatski, who — figuratively, at least — pried more than one razor blade from my fingers. Thanks also go to Allison Strine, whose work on the first edition of this book was second to none. And of course, thanks to Tracy Boggier for giving us the opportunity to tackle this exciting project; to Chrissy Guthrie for her dedication and patience in guiding this project from start to finish; to technical editor Caroline Vasquez, who skillfully checked each step and offered valuable input along the way; to copy editor Jennette ElNaggar for attempting to ensure that we didn't look like idiots; and to the Composition Services team at Wiley for their able efforts. Finally, thanks to the Etsy sellers and talented photographers who graciously allowed us to feature their gorgeous photographs, and to Etsy itself for enabling craftspeople the world over to make a living by selling their work online.

On a personal note, many thanks and much love to my beautiful and brilliant daughter, Heidi Welsh; to my darling husband, Olivier Boisson; to my incredible parents, Barb and Steve Shoup; to my wonderful sister, Jenny Shoup; to my delightful brother-in-law, Jim Plant; and to my crazy-cool nephew, Jake Plant. I love you all so much it makes me wheezy sometimes.

Kate Gatski: Thanks foremost to my brilliant coauthor Kate Shoup. Writing this book was a snap, thanks to you! Thank you to Chrissy Guthrie for her steadfast work and to Tracy Boggier for making the process simple and smooth. Thanks to Ben for picking up the slack while I worked on the book. And to Ivan, Hazel, and Evelyn, the best creators I've ever known: You're my inspiration!

Publisher's Acknowledgments

Senior Acquisitions Editor: Tracy Boggier

Editorial Project Manager and Development Editor: Christina N. Guthrie

Copy Editor: Jennette ElNaggar

Technical Editor: Caroline Vasquez

Art Coordinator: Alicia B. South

Production Editor: Vasanth Koilraj

Cover Photos: © sjhuls/iStockphoto

Leverage the power

Dummies is the global leader in the reference category and one of the most trusted and highly regarded brands in the world. No longer just focused on books, customers now have access to the dummies content they need in the format they want. Together we'll craft a solution that engages your customers, stands out from the competition, and helps you meet your goals.

Advertising & Sponsorships

Connect with an engaged audience on a powerful multimedia site, and position your message alongside expert how-to content. Dummies.com is a one-stop shop for free, online information and know-how curated by a team of experts.

- Targeted ads
- Video
- Email Marketing
- Microsites
- Sweepstakes sponsorship

20 MILLION PAGE VIEWS EVERY SINGLE MONTH

15 MILLION UNIQUE VISITORS PER MONTH

43% OF ALL VISITORS ACCESS THE SITE VIA THEIR MOBILE DEVICES

700,000 NEWSLETTER SUBSCRIPTIONS TO THE INBOXES OF

300,000 UNIQUE INDIVIDUALS EVERY WEEK

# of dummies

Custom Publishing

Reach a global audience in any language by creating a solution that will differentiate you from competitors, amplify your message, and encourage customers to make a buying decision.

- Apps
- Books
- eBooks
- Video
- Audio
- Webinars

Brand Licensing & Content

Leverage the strength of the world's most popular reference brand to reach new audiences and channels of distribution.

For more information, visit dummies.com/biz

PERSONAL ENRICHMENT

Staying Sharp

9781119187790
USA $26.00
CAN $31.99
UK £19.99

Facebook

Carolyn Abram

9781119179030
USA $21.99
CAN $25.99
UK £16.99

Guitar

Mark Phillips
Jon Chappell

9781119293354
USA $24.99
CAN $29.99
UK £17.99

Investing

Eric Tyson, MBA

9781119293347
USA $22.99
CAN $27.99
UK £16.99

Beekeeping

Howland Blackiston

9781119310068
USA $22.99
CAN $27.99
UK £16.99

Digital Photography

Julie Adair King

9781119235606
USA $24.99
CAN $29.99
UK £17.99

Meditation

Stephan Bodian

9781119251163
USA $24.99
CAN $29.99
UK £17.99

Pregnancy

9781119235491
USA $26.99
CAN $31.99
UK £19.99

Samsung Galaxy S7

Bill Hughes

9781119279952
USA $24.99
CAN $29.99
UK £17.99

iPhone

Edward C. Baig
Bob "Dr. Mac" LeVitus

9781119283133
USA $24.99
CAN $29.99
UK £17.99

Crocheting

Karen Manthey
Susan Brittain

9781119287117
USA $24.99
CAN $29.99
UK £16.99

Nutrition

Carol Ann Rinzler

9781119130246
USA $22.99
CAN $27.99
UK £16.99

PROFESSIONAL DEVELOPMENT

Windows 10

Andy Rathbone

9781119311041
USA $24.99
CAN $29.99
UK £17.99

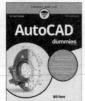
AutoCAD

Bill Fane

9781119255796
USA $39.99
CAN $47.99
UK £27.99

Excel 2016

Greg Harvey, PhD

9781119293439
USA $26.99
CAN $31.99
UK £19.99

QuickBooks 2017

Stephen L. Nelson, MBA, CPA, MS in Taxation

9781119281467
USA $26.99
CAN $31.99
UK £19.99

macOS Sierra

Bob "Dr. Mac" LeVitus

9781119280651
USA $29.99
CAN $35.99
UK £21.99

LinkedIn

Joel Elad, MBA

9781119251132
USA $24.99
CAN $29.99
UK £17.99

Windows 10

Woody Leonhard

9781119310563
USA $34.00
CAN $41.99
UK £24.99

SharePoint 2016

Rosemarie Withee
Ken Withee

9781119181705
USA $29.99
CAN $35.99
UK £21.99

Fundamental Analysis

Matt Krantz

9781119263593
USA $26.99
CAN $31.99
UK £19.99

Networking

Doug Lowe

9781119257769
USA $29.99
CAN $35.99
UK £21.99

Office 2016

Wallace Wang

9781119293477
USA $26.99
CAN $31.99
UK £19.99

Office 365

Rosemarie Withee
Ken Withee
Jennifer Reed

9781119265313
USA $24.99
CAN $29.99
UK £17.99

Salesforce.com

Liz Kao
Jon Paz

9781119239314
USA $29.99
CAN $35.99
UK £21.99

Coding

Nikhil Abraham

9781119293323
USA $29.99
CAN $35.99
UK £21.99

dummies.com

dummies®
A Wiley Brand

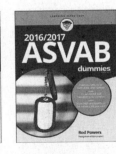

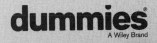